The Science Fiction *of* Poetics *and the* Avant-Garde Imagination

The Science Fiction *of* Poetics *and the* Avant-Garde Imagination

MICHAEL GOLSTON

THE UNIVERSITY OF ALABAMA PRESS
Tuscaloosa

The University of Alabama Press
Tuscaloosa, Alabama 35487-0380
uapress.ua.edu

Typeface: Warnock Pro

Cover image: *The Isolator*, cover illustration of *Science and Invention in Pictures*, July 1925, No. 3
Cover design: Danielle Guy

Cataloging-in-Publication data is available from the Library of Congress.
ISBN: 978-0-8173-6100-6
E-ISBN: 978-0-8173-9468-4

This book is for
Bernhard Rast (grandfather)
and
Jacob Krovatin (grandson)

I beg your pardon coach I thought you were a wheelbarrow.

—Molly Bloom, *Ulysses*

Contents

Illustrations

Acknowledgments

The following people contributed, wittingly or unwittingly, to the making of this book, for which they have my deepest gratitude: Bruce Andrews; Sarah Arkebauer; Veronica Belafi; Charles Bernstein; Gabriel Bloomfield; Charles Borkhuis; Jeff Bryant; Dennis Büscher-Ulbrich; Alejandro Crawford; Kyle Dartnell; Katie Degentesch; Craig Dworkin; Katrina Dzyack; Brent Hayes Edwards; Dylan Furcall; Drew Gardner; Anne-Marie and Serge Gavronsky; Anatole, Nancy, and Sam Gershman; Alan Gilbert; Chris (Cork) Golston; Chris (Lorly) Golston; Julius Greve; Paul Grimstad; Ursula Heise; Matthew Hofer; Peter Inman; Sean Killlian; Chris Krovatin; Marty Larson-Xu; Max Lawton; Hank Lazar; Roger Luckhurst; Naomi Michalowicz; Peter Middleton; Anahid Neressian; Peter Nicholls; Amber Noe; Evelyn Reilly; Aled Roberts; Matt Sandler; Andrew Schelling; James Sherry; Toni Simon; Paul Stephens; Dennis Tenen; Eugene Vydrin; Caroline Wallenberg; Aaron Winslow; Grant Wythoff; and the students who attended my spring 2016 and fall 2017 Science Fiction Poetics lecture courses at Columbia University.

Special thanks to Leif Rustebakke, at whose adobe hacienda in Placitas, New Mexico, this book was completed during the year of our COVID 2020. Also thanks to Leslie Jean, at whose jungle hale on the Big Island of Hawai'i revisions were begun during the summer of 2022.

The Science Fiction *of* Poetics *and the* Avant-Garde Imagination

Introduction

> A book of philosophy should in part be a kind of science fiction. How else can one write but of those things which one doesn't know, or knows badly? It is precisely there that we imagine having something to say. We write only at the frontiers of our knowledge, at the border which separates our knowledge from our ignorance and transforms the one into the other.
>
> —Gilles Deleuze, *Difference and Repetition*

> The universe is a site of lingering catastrophes.
>
> —Walter Benjamin, *The Arcades Project*

CAVEATS AND QUALIFICATIONS

This book examines experimental and avant-garde poetry and poetics that are motivated or inspired by science fiction, especially varieties of popular, pulp, and B-grade sci-fi. It is *not* about the poetics of science fiction prose narratives, a topic that has been written about frequently and well. I approach the issue from the other direction: How has science fiction influenced poetics? I deal primarily with poetry, although I occasionally turn to a relevant novel, short story, film, or piece of music. This book is also not about science fiction poetry comprised of outer space adventure vignettes broken into lines, stanzas, verses, or otherwise utilizing standard poetic devices. The book thus treats neither science fiction narrative poetry nor the poetics of science fiction prose works. In examining the influence of science fiction on developments in innovative poetry and poetics over the past hundred plus years, I set out to uncover a hitherto underexamined but nonetheless major strain of influence on modernist, postwar, avant-garde, and contemporary writing.

In shifting focus from the poetics of science fiction to the science fiction in poetics, my work sets out to challenge several critical canards regarding science fiction and poetry, the principal one of which is the general perception, in the words of Seo-Young Chu, of "the virtual non-existence of science fiction poetry."[1] What I aim to show is that there exists a vigorous and even a rigorous branch of science fiction poetry, although it does not typically appear in traditional lyrical or otherwise subject-centered poetic modes, nor does it necessarily involve stories or fiction. In this poetry, the tropes of science fiction play out not at the level of narrative or meditative soliloquy but in the poetic texture itself: in the poem's language—its vocabulary, syntax, grammar—certainly, but also in its lineation, stanza shape, and verse form. A science fiction poem can become a kind of science fiction *object*—something like William Carlos Williams's "machine made out of words"[2]—or a gadget, like the weird extraterrestrial toys in Lewis Padgett's "Mimsy Were the Borogoves":

> The "abacus," unfolded, was more than a foot square, composed of thin, rigid wires that interlocked here and there. On the wires colored beads were strung. They could be slid back and forth, and from one support to another, even at the points of juncture. But—a pierced bead couldn't cross interlocking wires. . . . So, apparently, they weren't pierced. Paradine looked closer. Each small bead had a deep groove running around it, so that it could be revolved and slid along the wire at the same time. Paradine tried to pull one free. It clung as though magnetically. Iron? It looked more like plastic. The framework itself—Paradine wasn't a mathematician. But the angles formed by the wires were vaguely shocking, in their ridiculous lack of Euclidean logic. They were a maze. Perhaps that's what the gadget was—a puzzle.[3]

Poet Clark Coolidge uses just such science-fictional devices as models for building his poems, and conceptual artist Robert Smithson thinks of them as prototypes for his sculptures and writings. It is these sorts of overlaps and influences that I am interested in tracing here.

The question is, what happens when the tropes and strategies of science fiction migrate into poetic writing or for that matter into other non- or anti-narrative arts? What happens to the *fiction* in science fiction when the latter is projected into nonfiction friendly media or genres? Can terms like *alien, experiment, laboratory, novum, entropy, alternative dimension,* or *time travel* be brought to bear on the poetry of the past hundred years? What role might speculative or futuristic technology play in a poem? And I am not talking about facile or obvious analogies between sci-fi and poetry, which, as several entries on the list above suggest, might easily enough be made. What sorts of links exist between science fiction and the poetry of the past century and the last twenty years, and how do they manifest themselves? And if there are poetics and poetry modeled on science fiction, can we also articulate a critical practice modeled on sci-fi? In other words, can we imagine, not a "science fiction" fiction, but a "science fiction" *poetics*, where *poetics* qualifies or even negates or replaces fiction, and "science fiction" plays out in poetic registers rather than in narrative plots and storylines? Were the tropes of science fiction to filter into and inform critical practice, what sorts of insights might be gained, methods developed, models of intelligibility articulated and mobilized? If philosophy, to cite Deleuze, should be a kind of science fiction, can we imagine a science fiction *criticism*?

At this point the long history of the critical reception of science fiction as fatally popular, secondary, minor, or otherwise degraded is firmly in our cultural rearview mirror, due to decades of serious scholarship as well as the ongoing production of sci-fi novels, short stories, movies, television shows—and poetry, the unacknowledged poor relation of the family. While the volume of scholarship on science fiction at this point is impressive, nothing substantial has been written about science fiction poetry or about poetics that are motivated by science fiction: thus, while there is a lengthy entry in *The Princeton Encyclopedia of Poetry and Poetics* titled "Science and Poetry," there is none on "Science Fiction and Poetry." The purpose of this book is to write the conditions for that entry. If, as the *Princeton Encyclopedia* says, "science may appear in poetry as theme, as underlying world view, and as a model for poetics," why may not *science fiction* appear in poetry "as theme, as underlying world view, and as a model for poetics"?[4] And why should science fiction not operate as a model for criticism? In what follows, I lay out the terms for such a project, in the hopes of bringing sci-fi into the folds of both modern poetics and criticism, where, I argue, it has anyway always been hidden.

All of this leads immediately into the twin quicksands of Planet Scholarship: Taxonomy and Categorization. What exactly is science fiction? What are the tropes of sci-fi? What, for that matter, is science? What is fiction? Where are the boundaries between the two? Then, what is poetry? What is the relationship between fiction and poetry? Can fiction be non-narrative? Can you have a science "fiction" *poem*? How about a non-narrative science fiction poem? What is non-narrative fiction? Concerning such matters I tend to side with Fredric Jameson, who in *Archaeologies of the Future* writes of

> the standard aim of traditional aesthetics, namely to identify the specificity of the aesthetic as such: in other words, for standard literature, to differentiate fiction from other discourses; or, in the case of Sci-fi, to differentiate its narrative sentences and their content, not only from realism, but also from the literary fantastic or "maravilloso" as well as from fantasy, horror and other paraliterary forms. In my opinion, this is not in the long run a very interesting or productive line of inquiry, although it can certainly throw off many useful or striking insights in the process. Indeed, the sterility of the approach documents the structural

> limits of aesthetic philosophy as such and confirms its obsolescence. (I am inclined to make an exception for the study of the specificity of poetic language).[5]

It is "the study of the specificity of poetic language" for which Jameson was inclined to make his exception that I am interested in pursuing here: that is, *the study of the specificity of poetic language as it is filtered through science fiction as a model for poetics.*

In what follows, I take some account of the ongoing controversies and discussions involving exactly what science fiction is, where its generic boundaries lie, when it starts fading into other speculative literatures like fantasy or horror, and so on. But I also maintain that generic defining and boundary making are fluid and ongoing processes, especially when it comes to an aesthetic sensibility and a set of practices as recently evolved and as multiplatform as is modern science fiction, which was born at the beginning of the age of mechanical reproduction and has as important a lineage in film and visual art and music as it does in literature. If there is any genre that categorically warps categories, redefines definitions, and constantly delimits limits, it would have to be science fiction, which, as Darko Suvin pointed out nearly half a century ago, is premised on necessary ongoing estrangement and defamiliarization. For one thing, science fiction continually has to change, *by definition*, since it inevitably deals with the fictions of science, whatever those happen to be at the historical moment that a particular work is conceived.[6] Science fiction at the turn of the twentieth century dealt with racialist science and eugenics and with the theory of the Hollow Earth; at midcentury, it tackled Freudian psychology and psychoanalysis; in the 1970s, it took on entropy and the heat death of the universe; later in the century, it became preoccupied with identity politics and climate change; and so on. Just as much if not more than any other genre, science fiction acts as a distorted mirror to the times, reflecting both on what science knows and wants to know or thinks it might one day be able to know, and simultaneously on the social and political circumstances of the day. Reading Edgar Rice Burroughs on the "races" of the Lost Continent of Caspak or watching Jane Fonda parry sexual advances in *Barbarella* can grant one real insight into the social pathologies of the 1920s or the gender dynamics of the 1960s. This is not to say anything new or surprising, only to point out that a necessary urgency to update and revise itself constantly is built into sci-fi.

This leads to one of the more profound and entertaining characteristics of science fiction: the speed with which it goes out of fashion. Nothing feels more corny or obsolete than the hair-dos, crew outfits, aliens, machinery, robots, production values, and politics of the science fiction of a decade—or even a few years—ago. This is especially true when it comes to film, a medium that was born at the same time that modern science fiction appeared and has co-evolved with it. Sci-fi literature and the movies and visual arts have fed off one another over the decades, offering each other prompts in the forms of concepts, pretenses, plot lines, and visuals. Science fiction is a genre parasite, a Blob that squeezes through the sundry ventilation systems of the arts, absorbing and distorting everything it touches, and in touching anything immediately rendering it obsolete. The original Time Machine, sci-fi projects a future that is the product of a past into which the present immediately fades; it thus has the configuration of dream and bears the dialectical structure of awakening.[7] In science fiction, the past impinges upon the present *as* a future: hence the atmosphere of kitsch that drapes and dooms sci-fi. Science fiction produces the most dialectical of dialectical images, *doubled* dialectical images, future moments conceived in the past that explode into the present already carrying with them the whiff of junk shops and used book stores filled with degraded fetishes embodying the dreams of last season's intellectual fashions.[8] Sci-fi is the graveyard of the future, its mod paperback book covers its tombstones. As the premier site of catastrophes that linger forever, it eventually drifts into Walter Benjamin's entropic universe of the Petrified, the Passé, and the Boring—the melancholic realm of the Collector.[9]

And inevitably it floats into the spheres of the Comic, the Satiric, and the Ridiculous. In the end, there is something ludic about science fiction: based on fantasy and flights of fancy, it lends itself readily to parody and ridicule:

> We should, however, also keep in mind that sci-fi has always invited satirical, parodistic, and extravagantly whimsical thought. Every sci-fi text plays with cognitive dissonance, and most sci-fi texts are tacitly aware of the enormous range of styles of incongruity-management used in the history of the genre, from outright satire and parody, comedy, pornography, and allusion, to near-surrealistic arbitrariness of imagery. . . . With regard to the rational impossibility—and hence irrationality—of giant creatures, instant evolution, and superheroes of sci-fi movies, science often functions for sci-fi as a contemporary package for archaic dreams and myths. The rationality of such novums, such as it is, lies not in the texts themselves, but in the often impossible effort to make them fit into a consistent and coherent world-picture. . . .
>
> Even so, sci-fi continues to construct "sentimental" myths that simultaneously satisfy readers' needs for complete world-pictures, and call ironic attention to their ludic and constructed character.[10]

Seriousness is a poison gas turning science fiction into kitsch and false consciousness; profundity and self-importance make it phony and funny, with its ray guns and aliens and weird shoes (see *Space is the Place*). Part of this has to do with the genre's acute susceptibility to the passage of time: made-up histories of made-up places, themselves made-up at particular historical moments, sci-fi stories generally do not age well, and it takes only a slightly skewed eye to see them as willful if not downright dopey. Northrop Frye classified science fiction as a form of late romance, equal parts utopian and satiric.[11] Due to its ongoing obsolescing, sci-fi that forgets its ludicrous side risks becoming pompous and sententious, although its self-effacing aspects are part of its power, if not its charm. Science fiction was born in the crucible of modernism, with its savage ironies and acrobatic formal distortions: it was always already avant-garde.

In what follows, I use Benjamin, along with Roman Jakobson and Gilles Deleuze and Félix Guattari, to construct a three-part critical structure, a regular Rube Goldberg machine (what is science fiction if not a junkyard of Rube Goldberg machines?), for modeling a science fiction poetics. After all, the "science" of poetics has always been fictional, from early modern exercises in construing English prosody according to classical Greek and Latin metrical systems, to nineteenth-century attempts to hook up poetic rhythms to bodily metabolisms and racial types, to formalist typologies and catalogs of prosodic figures and tropes, and on to the myriad of other scientific "systems" for explaining poetics. The history of modern criticism itself parallels the history of science fiction, and each phase or mode of sci-fi has its theoretical counterpart: there are futurist and constructivist science fictions; sci-fi based on Freud or Marx or inspired by structuralism and various brands of poststructuralism; ethnic studies, postcolonial, and Indigenous science fictions; and ecopoetic and Anthropocene sci-fis. Pillaging the scientific and philosophical worlds around it, science fiction, like critical theory, is always about *something else*, although science fiction poetry might just be about science fiction.[12]

The idea for this book originates in a statement made by Robert Smithson in his essay "Entropy and the New Monuments," published in *Artforum* in 1966. Speaking of his compatriot minimalist and conceptualist artists, Smithson writes:

> Some artists see an infinite number of movies. [Peter] Hutchinson, for instance, instead of going to the country to study nature, will go to see a movie on 42nd Street, like "Horror at Party Beach" two or three times and contemplate it for weeks on end. The movies give a ritual pattern to the lives of many artists, and this induces a kind of "low budget" mysticism, which keeps them in a perpetual trance. The "blood and guts" of horror movies provides for their "organic needs," while the "cold steel" of Sci-fic movies provides for their "inorganic needs." Serious movies are too heavy on "values," and so are dismissed by the more perceptive artists.[13]

Tongue in cheek as this passage may be, Smithson's claim that a "'low budget' mysticism," a kind of kitsch spirituality spurred by horror and sci-fi flicks, lurks behind the innovations in the visual arts of the late 1960s and early 1970s, opens on to the literary terrain that I aim to explore. If the "cold steel" sensibilities of B-grade sci-fi movies in the 1960s migrate into the cryospheres and lattice structures of midcentury sculpture, what do they do to the poetry and poetics of the period? When exactly did these cross-fertilizing impulses between science fiction, the visual arts, and poetry begin? And how did they change and evolve?

While answering these questions in any systematic manner is not the primary purpose of this book, I will at points return to them in what follows. Before going any further, however, we need to look at the most recent state of the critical conversations around the discussion of the "poetics" of sci-fi. I reiterate here that this latter is not the subject of the present study: in fact, it is its diametrical opposite. I am not searching for the poetics in science fiction but for the science fiction in poetics. I therefore deal below with the two critics most immediately relevant to my topic—Darko Suvin and Seo-Young Chu, both of whom explicitly treat the question of poetry and sci-fi—and then later with Istvan Csicsery-Ronay Jr., whose *The Seven Beauties of Science Fiction* I make use of throughout for a somewhat different reason.[14]

DARKO AT THE BREAK OF NOON

Suvin's definition in 1979 of science fiction as "the literature of cognitive estrangement" in his landmark *Metamorphoses of Science Fiction* initiated a half century of ongoing critical discussion. It has been challenged, revised, torqued, and twisted, but this only attests to its flexibility and the fact that there is something fundamentally right about it: as general and loose as the description may be, surely science fiction, of all genres, *estranges*, and surely by doing so it makes one "think."[15] The fact that other genres do some version of the same does not detract from the basic truth of the definition, although it might be conceded that sci-fi, with its weird planets and exotic extraterrestrials, employs a kind of *enhanced* estrangement. I do not want to wade into the arguments, pro or con, about the issue, and anyway, the definition so nicely fits the tenor of the present book that I will make partisan use of it. Suvin buttons together modernist poetics and science fiction by deriving his notion of cognitive estrangement from Viktor Shklovsky's Russian formalist trope of *ostranenie*, often translated into English as "defamiliarization." According to Shklovsky, estrangement is a tool of art in the service of liberating perception from automatism and hence of "making the stone stony" in order to "lead us to a knowledge of a thing through the organ of sight instead of recognition": in essence, art that is estranged gives the reader or viewer a new pair of eyes by rendering its objects unfamiliar and hence palpable.[16] By employing the tool of estrangement in constructing its fantastic worlds, sci-fi de-automatizes perception, making the "real," present world visible once again.[17] (Note here that "estrangement" and "automatization" fit the rubric of the robot, which is nothing if not an estranged automaton: a robot is an uncanny conflation of the two halves of the formalist figure, one whose automatization *produces* its estrangement.)

In his book, Suvin goes about applying formalist poetics of *ostranenie* to science fiction—a genre that he counterintuitively traces back to Hellenic Greece (the bulk of his discussion ranges from the early sixteenth century to the late nineteenth century and includes writers like Jonathan Swift and Percy Bysshe Shelley)—but he nowhere treats poetic form or poetry as such.[18] He focuses entirely on the poetics of science fiction, not at all on the science fiction behind poetics. But the idea that one should turn to the formalists of the early twentieth century in order to find a critical hook into the literature of earlier times suggests something anachronistic about Suvin's formulation. For one thing, the concept of *ostranenie* only rounds into view during the early modernist period of the late 1910s, and this should come as no surprise. The Russian formalist critics were closely affiliated with the Russian futurist poets, avant-gardists whose work explicitly set out to be cognitively estranging and who wrote their own brand of science fiction (see for instance Velimir Khlebnikov's "The Trumpet of the Martians" from 1916). The question poses itself: Did formalism, arguably the first fully modern literary critical practice, derive its methodological principles from science fiction?

Suvin ends his book with short chapters on H. G. Wells, Russian sci-fi, and Karel Capek, the inventor of the term *robot*. This is precisely where my book begins, at what Suvin calls "*the threshold of contemporary Sci-fi, which can be said to arise between the World Wars, after the October Revolution and before the atomic bomb, with the modern 'mass culture' of movies, radio, and specialized magazines and paperback book lines for commercial literary 'genres'—one of the most prominent of which Sci-fi has become.*"[19] Suvin declares Wells the "turning point of the Sci-fi tradition": the author of *The War of the Worlds* is the wellspring, so to speak, of a move into the "paraliterary" age described above, during which science fiction underwent a sea change in the general muddling of elite and popular forms and genres under the pressures of full-blown mechanical reproduction. This is the arid Martian seabed that I intend to terraform in the present study. Suvin is at once dismissive of what he calls "the compost heap of . . . juvenile or popular subliterature" while exhorting critics to study it; this along with other "popular, 'low,' or plebeian" paraliterature make of modern science fiction something altogether different from earlier instantiations of the genre.[20] The idea of rummaging through this cultural mulch recalls the foragings of Benjamin's surrealists for totems of kitsch in the rich middens of Paris's arcades and flea markets of the 1920s: after all, what is surrealist strange-making in the service of desublimation but a version of science fiction projected beneath the lunar surface of the psyche?

Suvin thus serviceably weds science fiction and modernist poetics, providing a basic definition of the poetics of sci-fi by using an enhanced version of Shklovsky's *ostranenie* to describe the genre's fundamental formal armature *as it appears in narrative*: as Suvin puts it, in science fiction "the cognitive nucleus of the plot codetermines the fictional estrangement itself."[21] In what follows, I instead explore the mutually reciprocal relations between cognitive estrangement and poetics as they play out in sci-fi poetry and poetic form by reformulating Suvin's statement: *the cognitive nucleus of sci-fi poetics codetermines the poetic estrangement itself.* Again, instead of the poetics of science fiction, I seek the science fiction in poetics: at the center of Suvin's cognitive nucleus is poetic estrangement, which produces sci-fi; at the center of my cognitive nucleus is science fiction, which produces poetic estrangement.

SEO-YOUNG CHU'S LYRICAL SCI-FI

Seo-Young Chu writes a sort of mirror image of my book; building on Suvin, she argues that what makes science fiction cognitively estranging is its use of the tropes of lyric poetry, which sci-fi literalizes and incorporates into the very textures of its prose narrative:

> For example, *apostrophe*—a lyric trope whereby a speaker addresses an absent or inanimate person as though the "you" were alive and attendant—is routinely literalized in Sci-fi as *telepathy*, whereby a speaker addresses an absent person who is actually alive, mentally present, and capable of listening to the speaker without the aid of telephones or even ears. *Synesthesia*—the poetic description of one kind of sensory experience via words that ordinarily describe another—is routinely literalized in Sci-fi as a *paranormal sensorium*, for example, the mutant anemone who hears photons as music in J. G. Ballard's 1962 story "The Voices of Time." *Personification*—a lyric figure whereby an abstraction or inanimate object is characterized as if endowed with human attributes—is routinely literalized in Sci-fi as the *animation of a humanoid artifact.*[22]

The whole of science fiction is a literalization of *catachresis*; hence "every science-fiction world is a metaphysical conceit literalized as ontological fact within a narrative universe": reading science fiction is like reading John Donne *literally.* Only "poetic" language, with all of its poetic license, can achieve the estrangement necessary for describing sci-fi's "elusive referents" and unrepresentable representations:

> As I hope to demonstrate, only a narrative form thoroughly powered by lyricism possesses enough torque—enough twisting force, enough *verse* (from "vertere," Latin for "to turn")—to convert an elusive referent into an object available for representation. Only a form in which poetic *tropes* (from "tropos," Greek for "turn") are systematically turned into narrative literalities can accommodate referents ordinarily averse to representation. By literalizing poetic figures, science fiction transcends the literal/figurative dichotomy. In transcending the literal/figurative dichotomy, science fiction provides a representational home for referents that are themselves neither purely literal nor purely figurative in nature.[23]

Chu classifies science fiction as "lyric mimesis": sci-fi imitates the tropes of lyric poetry by extrapolating them from poetic registers and projecting them into the narrative modes of fiction.

I rewrite Chu's passage above, reversing its key terms:

> As I hope to demonstrate, only a poetic form thoroughly powered by science fiction possesses enough torque—enough twisting force, enough verse (from "vertere," Latin for "to turn")—to convert an elusive referent into an object available for representation. Only writing in which science fiction tropes (from "tropos," Greek for "turn") are systematically turned into poetic forms can accommodate referents ordinarily averse to representation. By formalizing science fiction literalities, sci-fi poetics transcends the literal/figurative dichotomy. In transcending the literal/figurative dichotomy, sci-fi poetics provides a representational home for referents that are themselves neither purely literal nor purely figurative in nature.[24]

As I note earlier, Chu mentions "the virtual non-existence of science fiction poetry," and she seeks to make good on her claim by listing some twenty-six major critical works on sci-fi, in the indexes of which the terms "'lyric,' 'poem,' 'poetry,' and 'verse' are nowhere to be found" (one of these works is Suvin's *Metamorphoses*). Wikipedia's entry for "science fiction" does not mention poetry at all, and most literary reference books typically characterize the genre as a branch of prose fiction.[25] Poetry is thus either utterly absent from sci-fi, or it is literally hiding in plain sight, in the rhetorical armatures of the writing itself: "Lyric qualities are so prevalent in science fiction, so thoroughly characteristic of Sci-fi, that their collective presence need not take the physical form of verse to make itself felt to the reader of Sci-fi narratives."[26] In other words, according to Chu, the tropes of lyric poetry appear in science fiction, but the tropes of science fiction do not appear in lyric poetry. Why not?

Chu claims that, aside from the "absent omnipresence" of lyric tropes in science fiction prose and hence the lack of a real need for sci-fi poetry,[27] there are two other reasons for the nonexistence of science fiction poetry: people who study poetry tend not to "overlap" with those who study fiction, and poetry is generally considered a "high" art and science fiction a "low" one. But I would like to propose another reason: to wit, *lyric poetry cannot bear the burden of the science fiction project.* It is easy enough to see how the tropes of lyric poetry might migrate into narrative registers in fiction; we are talking about rhetorical and stylistic issues here. Chu makes a reasonable argument for cognitive estrangement torqued by the extravagances of poetic language.[28] But think of it the other way around: How exactly might the tropes of sci-fi migrate into lyric poetry? Science fiction is neither a mode of address nor a style of rhetoric; it is a more or less loose set of narrative conventions: plots, settings, objects, aliens. If you project a set of narrative conventions into a lyric poem, you get lineated fiction, which is what 99 percent of what is known as science fiction poetry consists of, and one reason why it is so unsatisfying: the estrangement does not go deep enough. Line breaks do not a poem make. Something *structural* needs to occur; the spaceship must somehow *appear* in the poetic texture; the alienness needs to be palpable in the writing itself. Otherwise, what is the point of writing sci-fi into a poem?

But I submit that there is another problem, specifically with lyric poetry, and especially with *traditional* lyric poetry: Chu remains blind to or stays silent on the innovations that poetry has undergone over the past century or so, particularly in its relations to the lyric subject, that ghost in the machine whose main proscenium for the past several hundred years has been the monologic poem. Chu's privileging of conventional lyrical tropes and modes carries along with it the whole unwieldy apparatus of the Western self: the unitary, singular presence staged in its narrative arcs and patterns and sentiments, the creature of both romanticism and realism, each of which, I argue, sci-fi simultaneously absorbs and decenters.[29] Taken to its logical conclusions, science fiction is aggressively *non*realist: sci-fi is a thoroughgoing examination and deconstruction of realism, and hence by extension of narrative, and hence of the self that realist narrative interpolates.[30] Science fiction thus ultimately insists on postidentity formations: present at the theoretical beginning of the end of the subject and the appearance of the robot as the new systems-based organization of the human, sci-fi's proper home is the algorithmic world of distributed intelligence. Science fiction unseats or destabilizes the human "I" and replaces it with the digital electronics of the intelligent machine, which is not a self, but a system, and it is this insight—that the human being is what Lyn Hejinian calls a "zone"—that recalls poststructuralist versions of the self as well as the "I am an other" of modernism, and specifically of avant-garde groups like the futurists and the surrealists.[31] This is where sci-fi becomes a critical integer in the critique of realist narrative as the coherent plotting of a cohesive self through time and space, both of which are *warped* in science fiction. How can you have a "normal" human being wandering through warped space and time? The warping would presumably be comprehensive; the nonreal that sci-fi indexes reaches into the body and the mind just as it recasts the categories of time and space. Sci-fi is ultimately antilyrical and antinarrative, since its very target is the "normal," the quotidian, the human as depicted in realism and its house of mirrors. For science fiction to extend fully into writing, it would need to reconceptualize the "real" as it has traditionally been staged and construed altogether. Science fiction is a genre explicitly designed to interrogate the Western self—the rugged individual found in its most distilled form, in fact, in Westerns, out of which sci-fi partly evolved—by placing that self into nonrealist environments and watching it deform. Science fiction poetry cannot be "lyrical" because the singer is gone, the subject warped, alienated, and finally dissolved by the strange and estranging forces around it. A human is a robot that screams.

And what it screams at, more often than not, is an alien: the inexplicable other, whose subjectivity—if it even has one—is so different, so unhuman, that it can only be experienced as an existential threat. The sci-fi alien is a legacy of romanticism, with its exotic peasants, Indians, islanders, idiot boys, and other others. If you project the trappings of romanticism—the voyage, the encounter with the native, the frontier—into outer space, you get the settings of science fiction. The romantic encounter with the other typically causes an initial shock to one's sense of self, but more often than not this shock leads to a recovery and a deepened sense of shared humanity: Romantic encounters with the other are a species of the sublime. But space aliens are not deep humans—they are not humans, at all—and so encounters with them play out in shades of terror as they rock the subject to its core. Science fiction oscillates between the robot and the alien as models for radically estranged subjectivity. Lyric poetry has no purchase on the songs—or even the sounds—that might emit from such creatures.[32]

Another book in the index of which the terms *lyric, poem, poetry,* and *verse* are nearly nowhere to be found is Csicsery-Ronay's *Seven Beauties.* A word search finds that in its nearly four hundred pages, *poetry* shows up twice (once in the bibliography); *poem* also shows up twice; and *verse* appears not at all. Some version of *lyric* (*lyricism, lyrical,* etc.) appears seven times, and *poetics* turns up twice in the main body of the text and several times in the notes and the bibliography, where it appears exclusively in the titles of other books. This is also clearly not a study that involves science fiction poetry. It is, however, a fascinating and comprehensive look at science fiction as "a particular, recognizable mode of thought and art,"[33] and Suvin's term *estrangement* appears some twenty-five times in the body text and eight times in the notes. Csicsery-Ronay explores Suvin's poetics of the genre under seven rubrics: in what follows, I maintain this scheme while selectively revising it to fit my topic of science fiction poetry and poetics. I deal with Csicsery-Ronay's "beauties" as they crop up in the parallel titles of my chapters.

A CRYSTAL THEORY OF SCI-FI POETICS

> The Russian Futurists looked at the skies through the telescope of science fiction.
>
> —Anna Lawton, *Russian Futurism through Its Manifestos*

At this point, I need to describe my own Rube Goldberg theoretical apparatus, modeled on a mix of Jakobson's formalism, Benjamin's theory of the dialectical image, and Deleuze and Guattari on the rhizome. The first extends into space, the second into time, and the third collapses these categorical dimensions into what I call the sci-fi mess.

Sci-fi Space: Roman Jakobson's Galaxes

Science fiction takes place in three narrative spaces, set along three cardinal directions: up, into outer space; down, toward the center of the Earth; and sideways, along the world's circumference, toward lost continents and hidden islands. It is no coincidence that these three spatial vectors also define the structure of Dante's *Divine Comedy*: Paradiso, Inferno, and Purgatorio; and behind that the Christian cosmos of heaven, hell, and Earth. They also map onto the axes of Roman Jakobson's linguistic model, based on his studies of aphasia and comprised of a vertical, metaphorical, spatial axis and a horizontal, metonymical, temporal axis. According to Jakobson, the poetic function of language projects the vertical axis, based on substitution and equivalence, into the horizontal axis, based on contiguity and combination. One way to understand science fiction is to see it as science *projected* or *extended* into fiction: that is, in order to make science fiction, you take the concepts and "equivalencies," the conceptual objects and equations, of science and use them in building and constructing narrative; you introduce the facts and theories of science into the continuous series of plot, where they act as the gears and levers behind the temporal unfolding of a story. This is another way to think of the "poetics" of science fiction: not as lyrical tropes and figures projected into fiction in order to make it strange but as scientific tropes and figures projected into fiction in order to make it "science."[34]

For a sci-fi poetics, however, this gets more complicated. In this case, it is not science, but *science fiction*, that is projected from the vertical axis into the horizontal axis. In other words, for such a poetics, science fiction has become its own object; as a freestanding literary modality, it has little or nothing to do with science per se. Sci-fi is comprised of a specific set of literary tropes and themes, narratives and scenarios, modes and styles. (At this point, we can even speak of *science fiction fiction*: that is, fiction that is generated according to the precepts and conventions of the literary genre and hence no longer in the service of exploring or interrogating science as such.) In other words, artists like Smithson and poets like Coolidge are not interested in *science* as a model for their art; they are interested in *science fiction* as a model for their art—that is, they are interested in sci-fi "as theme, as underlying world view, and as a model for poetics." Smithson's fellow conceptualists were not studying science textbooks, they were watching B-grade sci-fic flicks; and Coolidge was reading *Astounding Science Fiction Magazine* from 1948.[35]

Along with Shklovsky's *ostranenie*, Jakobson's formalism is, properly speaking, a science fiction poetics: that is, if I extend futurist science fiction into theoretical linguistics, I get something like Russian formalism.[36] In other words, project the metaphorical axis of sci-fi into the metonymical axis of litcrit, and you get a poetics based on sci-fi tropes like estrangement, defamiliarization, automatization, dissociation, projection, alienation, neologism, and the "realization of verbal constructions in abrogations of boundaries between real and figurative language," as Jakobson puts it.[37] This is (formalist) poetics looked at through the telescope of (futurist) science fiction.[38] Jakobson after all was close with Khlebnikov, who he met in 1913 ("The Trumpet of the Martians" appeared in 1916), and in 1914, he tried his hand at sci-fi poetry himself:

> In the electro your costumechik's electric
> So silhouettic in fact now eyes there curls dream bra
> Bold hand partner screen quickflicking each stroke
> So jealous jocks grab fidgetty ball love each trick.[39]

Here the *ostranenie* reaches into the poem's very words, which move close to the neologic beyondsense of *zaum*: in order to conflate the robotic "costumechik" with its masturbatory electronics, language itself warps and twists. This is science fiction driven into the syntagmatic chain, the dynamics of outer space extended into grammar and semantics. Not only has the romantic subject been crimped into a cubo-futurist portrait, but the lyrics it utters are themselves fragmented and bent. In a letter from 1913 to futurist Aleksi Kruchenykh, Jakobson mentions the latter's science fiction opera *Victory over the Sun*, with its sci-fi "f-ray," as a key battle in the modernist war against romanticism: "You know, poetry up to now was a stained-glass window (Glasbilder), and like the sun's rays passing through the panes, romantic demonism imparted picturesqueness to it. But here's victory over the sun and the f-ray (from your own works). The glass is blown up, from the fragments . . . we created designs for the sake of liberation."[40]

Sci-fi Time: Walter Benjamin's Arcadean Dialectics

> The smallest act of political reflection makes for an epoch in the antiques business. We construct here an alarm clock that rouses the kitsch of the previous century to "assembly."
>
> —Walter Benjamin, *The Arcades Project*

Another messianic futurist who blew up windows and used their fragments to create designs for liberation was Walter Benjamin, whose *Arcades Project* is explicitly conceived as a literary montage comprised of thousands of fragments of quoted text mixed in with commentary written by Benjamin himself.[41] The book is an extended study of the commercial arcades of nineteenth-century Paris and the role they played in the culture of commodity fetishism. Long past their heyday—diminished, degraded, shabby, déclassé, and awaiting demolition—the arcades had by the late 1920s fallen on hard times, and their melancholy junk shop atmosphere became an occasion for Benjamin to meditate on the dynamics of fashion, urban *flanerie*, surrealism, decadence, boredom, prostitution, and kitsch, all driven through his theory of the dialectical image and its literary corollary, allegory. What fascinated Benjamin about the arcades was, first, the arbitrary and random arrangements in which commercial wares and shoddy businesses were collected and organized there—the arcades were themselves collages that invited allegorical readings—and second, the fact that, in the arcades, one encountered what he calls dialectical images, which for Benjamin were outmoded, obsolete, and even antique objects that had gone out of fashion but hearkened back to earlier capitalist formations, and notably to the childhood of the onlooker, who upon recognizing them came to realize his or her nature as a malleable creature of market forces.[42] Dialectical images are dream fetishes that "explode" into the present bearing traces of the past; they make us aware of ourselves as products of material history and hence as historical beings.[43] The kitsch of former times, assembled and constellated in the arcades, acted as an alarm clock for rousing Benjamin's contemporaries from the somnambulist dream of the nineteenth century. The surrealists were archaeologists of this arcadean kitsch, which they understood to stimulate the unconscious and produce their famous waking dream states.[44] Benjamin saw the arcades as the panoramic unconscious of society itself.[45] Peregrinating through them was to look into a phantasmagorical and ambiguous house of mirrors.[46]

If Jakobson provides the spatial axes of science fiction, Benjamin gives us its temporal coordinates. Sci-fi is its own arcade of dialectical images conceived in the past that "explode" into the present, but the mirror arrives ostensibly from the future: the explosion produces a *doubled* dialectical image, a mirror reflected in a mirror. What appears when we peer into science fiction? According to Benjamin, "precisely the modern, *la modernité,* is always citing primal history. Here, this occurs through the ambiguity peculiar to the social relations and products of this epoch. Ambiguity is the appearance of dialectic in images, the law of dialectics at a standstill. This standstill is utopia and the dialectical image, therefore, dream image. Such an image is afforded by the commodity per se: as fetish. Such an image is presented by the arcades."[47] The ambiguity of the dialectical image lies in the uncanny temporal displacement at its core, the very displacement of dream.[48] In it, we watch the past crash into the present, but in science fiction, this past is troped as what is yet to come: the phantasmagoria of former days are the trappings of the future in science fiction, which becomes an antique store with the face of an alarm clock that in each minute rings for sixty seconds.[49]

Hence the urgency for novelty in sci-fi and the accelerated tempo of its obsolescing: science fiction demands ongoing innovation while going out of fashion at the speed of light. Sci-fi is a weird motley of "immemorial antiquity parading as up-to-date novelty [that] turns out to be the phantasmagoria of history itself"[50]: "Newness . . . is the origin of the semblance that belongs inalienably to images produced by the collective unconscious. It is the quintessence of that false consciousness whose indefatigable agent is fashion. This semblance of the new is reflected, like one mirror in another, in the semblance of the ever recurrent. The product of this reflection is the phantasmagoria of 'cultural history,' in which the bourgeoisie enjoys its false consciousness to the full."[51] If sci-fi is the dream kitsch of the future, then reading a sci-fi anthology is like strolling through an arcade with Louis Aragon.[52] The temporal disjuncture specific to the genre jars readers into experiencing a singularly unsettling vision: *When* is science fiction? Ahead of us, still to come? Now, in the present? Behind us, long ago? Like Paul Klee's *Angelus Novus,* which Benjamin called the angel of history, sci-fi flies with its back to the future, its face turned to the catastrophes of the past.[53] This is what Jameson means by sci-fi's essentially epistemological function, torqued by Suvin's *ostranenie*: science fiction liberates us from automatism by giving us a cognitively estranging experience of time.

And experience and its relationship to science fiction are explicitly the issues in "Experience and Poverty," Benjamin's 1933 essay in which he addresses a crisis in postwar consciousness: "Experience has fallen in value, amid a generation which from 1914 to 1918 had to experience some of the most monstrous events in the history of the world."[54] Modern life is marked by a "poverty of human experience in general," but the good news is that this condition has given rise to "a new, positive concept of barbarism. For what does poverty of experience do for the barbarian? It forces him to start from scratch; to make a new start; to make a little go a long way; to begin with a little and build up further, looking neither left nor right. Among the great creative spirits, there have always been the inexorable ones who begin by clearing a tabula rasa. They need a drawing table; they were constructors."[55] Modernist barbarian constructors include great creative spirits like Albert Einstein and artists like the cubists and Paul Klee, whose

> figures too seem to have been designed on the drawing board, and even in their general expression they obey the laws of their interior. Their interior, rather than their inwardness; and this is what makes them barbaric. A complex artist like the painter Paul Klee and a programmatic one like [Adolf] Loos—both reject the traditional, solemn, noble image of man, festooned with all the sacrificial offerings of the past. They turn instead to the naked man of the contemporary world who lies screaming like a newborn babe in the dirty diapers of the present. No one has greeted this present with greater joy and hilarity than Paul Scheerbart.[56]

Scheerbart was the visionary author of *Lesabéndio: Ein Asteroïden-Roman*, one of the first works of modern German science fiction (1913) and a text, Benjamin suggests, in the vanguard of the new sensibility. Benjamin first read the book in 1917. His call in "Experience and Poverty" for a constructivist, posthuman barbarian who has a constructed *interior* rather than a humanist *inwardness* is answered in spades by Scheerbart's asteroidal novel: "Scheerbart is interested in inquiring how our telescopes, our airplanes, our rockets can transform human beings as they have been up to now into completely new, lovable, and interesting creatures. Moreover, these creatures talk in a completely new language. And what is crucial about this language is its arbitrary, constructed nature, in contrast to organic language. This is the distinctive feature of the language of Scheerbart's human beings, or rather 'people'; for human likeness—a principle of humanism—is something they reject."[57] The elastic, rubbery *people*—NOT "human beings"—of the asteroid Pallas use their single suction-cup foot to stick to the sides of cliffs while they stretch their bodies fifty meters into the air. Their mobile faces feature retractable telescopic eyes, as we see in Scheerbart's initial description of the novel's eponymous hero: "A great transformation took place as Lesabéndio's head rose into the air: the rubbery skin of his head began to unfurl like an umbrella. Then it slowly shut itself up again, hiding his face, and his scalp began to turn into a pipe, open at the front. His face appeared on its back-surface, from which two long telescopic eyes protruded, eyes which Lesabéndio could use to effortlessly gaze at the green stars, just as if he were near them."[58]

If this sounds like a surrealist portrait—complete with Magritte's umbrellas and pipes—of Benjamin gazing at the constellations of the nineteenth century through the telescopic mirror lenses of the arcades, there is some reason to consider it so.[59] In a 1935 letter to Werner Kraft, in which he "uses metaphors from *Lesabéndio* to characterize his current work on the arcades project," we can see the complicated temporal dynamics that characterize the sci-fi dialectical image for him: "I am busy pointing my telescope through the bloody mist at a mirage of the nineteenth century that I am attempting to reproduce based on the characteristics it will manifest in a future state of the world, liberated from magic."[60] Using the futurist telescope of a sci-fi text written twenty years earlier in order to reflect back on the nineteenth-century past in the service of liberating a utopian future, this is Benjamin gazing at the arcades through the dialectical telescope of science fiction, in the process constructing a complicated geometry of sci-fi reading as a deliberate mirroring back and forth through time.

It is precisely the idea—or the *image*—of "a future state of the world, liberated from magic," that Benjamin discovers in Scheerbart's *Lesabéndio*: "This idea—or rather, this image—was of a humanity which had deployed the full range of its technology and put it to humane use. To achieve this state of affairs, Scheerbart believed that two conditions were essential: first, people should discard the base and primitive belief that their task was to 'exploit' the forces of nature; second, they should be true to the conviction that technology, by liberating human beings, would fraternally liberate the whole of creation."[61] The implications of the novel for Benjamin's political thinking are profound. *Lesabéndio* disenchants technology, which people tend to think of as magic designed to give human beings dominion over nature by granting them the means to exploit and commodify it. Instead, Scheerbart depicts the *transformational* effects of technology, the liberated and creative use of which will produce the new posthuman person, designed on the constructivist drawing-table to "reject the traditional, solemn, noble image of man, festooned with all the sacrificial offerings of the past."[62] This asteroidal being will integrate itself with nature in a technological symbiosis that will do away with the human subject, whose "inwardness" has always stood between it and the cosmos. Instead, the *interior* of such a creature shifts and changes according to the worlds that it encounters through its enhanced senses and sensibilities in the same way that the gravitational fields of Pallas warp when its inhabitants finish building the giant tower that permits them to pierce the mysterious cloud above them. At the end of the novel, Lesabéndio messianically launches himself into outer space from the tip of this tower and becomes a star in a system with other stars. Benjamin summarizes:

> Lesabéndio's tower is designed to connect the body of the asteroid with its head, which floats above it in the form of a luminous cloud. But the *restitutio in integrum* of Pallas can succeed only at a price: Lesabéndio must allow himself to be dissolved in the body of the asteroid. . . . The tower which grows higher day by day through the zeal of the Pallasians, will bring about changes in the stellar order. At the same time, the dissolution of its architect in the asteroid will begin to change the rhythm of this heavenly body. It will reach out to its brother stars. It will dream only of uniting with them, forming a link in the chain of asteroids which one day will encircle the sun.[63]

The futurist utopianism of the novel is leavened, Benjamin says, by the "freshness" and "transparency" of its style, which assists it "in shedding the dross of sentimentality" while nonetheless expressing a serious political sentiment.[64] *Lesabéndio* is thus a fully realized modern piece of science fiction, one in which the sci-fi impulse reaches into the very textures of its prose, where posthuman people talk in a new, artificial, arbitrarily constructed language. Somewhere between an estranged human being and an engineered one, the Pallasian is part alien and part robot, wrapped up in a sort of lovable extraterrestrial gummi bear. The book is the work, Benjamin says, of a "humorist . . . who seem[s] never to forget that the earth is a heavenly body."[65] This potent combination of humor and theology accords with Csicsery-Ronay's sense that sci-fi typically "construct[s] 'sentimental' myths that simultaneously satisfy readers' needs for complete world-pictures, and call[s] ironic attention to their ludic and constructed character." Through encounters with the work of Scheerbart, who greets the naked man of the modern world with greater hilarity than any of his fellow constructors, Benjamin's contemporaries learn to "adapt—beginning anew and with few resources. They rely on the men who have adopted the cause of the absolutely new and have founded it on insight and renunciation. In its buildings, pictures, and stories, mankind is preparing to outlive culture, if need be. And the main thing is that it does so with a laugh. This laughter may sound barbaric. Well and good."[66] There is something in the double-mirror dialectical image of science fiction that provokes the barbaric laughter that always signals the end of empire. Seeing ourselves reflected in the gelatinous, elongated cartoons in Scheerbart's house of mirrors, we come to know ourselves as pliable constructions capable of seemingly endless metamorphoses. *Lesabéndio* plays a *weak* messianic role in the origins of Benjamin's dialectical image: as with Jakobson's formalism, the dialectics of the *Arcades Project* are grounded in the estranging optics of science fiction.[67]

Mass and Mess: Deleuze and Guattari's Sci-fi Rhizometrics

The rubbery Lesabéndio is strange for another reason: he is perhaps the first entirely rhizometric character in science fiction, if not in literature altogether. His astonishing transformation at the end of the novel from an ambitious Gumby into a celestial body without organs able to communicate telepathically with stars, comets, asteroids, planets, and the sun, calls upon every resource in Scheerbart's literary lab for inventing the completely new language of his book. It is a language, the author tells us, that consists entirely of "different pressures."[68] After Lesabéndio launches himself, "like a long brown beam, straight into the heaving sea of the glowing yellow snake-bodies" that appear in the cloud above Pallas, he is completely deterritorialized, feeling "that his entire body was decomposing, and—spreading out—spreading far out on all sides."[69] Like a cosmic potato, Lesabéndio begins sprouting fascicular roots that stretch into new senses and expanded sensitivities:

> It seemed to him as if tiny feelers were extending from every part of himself—tiny, extremely fine ones. They grew longer, longer, and even longer. The delicate tips of his feelers were becoming sensitive, and, he believed, they were feeling all around great fine and shivering glass basins. The tips of the feeler threads bonded with the glass basins, and, together, became enormous glass balls through which he could suddenly see everything in the solar system much better than he could previously.
>
> He looked again through the big glass balls, and found he could enlarge or shrink them at will. He could also give them other shapes, and pull them in toward himself or send them out far away. And he felt no obstacles or restraints *anywhere*.[70]

As he slowly expands, Lesabéndio begins rotating without volition and understands himself as a wheel within countless other asteroidal and planetary wheels. Intoxicated with his enhanced vision, he develops the ability to see into the interiors of stars, and then "something spoke near him—in a secretive sign language": he is told to look into the sun, and "as he did so, he felt as if the great Sun spoke directly to him. . . . After a while, Lesa heard a clear tone, and then the following messianic words: '*All of you, don't fear pain—and don't fear death either.*'"[71] Lesa becomes able to communicate directly with other stellar beings in "strange new tones" until he "sensed more and more that he no longer perceived or thought in the ways he had before the transformation. Gradually, the comet-system's striving became more and more forcefully entrenched within him."[72] After dissolving himself into the asteroid's body, he "had the sense that he was gradually turning into a star. The interests of the Pallasians no longer touched him. He also noticed that he was developing new organs again. Gradually, he was able to see by means of the atmosphere of his star—the atmosphere functioned on all sides for him like a colossal telescope." The novel ends in a scene of cosmic synthesis:

> He powerfully stretched out his entire body—and realized that his body was the entire torso-system of Pallas. . . .
> The asteroids greeted the double star that had awakened to new life with glittering electric lights.
> Lesa dreamed that he was completely free and could go wherever he
> wanted—now that he had the strength of a star. . . .
> And the green Sun radiated so much more brightly, all of a sudden, that it
> seemed as if there, too, new life was awakening.[73]

Lesabéndio effects a world-altering transformation of the planet and its inhabitants and beyond them of the galaxy itself, which eventually forms into concentric series of giant rings of meteors, asteroids, planets, stars, and peoples, all communicating, communing, and rotating with burning cosmic desire around the green sun.[74] Thus one model for what I call the sci-fi *mass*—the rhizomic, utopian, multiple, nomadic, interpenetrating, nonhierarchical, heterogeneous, inwardless, ultimately *musical* constellation of points of creative and liberating interconnection between beings, technologies, and the universe.[75]

A rhizome book, according to Deleuze and Guattari, is made of "plateaus," a word that designates "a continuous, self-vibrating region of intensities whose development avoids any orientation toward a culmination point or external end. . . . We call a 'plateau' any multiplicity connected to other multiplicities by superficial underground stems in such a way as to form or extend a rhizome."[76] "The fabric of the rhizome is the conjunction "and . . . and . . . and. . . ."["77] The last page of *Lesabéndio* as originally printed is comprised of a list of twelve sentences, each end-stopped, separated from one another and indented: a series of sentential plateaus. Six of them begin with "And" (German "Und"). Listen for the biblical cadences:

> Und es war ihm dann, als spräche er mit den Saturnringen und mit den Monden des Saturn—und da kam der Quikko und sagte: »Bleibe bei uns.«
> Und da kehrte Lesa zurück.
> Und er sah den ganzen Stern Ouikko—auch sein Inneres—das war so milde—als war's aus lauter streichelnden Händen zusammengesetzt.
> »Wir kommen immer weiter!« hörte Lesa leise aus dem Ouikko heraustönen.
> Doch donnernd rief die Sonne dazwischen:

»Wenn wir Schmerz und Tod nicht fürchten!«
Lesa hörte Beides.
Und er drehte sich ruhig weiter und empfand eine große Ruhe.
Und es kam ihm so vor, als ginge er leicht hinüber in ein neues Reich, in dem alles ganz sanft hin und her schwankte—wie flüsternde Manesiranken—unten am großen Turm.
»Mit Allen zusammen!« sagte Lesa ganz still.
Und die grüne Sonne strahlte so hell auf—als wäre auch auf ihr ein neues Leben erwacht.[78]

(And it was then as if he were speaking with Saturn's rings and with the moons of Saturn—and Quikko came and said:
"Remain with us."
And Lesa turned back.
And he saw all of the star Quikko—including its interior—which was so calm—as if it were composed of caressing hands.
"Forever onward!" Lesa heard Quikko quietly intone.
And at the same time the Sun thundered:
"As long as we fear neither pain nor death!"
Lesa heard them both.
And he rotated quietly and discovered a great peace.
And it seemed to him that he went lightly over into a new realm, in which everything swayed gently back and forth—like Manesi's fronds—on the great tower below.
"One and all together!" said Lesa, quietly.
And the green sun flared and shone brightly—as if a new life were beginning for it too.)[79]

Hence a rhizometric prosody echoing both Genesis and Revelation, lifted in a plateaunic paean to the new life of the cosmos: but this science fiction universe is decidedly secular, motivated and mobilized by human technology in the service of profane illumination and communion with the material world. Lesabéndio is a *people* messiah, neither god nor son of god, but literally an *astro-naut*: a star sailor.

Mess

The rhizome includes the best and the worst: potato and couchgrass, or the weed.

—Deleuze and Guattari, *Thousand Plateaus*

There is another facet or face of the rhizome that makes of it a useful model for science fiction: the rhizome can be used to conceptualize the sci-fi *mess*, the opposite of the mass. The mess as I define it is the condition of collapse, of systems failure, where "the world has lost its pivot. . . . The world has become chaos": rank crabgrass over nutritious potato, the disintegration of time and space, cataclysm and *dis-aster* (the end of stars).[80] The Blob is the worst rhizome, seeping and absorptive, an organ without a body, a monstrous version of the swelling Lesabéndio. Its formal opposite is the crystal, as in the entropic heat-death freezing of the universe into glassy shards. Science fiction has a genius for imagining holocaust and ruin, "quantum entanglement," often on a cosmic level, as in the film *The Cloverfield Paradox*: "That accelerator is 1000 times more powerful than any ever built. Every time they test it, they risk ripping open the membrane of space-time, smashing together multiple dimensions, shattering reality, and not just on that station—everywhere. This experiment could unleash chaos, the likes of which we have never seen. Monsters, demons, beasts from the sea . . . And not just here and now . . . In the past. In the future. In other dimensions."[81] After all, Deleuze and Guattari's "acentered systems, finite networks of automata in which communication runs from any neighbor to any other, the stems or channels do not preexist, and all individuals are interchangeable" could just as easily describe the Borg as the decentered 1970s vegetable utopia of "underground stems and aerial roots, adventitious growths and rhizomes. Amsterdam, a city entirely without roots, a rhizome-city with its stem-canals."[82] The sci-fi rhizome can either effloresce into symphonies of cosmic connection or collapse into the roaring mulch of undifferentiated reality.

Csicsery-Ronay's sixth science fiction beauty, the "science-fictional grotesque," elaborates this latter condition quite well: the science-fictional grotesque "represents the collapse of ontological categories that reason has considered essentially distinct, creating a spectacle of impossible fusions. This is the domain of monstrous aliens, interstitial beings, and anomalous physical phenomena. . . . The grotesque is implosive, accompanied by fascination and horror at the prospect of intimate category-violating phenomena discovered by human science."[83] The spatial axes of science fiction and its dialectically mirroring temporal coordinates warp and fuse in the mess; the universe shudders off its foundations, its inhabitants congeal and smear. What are the poetics of the mess? What strophes nail catastrophe? In "Entropy and the New Monuments," Smithson writes of some artists' "hyper-opulence":

> [Paul] Thek's sadistic geometry is made out of simulated hunks of torn flesh. Bloody meat in the shape of a birthday cake is contained under a pyramidal chrome framework—it has stainless steel candles in it. Tubes for drinking "blood cocktails" are inserted into some of his painful objects. Thek achieves a putrid finesse, not unlike that disclosed in William S. Burroughs' *Nova Express*. . . . Something of the primal nightmare ex-

> ists in both Thek and [Craig] Kauffman. The slippery bubbling ooze from the movie "The Blob" creeps into one's mind. Both Thek and Kauffman have arrested the movement of blob-type matter. The mirrored reflections in [Larry] Bell's work are contaminations of a more elusive order. His chrome-plated lattices contain a Pythagorean chaos. Reflections reflect reflections in an excessive but pristine manner.[84]

Here again we see the science fiction poetics behind midcentury avant-garde art, inflected through Burroughs's sci-fi surrealism and the goo of the Blob, an extraterrestrial that drops to the Earth from outer space. Smithson's cover word for the mess is "entropy" or "energy drain": "In a rather roundabout way, many of the artists have provided a visible analog for the Second Law of Thermodynamics, which extrapolates the range of entropy by telling us energy is more easily lost than obtained, and that in the ultimate future the whole universe will burn out and be transformed into an all-encompassing sameness."[85] The "visible analogs" of this entropic condition are either Thek's and Kauffman's ooze and hunks or "contaminations of a more elusive order": the crystalline lattices of Bell and Sol Lewitt, and Donald Judd's "crystallographic boxes [which] come in a variety of surfaces from Saturnian orchid-plus to wrinkled-textured blurs and greens—alchemy from the year 2000."[86] It is important to note that Smithson's notion of entropy is highly literary, derived as much from sci-fi novels like Damon Knight's *Beyond the Barrier* and *The Reefs of Space* by Frederik Pohl and Jack Williamson as they are from P. W. Bridgman's *The Nature of Thermodynamics*. Blob and crystal, grid and puddle, bubble and rock, angle and opulence—the sci-fi universe dichotomizes into a negative dialectic that constantly threatens to sublate into a spectacle of impossible fusions.

When does science become science fiction? And when does science fiction become science fiction poetics? The key for a visual artist like Smithson is the word *analog*: if I take the science of crystal entropy as derived from the Second Law of Thermodynamics and project it into fictional narrative, I get a sci-fi novel like J. G. Ballard's *The Crystal World*, in which the universe slowly crystallizes as entropy increases. If I take Ballard's fictional conceit and apply it to non-narrative art such as Thek's "sadistic geometry" or Bell's "Pythagorean chaos"—if I *formalize* science fiction as "visible analog" in the chunks and grids of postmodern sculpture—I get a sci-fi poetics, something like Csicsery-Ronay's "mode of thought and art," although closer to what he characterizes as a "set of rules and devices."[87] Furthermore, if I use a science-fictional conceit like the "dim lattice of crystals, growing more shadowy and insubstantial as it swelled [into] a vast three-dimensional array" in Knight's novel or the long parallel lines of "monuments" in John Taine's "The Time Stream" as analogies to modern American suburbia, I get something like sci-fi critical theory.[88] For

Smithson, science becomes science fiction when we analogically apply entropy to sociology:

> The slurbs, urban sprawl, and the infinite number of housing developments of the postwar boom have contributed to the architecture of entropy. Judd, in a review of the show by Roy Lichtenstein, speaks of "a lot of visible things" that are "bland and empty," such as "most modern commercial buildings, new Colonial stores, lobbies, most houses, most clothing, sheet aluminum, and plastic with leather texture, the formica like wood, the cute and modern patterns inside jets and drugstores." Near the super highways surrounding the city, we find the discount centers and cut-rate stores with their sterile facades. On the inside of such places are maze-like counters with piles of neatly stacked merchandise; rank on rank it goes into a consumer oblivion. The lugubrious complexity of these interiors has brought to art a new consciousness of the vapid and the dull.[89]

The historical migration of fetish commerce from modern arcade to postmodern facade is not difficult to trace; like Benjamin, a postwar sci-fi artist/critic like "Peter Hutchinson, author of 'Is There Life on Earth?' (*Art in America*, Fall 1966), uses the discards of last year's future in order to define today's present."[90] The dialectical mirrors are firmly in place.

"Entropy and the New Monuments" concludes with Csicsery-Ronay's sense of sci-fi's parodic, satiric, and ludic endgame: science fiction for Smithson crystallizes finally into Benjamin's barbaric laughter:

> [Buckminster Fuller] was told by certain scientists that the fourth dimension was "ha-ha," in other words, that it is laughter. Perhaps it is. It is well to remember that the topsy-turvy world revealed by Lewis Carroll did spring from a well ordered mathematical mind. Martin Gardner in his "The Annotated Alice," notes that in the science-fiction story "Mimsy Were the Borogoves," the author Lewis Padgett presents the Jabberwocky as a secret language from the future, and that if rightly understood, it would explain a way of entering the fourth dimension. The highly ordered non-sense of Carroll, suggests that there might be a similar way to treat laughter. Laughter is in a sense a kind of entropic "verbalization."[91]

The laughter that sci-fi provokes *verbalizes entropy*: the cognitive estrangement of science fiction leads either to the assonance of the mass or the dissonance of the mess. Benjamin calls such laughter "shattered articulation," words themselves splintering into crystal shards under the epistemological stresses of astounding tales. The futurist *ostranenie* of the Jabberwocky's nonsense language can lead directly to the fourth dimension, the world of Lewis Padgett's distorted gadgets, where poems are objects for creating what Smithson calls "solid-state hilarity"[92]: the laughter that can bring down a universe.

The Science Fiction Crystal

Smithson ends his essay with a question—"How could artists translate this verbal entropy, that is 'ha-ha,' into 'solid models'?"—and a proposal: "The order and disorder of the fourth dimension could be set between laughter and crystal-structure, as a device for endless speculation. Let us now define the different types of Generalized Laughter, according to the six main crystal systems: the ordinary laugh is a cubic or square (Isometric), the chuckle is a triangle or pyramid (Tetragonal), the giggle is a hexagon or rhomboid (Hexagonal), the titter is prismatic (Orthorhombic), the snicker is oblique (Monoclinic), the guffaw is asymmetric (Triclinic)."[93] Transcoding crystallography and laughter, Smithson comes up with a "device for endless speculation": a generative poetics for the fourth dimension, a grammar of entropic verbalization founded firmly on science fiction. What such a poetics does for poetry is the question that this book explores.

Meanwhile, my own sci-fi poetics crystal is modeled on Smithson's isometric cube of the ordinary laugh (see figure 1). The vertical and horizontal axes forming the two-dimensional + at the center of the crystal represent Jakobson's metaphoric and metonymic poles—the armatures of the poetic function—as well as the spatial axes of the science fiction universe—up, outer space/down, inner earth/lateral, along the planet's surface. The third line, intersecting the first two at right angles and creating the third dimension of the crystal, represents the axis of Benjamin's temporal coordinates, along which past, present, and future are strung like beads or stars. Any work of science fiction can be plotted along these axes. The ensemble taken together constellates the sci-fi cosmos. The crystal itself is the laugh, a single shard of shattered articulation, the verbalized entropy that threatens the sci-fi space/time continuum constellated by the three axes. It is the gelotological blast that explodes the petrified image of sci-fi dialectics at a standstill and expels it violently from the continuum of history.[94]

STAR CHART

This book is comprised of six chapters loosely organized along the lines of Csicsery-Ronay's *Seven Beauties of Science Fiction*, which he calls "a map of suggestions, made necessarily from a great distance, of possible paths that are still open to travel."[95] I make use of his map to travel further onward and outward: my chapters parallel his, but the themes have been changed. His seven beauties are "*fictive neology, fictive novums, future history, imaginary science,*

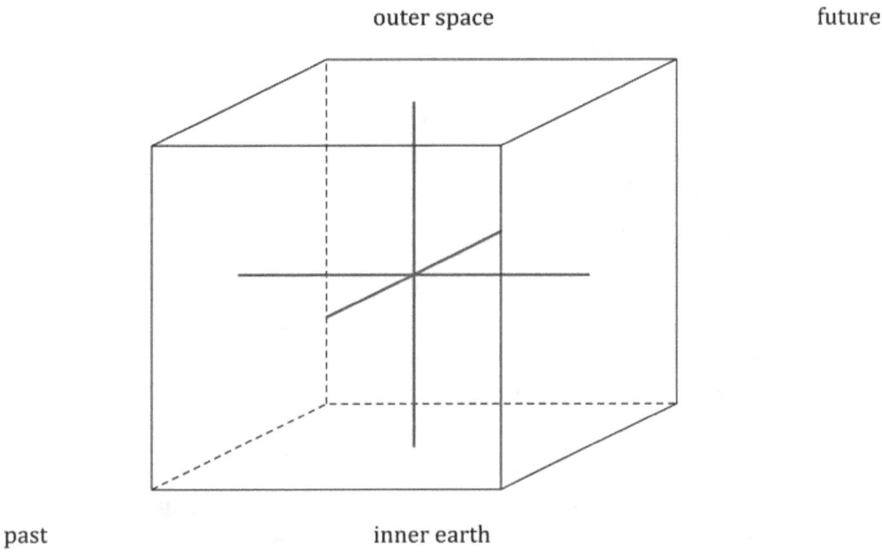

Figure 1. The sci-fi poetics crystal. Courtesy of the author.

the science-fictional sublime, the science-fictional grotesque, and the *Technologiade*."[96] My six beauties each include an object or topic and a corresponding critical or aesthetic mode (listed here next to their parallels in *Seven Beauties*):

Gadget	*Futurism*	*(Technologiade)*
Dream	*Surrealism*	*(The Sublime)*
New World	*Phenomenology*	*(The Novum)*
Mass: Mess	*Crystal: Rhizome*	*(Imaginary Science + The Grotesque)*
Diploetics/Aliennations	*First Encounter*	*(Future History)*
Language	*Translation*	*(Neology)*

Furthermore, every chapter has a snazzy sci-fi marquee title, which I list in the chapter descriptions below. Each focuses on one or more poets, who include Mina Loy, Edward Dorn, Clark Coolidge, Sun Ra, Evelyn Reilly, Sherwin Bitsui, Bruce Andrews, Amiri Baraka, and others. The treatment of each poet's work is framed by discussion of relevant novels, stories, films, scores, recordings, and critical texts—in short, the paraliterary galaxy around which science fiction poetry and poetics orbit. Since I deal primarily with works that have received scant, if any, critical attention, and that are not part of the high canon of science fiction, or might even in some cases not be classified as sci-fi at all, my book is not in any way an attempt at a comprehensive definition of the genre of sci-fi or of the subgenre of science fiction poetry and poetics. Like

Csicsery-Ronay's map of suggestions, it traces an inevitably idiosyncratic path through the ever-expanding and evolving universe of science fiction, charts of which become obsolete every time the coordinates of a new star are published. For that reason, in what follows I let the writers and the literature speak their own discoveries, categories, tropes, points of focus, and preoccupations. The possible paths are not only still open to travel, they continue to proliferate at an alarming rate.

I also insist on having fun in this book. I take seriously Csicsery-Ronay's sense that "sci-fi is the literature that takes thought-experiment as its given reality, which it then artistically and ludically exaggerates and estranges." Sci-fi is "a ludic framework, a wide-ranging culture of game and play."[97] I wish to play this game in the service of creating both pleasure and critical discourse. My poetics crystal is its own sci-fi ha-ha. Hence in what follows I take liberties: I go exploring, try to think experimentally, digress, take what I can use, light out for parts unknown, exaggerate and estrange and stretch things like the body of Lesabéndio, writing at the frontiers of what I do not know or know badly. The poets I treat do the same thing; to approach them with anything less than their own intrepid spirits of invention and discovery would be to render them a disservice. I do all I can to write a sci-fi criticism, one that actively uses the ludic tropes of science fiction to describe the poetics at play in science fiction poetry.

The chapters are roughly chronological and cover the last one hundred plus years, beginning with early twentieth-century pre–science fiction and ending with texts written in the past ten years. A through-line writer who appears in a number of places is Edgar Rice Burroughs, whose works I use to illustrate the cardinal directions of the sci-fi crystal. Burroughs wrote several series of novels that take place in fantastic lands in the three settings of science fiction: Barsoom (Mars); Pellucidar, in the hollow center of the Earth; and Caspak or Caprona, a lost continent near Antarctica. I treat passages regarding these settings in various parts of the book. I also use the demented science in his novel *Synthetic Men of Mars* in chapter 4 as a thematic parallel to the catastrophic burgeoning plastic and Styrofoam garbage of Evelyn Riley's *Styrofoam*, and in my discussion of Sun Ra in chapter 5, I salt passages from *The Gods of Mars* in which Burroughs describes the majestic Black race of Barsoom, whose kitschy pharaonic harness and noble mien I use as ironic mirrors to the Arkestra's spectacular outfits and Sun Ra's Afro Black stellar mythologies.

SPACECRAFT SCHEMATICS

Chapter 1 is titled "The Robot and the Egg" (*Gadget/Futurism: Technologiade*) and explores several key questions in the sci-fi repertoire: What is a thing? What is a self? When does a thing become a self? When does the self become a thing? Using texts by Filippo Marinetti, L. Frank Baum (*Ozma of Oz*), Viktor

Shklovsky, and Burroughs's *Chessmen of Mars*, I focus on issues of automaton and deautomatization, labor and kitsch, human consciousness and machine intelligence, and organicism and constructivism, in what are properly pre–science fiction works. The chapter then discusses Mina Loy, whose "Human Cylinders" (ca. 1915) I claim is the first properly science fiction poem written in English.

Chapter 2, "Inner Space" (*Dream/Surrealism: The Sublime*) moves from outer space (Mars) to the center of the Earth in Burroughs's *At the Earth's Core*, exploring the legacy of surrealism in science fiction poetics via André Breton's interest in Freud's interior worlds of the unconscious and dream. Picking up the subject of automatism from chapter 1, I examine automatic writing in Breton and Phillip Soupault's *Magnetic Fields* and then move on to questions of autonomy in cut up and fold over in William Burroughs's surrealist sci-fi epic *Nova Express*. I end with a short digression on the poet Ted Greenwald.

Chapter 3, "Riding the Tachyon Showers" (*New World/Phenomenology: The Novum*), explores the genetic evolution from cowboy to astronaut, both present in the figure of Ed Dorn's *Gunslinger*. It is here that the unified Western self (the character named I in *Gunslinger*) gets debased and distributed via structuralism and phenomenology in the generic move from the Western to science fiction. I warps in warped space, and narrative coherence, character, and temporality gyrate into the psychedelic and the surreal. Other texts include Edgar Rice Burroughs's *A Princess of Mars* and *The Phantom Empire*, the 1935 serial film that early on blended and bridged the classical Western and science fiction. This chapter also deals with sci-fi ecopoetics: the American West as it appears in these texts is a gigantic repository of precious metals, oil, and gas, and each of the works I deal with concerns the politics and trauma of resource extraction.

Chapter 4, "Spilling Time, the Poetics of Entropy" (*Mass : Mess/Crystal :Rhizome: Imaginary Science + The Grotesque*), conflates two of Csicsery-Ronay's beauties and is divided into three parts. The first part examines the trope of the crystal as both theme and formal model. The poet for this section is Clark Coolidge, whose decade-long writing of crystallography in the 1970s and into the early 1980s, along with his close sympathetic reading of the essays of Robert Smithson, culminated in *Smithsonian Depositions*, a hybrid text that illustrates many of the tenets of this present book, including Benjamin's arcadean time travel and the dialectical image, surrealism and collage, journeys to the Earth's core, and science fiction, from which Coolidge liberally quotes and which he sifts into his text as a dynamic part of its framing. Sci-fi is a primary sensibility for Coolidge. The experimental, investigative, and exploratory sides of his writing derive from it, but also the goofiness, the kitschiness, the otherworldly, the scientific, the galactic, the geological, and the alien all draw from sci-fi. This section also treats crystal entropy in J. G. Ballard's *The Crystal World* and other essays by Smithson. The second part examines the other side of entropy: the rhizomatic mess. The horrible billowing mash of human tissues, limbs, hair, and organs that threatens to take over the entire planet of Barsoom and then the universe itself in E. R. Burroughs's *Synthetic Men of Mars* (talk about a blob!) is cited throughout. The discussion then focuses on Evelyn Reilly's *Styrofoam*, a book-length series of poems that concern themselves with the proliferation of Styrofoam and other plastics in our present period of ecological crisis (and cites both *The Blob* and *The Thing*). The chapter ends with Bruce Andrews's *Lip Service*, a kind of profane comedy modeled after the crystal sphere geometries of Dante's *Paradiso*. Andrews's poem synthesizes the poetics of rhizome and crystal to produce a dialectical model of language frozen in the condition of entropy.

Chapter 5, "The Diploetics of AlienNations" (*Diploetics/Aliennations/First Encounter: Future History*), is divided into four sections: "Do Robots Scream in Electric Sleep?," "Ra-mañana: Afrofuturist Psalms and Parables from the Cosmo Sphere," "Feedback, Kalooka Kaleeka, Harmolodics," and "Athabascan Sci-fi." The idea here is that African Americans and Native Americans are always by default already aliens: writing them as characters into science fiction makes them *alien aliens*—an apt figure for a doubled double consciousness. The first three sections have to do with Black science fiction poetics, approaching the subject through music as well as poetry and lyric: How does science fiction *sound*? In the first section, Amiri Baraka's "An Agony. As Now" presents a human cylinder with a radical difference. In the second section, I discuss how Sun Ra's intensely distorted space jazz produces cognitive *dissonance*, estrangement sheerly at the level of sound. His poems present outer space as a kind of science-fictional borderland for Black liberation and music as the spaceship for traveling there. The next section involves three other Black musicians: Jimi Hendrix uses feedback and vocal distortion to create the dense sonic textures of songs like "EXP," "Astro Man," and "Third Stone from the Sun"; Yusef Lateef's "Robot Man" explores machine consciousness; and Ornette Coleman's "Science Fiction" examines racial dynamics. For these artists, sci-fi embeds in a complicated kind of sound, a liminal audio space that paradoxically opens up to the center, not the edge, of the cosmos. The last section of this chapter then examines sci-fi elements in the work of Navajo poet Sherwin Bitsui, who writes of life on reservation lands in Arizona and New Mexico, where decades of uranium and coal mining have devastated the landscape and the communities that live there. Native Americans are depicted as suffering ongoing alien invasion in the form of enhanced technology, germ warfare, concentration camps, structural poverty, ecological degradation, and cultural genocide.

Chapter 6 is called "Dancing at the Language Barrier" (*Language/Transla-*

tion: Neology). What is science fiction *as* language? What would an alien "say"? What would it talk about? If science fiction is cognitively estranging, then sci-fi poetic language should necessarily produce a parallel dissonance in grammar, syntax, narrative, and so on. This chapter looks at Clark Coolidge's *Alien Tatters,* a collection of texts based on alien abduction narratives and "translations" of alien speech—but what do its semantic tatters signify? The estrangement of science fiction works itself down into tongue and throat, which stutter and gargle as they relate weird and astounding tales.

The book ends with a coda called "Virus Alien Hoax Lasagne 2020," which includes a brief reflection on living and writing during our intensely science fiction year of COVID-19 and a poem trolled and collaged from Google's search engine on the morning of Sunday, November 9, 2020.

NYCTALOPIAN READING

Nyctalope is a technical medical term meaning "night blindness," but it is also the name of a pulp sci-fi hero created by French writer Jean de La Hire in 1911. An early kind of cyborg, the Nyctalope, whose real name is Leo Saint-Clair, is outfitted with both organic and mechanical body parts. In spite of his name, his special power is his excellent night vision. He spends his time fighting mad scientists, dictators, and space aliens and rides rockets to Mars.

This sounds like an altogether excellent model for a critic lighting out for Deleuze's new frontiers of knowledge. The Nyctalope is also a reader of H. G. Wells: in *The Nyctalope on Mars,* our eponymous hero encounters Martians straight out of *The War of the Worlds*:

> The Martians were much as the historian Wells had described them: a large round head, about 1.20 meters in diameter, formed the entire body. It was provided with a face of sorts, and on that face two large dark eye-sockets were hollowed out, immediately beneath which was a sort of cartilaginous beak. Behind the head, or body—for I hardly know which of the two terms to employ—was a single extended tympanic surface; which is to say, an ear. Finally, around the cartilaginous beak, 16 slender tentacles, reminiscent of whips, were disposed in two clusters of eight.[98]

As he spies on these *kephales,* Saint-Clair discovers that they communicate in a *visual language*: "In the middle of the fantastic creatures' black eyes, symbols inscribed in white appeared: rapid, successive symbols, phosphorescent in the darkness; they must presumably be of another sort during the day in order to remain visible. These tiny symbols were in the form of geometric shapes. The Martians obviously had nerves that could be activated at will within the transparency of their pupils, capable of assembling, separating and amalgamating in

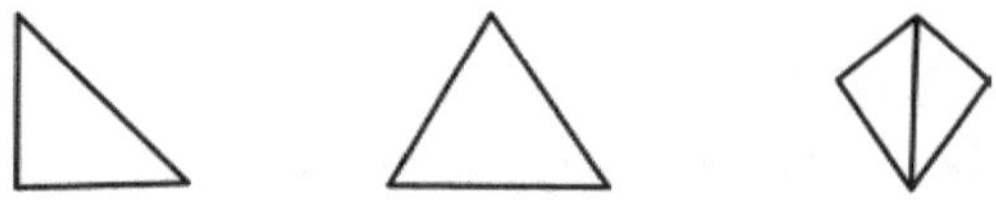

Figure 2. Three Martian language symbols from Jean de La Hire's *The Nyctalope on Mars*, 1911, redrawn by the author.

order to describe the minuscule figures."[99] The Nyctalope and his band of companions learn to read the weird Martian symbols by watching two captured kephales communicate and drawing the shapes on a blackboard[100] (see figure 2). Running like a ticker tape through the eyes of the aliens, these geometric characters resemble nothing less than Smithson's and Judd's crystal sculptures, symbols of entropic hilarity. These three would translate as two chuckles and a titter.

The Nyctalope is a bundle of contradictions. His name means "night blindness," but he is able to see in the dark. He is a character in a novel who reads symbols in the eyes of a character from an earlier novel who appears in the novel that he is in. What he reads there are the entropic crystals—Smithson's ha-ha language—in the eyes of an alien from a future written in the past. This alien is a giant head with a single large ear, slot machine eyes, and a beak with a goatee of tentacles. Saint-Clair translates the language of this startling dialectical image in order to predict his present future (the novel ends with Martian and Earthling making peace and forging a planetary union worthy of Scheerbart's asteroidal novel).

The Nyctalope suggests a special kind of reader and critic: the *science fiction* reader—not the reader *of* science fiction but the reader *in* science fiction. Such a reader figures as a cyborg with enhanced vision who does not see the "real world" but instead enters a funhouse of warped mirrors reflecting distorted spaces, weird planets, kitschy aliens, phantom empires, invisibilities, and impossibilities: humanity and the world estranged and thereby rendered palpable, subject to exaggerated cognition, and transfigured by laughter from the fourth dimension.

1

The Robot and the Egg

Futurism, Mina Loy

Another artist of highly ordered nonsense was Rube Goldberg, who like Lewis Carroll had a well-oiled mathematical mind that constructed solid models of ha-ha. His complicated gadgets are designed to perform the most mundane of tasks—in the case of figure 3, decrowning an egg. The humor of course lies in the insane ingeniousness of the gadget's construction, coupled with the utterly superfluous amount of work it requires to get the job done—in a perverse inversion of the modern labor-saving device, one step is turned into sixteen. Step H introduces a time warp into the whole thing, since we have to wait for the flower to grow before it can push up the rod to pull the string to fire the pistol to scare the monkey. Und so weiter. Goldberg stretches a mundane task into a ludicrous sequence of improbable events, a cause-and-effect narrative ostensibly stitched together by a mechanical tissue of wires, levers, and gears in a fiendishly complicated efficiency-parodying metonymy.

Goldberg's machine can serve as a flattened model for science fiction. It mimes science in its technological wizardry and the generally rational impulse motivating the logic behind the unlikely sequence of events that it construes, and it composes a coherent narrative in spite of the heterogeneity of the objects that it strings together. At the same time, it is incredible, impossible, ridiculous. To crib the words of Csicsery-Ronay, the conceit of the device is extravagantly whimsical, satirical, and parodistic, nearly surreal in the arbitrariness of its imagery, and it calls ironic attention to its ludic and constructed character. It certainly is cognitively estranging, making readers see their own social worlds, which are concealed from view by habit and ideology, with fresh eyes by presenting them with indirect images of the historical and material order of those worlds: in this case, the ever-increasing reliance of modern labor on technology and the hidden work behind convenience. And at its center, it screws

Figure 3. "Loosen an Egg from Its Shell," a Rube Goldberg cartoon, ca. 1931.

with time, introducing a temporal black hole into the scheme. Science fiction is just such an ensemble of devices, tropes, and themes.

Goldberg's machine can also be taken as a sketch for a primitive, pre-electronic robot: it is perhaps not yet a proper robot, but the principles underlying the logic of its construction are the same. A robot might be thought of as an assemblage of gadgets, with a twist: attach together and coordinate enough little machines, and at some point, you *might* get a robot. But you might just get a bigger machine: all robots are machines, but not all machines are robots. A locomotive is not a robot, but a self-driving car is. We can define a robot as a collocation of gadgets that achieves some degree of autonomy. You do not drive a robot, it drives you; a robot is a self-mobilizing device, programmed to perform a task without immediate human participation or interference. In Goldberg's sequence, step A, picking up the morning paper, is the only step that requires human doing; otherwise, the gadgetry motivates itself. The newspaper is like a key for winding up the machine or an electric switch for turning it on; once activated, it takes on a shambling "life" of its own and is subject at no further point to any directing or handling. Its alphabetical nodes are its programming, its system of what-happens-when-to-what. Like the jointed arm of a robotic welder in an automated assembly line, Goldberg's device, once triggered, sets out ineluctably to accomplish its single task, paradoxically saving labor while protracting time. It can break down but it cannot turn away. The word *robot,* after all, derives from the Czech word *robota,* meaning "forced laborer."

What follows in this chapter is my own Rube Goldberg sketch of several of what are properly speaking pre–science fiction moments, movements, and texts. I look briefly at sci-fi as it is prefigured in Russian and Italian futurism and then in two novels written for younger readers: Frank L. Baum's children's book *Ozma of Oz* (1907), which features one of the first—if not *the* first—robot in American literature; and Edgar Rice Burroughs's adolescent adventure novel, *The Chessmen of Mars* (1922), which along with Burroughs's other works is often described as "science fantasy" rather than science fiction. All of this is to frame a discussion of two poems—both from around 1914—by Mina Loy, feminist futurist extraordinaire. The delicate tension between egg and gadget in Goldberg's rickety machine is emblematic of several issues that early on become central to the science fiction repertoire: machines and the limits of machine intelligence; robots and things; acephalic bodies and asomatic heads; flesh and device; automatons, gender, time, and labor; and finally comedy: what Csicsery-Ronay calls "incongruity-management." First stop is Mars; we will end on the moon, murdering its shine with the help of a lunar Baedeker.

FUTURISM ON THE RED PLANET

> I. All the illustrious participants in Futurian publications are hereby promoted from the ranks of human beings to the ranks of Martians.
>
> Signed: Velimir I, King of Time
>
> II. The following are invited to become honorary nonvoting members of the Martian council: H. G. Wells and Marinetti.
>
> —Velimir Khlebnikov, *The King of Time*

Like Leo Saint-Clair, Velimir Khlebnikov was an avid reader of H. G. Wells, who he invites along with F. T. Marinetti to join his extraterrestrial council in "The Trumpet of the Martians," his futurian manifesto from 1916. Futurism—in both its Italian and its Russian iterations—is a simmering broth for science fiction, part of the same hot Martian soup that produced *Lesabéndio* and John Carter of Mars, the Nyctalope and *The War of the Worlds*. Conceived *avant la lettre*, futurism's tropes and concepts migrated handily to sci-fi: a fascination with technology and science; the figure of the artist/hero as creative barbarian engineer clearing the decks of the nineteenth century and refitting the schooner as a spaceship; and an ongoing preoccupation with the future itself as goal, prospective model, and fantastical theater for working out its myriad spectacles, many of which were staged on distant undiscovered islands and faraway planets. While it cannot be claimed absolutely that the Russian futurists wrote science fiction, they were sci-fi's avant-garde herald, blowing the klaxon of Mars as a clarion call to modernist writers, artists, and other speculators to the rich and unexplored fields of outer space.

"The Trumpet of the Martians" is a classic futurist text: in its unrelenting attack on the past, it declares all-out war by the young on the lumbering freight train of the present and the bougie schmucks who grease its wheels. The manifesto is grounded in the language of science fiction:

> *Here is the slogan for a new holy war.*
>
> Our questions are shouted into outer space, where human beings have never yet set foot.
>
> We will brand them in powerful letters on the forehead of the Milky Way, stamp them upon the circular divinity of businessmen—questions like how to free our winged engine from its fat caterpillar, the freight train of previous generations. *Let age groups separate and live apart!* We have broken open the freight cars attached to the locomotive of our daring—and they contain nothing but tombstones for the young. . . . Those who have drowned in the laws of the family and the laws of trade, those who know only the expression "I consume," they will not understand us, since none of those things concerns us.[1]

Khlebnikov conceptualizes this generational struggle as a "time war," a contest over the very fabric of time—figured as a lost continent that can be shaped and transformed—and a betrayal of space:

> We have studied the soil of the continent of time, and we found it fruitful. But unrelenting hands from back there grabbed us, and they keep us from carrying out our beautiful betrayal of space. Has there ever been anything more intoxicating than this betrayal? You! What better answer is there to the danger of being born a man than to carry off time? We summon you toward a land where the trees speak, a land where there are scholarly unions as regular as waves, a land of springtime armies of love, where time blossoms like the locust tree and moves like a piston, where a superman in a carpenter's apron saws time into boards and like a turner of wood can shape his own tomorrow.[2]

Khlebnikov follows this utopian vision with a reference to Kruchenykh's f-ray: "(Oh, equations of kisses—You! Oh death ray, killed by the death ray in the trough of the wave.) We young people were moving toward that land, and all of a sudden some bony figure, someone dead, grabs us and tries to keep us from losing the feathers of the idiot TODAY."[3]

A panoply of what will become generic features of science fiction—the apostrophe to outer space; the Milky Way as text; the land that time forgot or that forgot time; the superhuman engineer, shaping temporality; the death-ray war—frames Khlebnikov's declaration: Mars is fully the *occasion* for futurist vision.[4] Like his formalist friend Shklovsky, Khlebnikov wanted to give his readers fresh eyes; as he puts it in a later text, he writes "in order to arm the mind with new eyes, eyes of the intellect, that can make out events still in the distant future."[5] "The Trumpet of the Martians," he says, is "another sock in the eye for the vulgar inhabitants of space."[6] Showing his readers fantastic futuristic lands where trees speak and time moves like a piston, where each settlement will have Radio Reading-Walls—"enormous books, higher than houses, that stand in the center of each town, slowly turning their own pages"[7]—and cities that are "the marvelous monsters of the Futurian imagination," populated with wheeled mobile dwelling modules of molded glass tooling around gigantic public works—*bridge-buildings, poplar-tree-buildings, underwater auditoriums, steamship-buildings, filament-buildings that come in either single or double strands, checkerboard-buildings, swing-buildings, strand-of-hair-buildings, goblet-buildings, tube-buildings, book-buildings, and field-buildings*—this visionary element is properly the science fictional aspect of Russian futurism, which at its root is the renovation of seeing via the enhancement of the imagination, Khlebnikov's "eyes of the intellect," through artistic *ostranenie*.[8]

The Nyctalope is just such an enhanced human being but with a crucial difference: the sources of his futuristic powers are due not to the stimulation of his imagination but to actual mechanical supplements. His fabulous eyes, it turns out, are bionically engineered, and his heart is a cybernetic implant that gives him immense strength and endurance. He is a creature of prosthesis, one of the world's first cyborgs, and in this, he resembles the Italian version of futurism more than the Russian. Saint-Clair is what F. T. Marinetti calls a "multiplied man."

SHOOTING THE ITALIAN MOON

> I conclude in French improvising extremely light words-in-freedom on the scratchy metallic noise made by the inhabitants of Mars.
>
> —F. T. Marinetti

According to Marjorie Perloff, "Marinetti's writings—manifestos, fictions, political writings, memoirs, and his own inimitable *parole in liberta*—speak to our time with a sort of science fiction prescience."[9] Prescience fiction maybe ought to be its own genre—that is, the genre presciently preceding science fiction proper or at any rate Hugo Gernsback's coinage of the term "scientifiction" in 1926. Here, we find ourselves once again on Jameson's unproductive, sterile, obsolescent planet Aesthetic Philosophy, with its airless moon Taxonomy. Sir Walter Scotty beams Captain Crunch up from its desiccated surface to the hollow deck of the starship *Slipshod*. But if they did not write sci-fi, the futurists did provide it with plenty of philosophical and aesthetic lumber. The house of science fiction is built on a solidly futurist foundation.

Marinetti and his zany Italians declare war on the moon, the stars, and, finally, the Milky Way itself, all targets of their ambition and aggression after the world's first electrical war, the end of which will see the Earth covered by great futurist cities with smoking factory chimneys and the "the sick and weak, crushed, crumbled by the vehement wheels of intense civilization"—at which point the futuristas continue their relentless "marching along the Milky Way."[10] Italian futurism bequeaths to science fiction the prospect of a universe eternally at war and subject to the ongoing exploitation of its planets, moons, and asteroids by voracious and belligerent races of clown supermen competing for resources and Lebensraum at the far frontiers of time and space. Futurist man will be decidedly posthuman:

> It is certain that if we grant the truth of Lamarck's transformational hypothesis we must admit that we look for the creation of a nonhuman type in whom moral suffering, goodness of heart, affection and love, those sole corrosive poisons of inexhaustible vital energy, sole interrupters of our powerful bodily electricity, will be abolished. . . .

> This nonhuman and mechanical being, constructed for an omnipresent velocity, will be naturally cruel, omniscient, and combative.
>
> He will be endowed with surprising organs: organs adapted to the needs of a world of ceaseless shocks.
>
> From now on we can forsee a bodily development in the form of a prow from the outward swell of the breastbone, which will be the more marked the better an aviator the man of the future becomes.[11]

Marinetti's modernist neanderthal is a product of both accelerated evolution and technological enhancement: as his body and its organic functions become more mechanical, his sentiments and affections are streamlined into sheerly instrumental channels, transforming him into an automaton, more thing than human person. With his prow-shaped sternum and machined organs, he begins to resemble his tools, his turbines, and aeroplanes. Men who use gadgets lead to men who *are* gadgets, philosophical pistols to murder the great romantic moonshine. Outer space for these self-proclaimed madmen becomes the extraterrestrial object of their insatiable appetite for domination and control.

And poets who resemble gadgets produce a special kind of poetry: a gadget poetry. Marinetti takes writing apart as if he were fieldstripping a 9mm Luger, disarticulating and cleaning its parts, oiling and polishing and bluing the steel, and putting it back together with lockstep precision, building a whole new weapon, efficient, sleek: a death-ray gun. Poetry was never the same after 1912's "Technical Manifesto of Futurist Literature"; from then on, it would always have a wacky, incendiary, sci-fi member of the family: crazy *zio* Marinetti with his avant-garde armory. Already in the "Futurist Manifesto" (1909) we learn that poetry will be "conceived as a violent attack on unknown forces, to reduce and prostrate them before man"; it will consist of courage, audacity, and revolt; it will exalt "aggressive action, a feverish insomnia, the racer's stride, the mortal leap, the punch and the slap." It will "glorify war—the world's only hygiene—militarism, patriotism, the destructive gesture of freedom-bringers, beautiful ideas worth dying for, and scorn for woman."[12] Abjuring their symbolist masters, futurist poets will replace romantic sentiment and nostalgia with "the tragic lyricism of ubiquity and omnipresent speed."[13] Their only models for writing will be the relay panels in electrical plants "bristling with dials, keyboards, and shining commutators."[14]

The "Technical Manifesto" and "Geometric and Mechanical Splendor and the Numerical Sensibility" (1914) taken together provide a handbook for the new poetics. In the "Technical Manifesto," a talking propeller tells Marinetti that the futurist poet must destroy syntax; he will make free use of infinitives and compound nouns; abolish adjectives, adverbs, and conjunctions; substitute mathematical and musical symbols for punctuation; use ever remoter and more extensive chains of analogies; and destroy the *I* in literature in order "to substitute for human psychology, now exhausted, the lyric obsession with matter" and develop an "*intuitive psychology of matter*."[15] The second essay adds to the recipe free expressive orthography and typography, nine types of onomatopoeia, and random numbers that "have no direct significance or value" but "express the various transcendental intensities of matter and the indestructible correspondences of sensibility."[16]

Gadgets writing gadgets about gadgets for gadgets: a machine poetics for automatons. Here a fault line opens between the Russian and the Italian brands of futurism: if the Russians want to use *ostranenie* to deautomatize readers, the Italians want to use it to automatize them—in essence, to create a new automatization in the form of a human being who is totally automatic, a pugnacious robot who goes "through life almost without love, in a fine steel-colored atmosphere,"[17] "whose roots are cut . . . the multiplied man who mixes himself with iron, who is fed by electricity and no longer understands anything except the lust for danger and daily heroism,"[18]: a nonhuman, mechanical species, built for constant speed. If the Slavic *robota* becomes more of a human by becoming a revolutionary, the Italian human becomes more of a robot by becoming a reactionary.

There is of course a politics implicit in all this. Saint-Clair, with his prosthetic pump heart and bionically augmented eyes, is cut from futurist cloth, although in *The Nyctalope on Mars* he still fights for the good guys. But both Jean de La Hire and Marinetti became fascist sympathizers during the 1930s: Marinetti collaborated with Mussolini in the early days of the Italian Fascist party, and the Nyctalope winds up working for the Vichy regime. Technototalitarianism and dehumanization are endemic in science fiction; they might even be its principal and most enduring themes, in the form of twentieth-century political warfare projected into outer space and prefigured in the rapacious militants of Marinetti's loony theater of the skies.

It is important to acknowledge however that both Russian and Italian futurism are fundamentally *comic* at base; the laughter they cause might be barbaric, but after all, that is what Benjamin calls for in his modernist artist-heroes. With its bizarre exaggerations, puffed-up belligerence and insolence, adolescent love of cars and trains, schoolyard scrapping and posturing, and screwball sci-fi imagination, futurism also shatters articulation; that is how it grabs our attention. In fact, Khlebnikov writes a poem that is nothing but shards of entropic ha ha crystals:

> Hlahla! Uthlofan, lauflings!
> Hlahla! Uthlofan, lauflings!
> Who lawghen with lafe, who hlaehen lewchly,

Hlahla! Uthlofan hlouly!
Hlahla! Hloufish lauflings lafe uf beloght lauchalorum!
Hlahla! Loufenish lauflings lafe, hlohan utlaufly!
Lawfen, lawfen,
Hloh, hlouh, hlou! Luifekin, luifekin,
Hlofeningum, hlofeningum.
Hlahla! Uthlofan, lauflings!
Hlahla! Uthlofan, lauflings![19]

Whereas Marinetti deconstructs the blunderbuss of nineteenth-century poetics in order to repurpose its locks and pins into a modernist ray gun, Khlebnikov crystallizes futurism's main gear—the *laugh*—into its onomatopoeic and etymological permutations. Futurism is the art of lunatic science, as we shall see in the sci-fi poetics deployed in the poetry of Mina Loy. But before we go there, I want to detour briefly to the Land of Oz and the red planet, Barsoom: fantastical settings where science fiction spends its infancy and adolescence. While neither *Ozma of Oz* nor *The Chessmen of Mars* are in any sense poems, I use these novels to examine and describe themes and issues that resonate in the sci-fi poetry that follows and that will be important throughout this study.

SCI-FI IN THE LAND OF OZ

At this point, we leave outer space and digress along sci-fi's horizontal axis, laterally along the surface of the Earth—as Suvin puts it, "an island in the far-off ocean is the paradigm of the aesthetically most satisfying goal of the sci-fi voyage"[20]—off to lost worlds and into the realms of children's literature, where we can see sci-fi evolving out of earlier forms of fairy tale and fantasy, themes and tropes of which it carries into its own future. Published two years ahead of Marinetti's futurist manifesto, *Ozma of Oz* (1907) was the third book in L. Frank Baum's Oz series. While its setting—the Land of Ev, separated from the kingdom of Oz by a burning desert—has conventional trappings of magic and enchantment, it also features two robots, or "machine men." One of them is more of a machine than a robot, but the other—Tik-tok—is as far as I know the first bona fide robot in American literature: that is, he is a gadget with more than a modicum of autonomy. Neither magical nor enchanted, he is the product of turn-of-the-century industrial culture. A patent card hanging from a peg on his back comes straight out of machine-age advertising (see figure 4).[21] Because he is not technically alive, Tik-tok does not eat, sleep, or feel sorrow, joy, or kindness, but he does think: he speculates and reasons, makes his own decisions and plans, and acts of his own accord (as long as he is properly wound up). He has memories, keeps secrets, and understands injustice and the difference between right and wrong. As Tik-tok tells Dorothy in his mechanical

SMITH & TINKER'S

Patent Double-Action, Extra-Responsive,
Thought-Creating, Perfect-Talking

MECHANICAL MAN

Fitted with our Special Clock-Work Attachment.

Thinks, Speaks, Acts, and Does Everything but Live.

Manufactured only at our Works at Evna, Land of Ev.
All infringements will be promptly Prosecuted according to Law.

Figure 4. Patent card for Tik-Tok, from L. Frank Baum's *Ozma of Oz*, 1907.

stutter, "I am so com-pli-cat-ed. You have no i-de-a how full of ma-chin-er-y I am": the poetics of the robot shatters articulation at the level of the syllable.[22] Put enough gadgets together and presumably you can manufacture a thought. What does it mean to do everything but live?

In *Ozma of Oz*, we have a kind of hybrid text, one in which we see sci-fi cohabiting the isle with fairy tale, and this hybridity is reflected everywhere in Baum's novel. It polarizes the setting, where feudal castles share the landscape with industrial mines, but it also torques the relations between machines, objects, and flesh-and-blood beings: it is often difficult to say whether a character or a thing is sentient or insentient, living or dead, male or female, organic or inorganic. The novel describes an astonishing array of being: from the underground gnomes (written "Nomes" by Baum) of folk legend to futuristic robots, from human beings reduced to mute immobile objects to objects made of wood and straw that speak and move, from boys who find out that they are girls to a talking hen named Bill who is rechristened Billina and beats up roosters.[23] Much of this of course is the purview of fantasy, not sci-fi, where, strictly speaking, magic has no place, but it is as if Baum were exploring the very limits of genre and fiction making in this book, as well as grades of sentience and embodiment.

Tik-tok's generic origins go back on the one hand to clockworks—he "tells" time, literally by speaking—and on the other hand to locomotives, and especially to Edward S. Ellis's 1868 dime novel character the Steam Man of the Prairies (figure 5), to whom he bears an uncanny resemblance. Both characters are rotund; shaped like boilers, replete with rivets; and topped by round heads with staring metal eyes: Steam Man sports a smoking stovepipe hat, Tik-tok a bowler (figure 6).

The difference between the two machines though is telling. While Tik-tok has something of a mind of his own, the Steam Man possesses no intel-

Figure 5. Detail of cover illustration from *The Steam Man of the Prairies*, Edward S. Ellis, 1868.

Figure 6. Tik-Tok, illustration by John R. Neill in L. Frank Baum's *Ozma of Oz*, 1907.

ligence or autonomy whatsoever—he is simply a locomotive that looks and walks (and runs) like a human being. He must be steered manually, whereas Tik-tok decides for himself when and where to move. The latter's immediate patrimony is the firm of Smith & Tinker. Tinker is pure fairy tale; he picks stars out of the sky for the king's crown and builds a ladder to the moon, but Smith is a *Dorian Gray*–like artist who drowns in his own landscape, as Tik-tok explains to Dorothy: "Mr. Smith was an art-ist, as well as an in-vent-or, and he paint-ed a pic-ture of a riv-er which was so nat-u-ral that, as he was reach-ing a-cross it to paint some flowers on the op-po-site bank, he fell in-to the wa-ter and was drowned."[24] The issue of art and resemblance here raises questions of naturalism and mechanical reproduction that project back on to Tik-tok and look forward to science fiction itself: How "real" is a robot? How close to a human being is a machine that can do everything that a person can do except live? Conceived by a tinkerer and forged in a smithy, Tik-tok is a curious picture of aesthetic distance: a mind blended somehow into a tissue of machinery. "Where" is Tik-tok? What sort of artifice fools us so completely that we take it for real, at least until it becomes ludicrous?

Tik-tok has two foils in Ev, and the three taken together trace an arc of

Figure 7. A Wheeler, illustration by John R. Neill, in L. Frank Baum's *Ozma of Oz*, 1907.

machine-to-human possibility. The second of Smith & Tinker's creations is a nameless metal giant that guards the entrance to the subterranean kingdom of the Nomes. Like the Steam Man of the Prairies, it is an anthropomorphic machine that performs a single, simple, repetitive task: "They saw before them a huge form, which towered above the path for more than a hundred feet. The form was that of a gigantic man built out of plates of cast iron, and it stood with one foot on either side of the narrow road and swung over its right shoulder an immense iron mallet, with which it constantly pounded the earth."[25] Since the giant "has no think-ing or speak-ing at-tach-ment," as Tik-tok puts it, Dorothy and her party have little difficulty getting past it by timing their move to the moments when it raises its mallet. The iron giant is pure gadget, a blow-up of a child's mechanical toy. Like Tik-tok, its inner works are modeled on timekeeping—the former admires how it "works as stead-i-ly as a clock": it keeps time, but that is all that it does or can do. A clock is not a robot.

Tik-tok's other nemeses are the Wheelers, humanoids whose arms and legs end in keratinous wheels (see figure 7). These terrifying and hysterical creatures harass anyone who comes within their immediate vicinity, but their wheels render them entirely harmless; their only defenses against enemies are to threaten and bluster. Wheelers exist somewhere between human beings and gadgets, but the important thing is that *they do no work*: freeloaders, they live off of trees belonging to the king of Ev that grow well-stocked lunch boxes. Most remarkable is their appearance: aside from its weird limbs, a Wheeler is "clothed most gorgeously in embroidered garments of many colors, and [wears] a straw hat perched jauntily upon the side of its head."[26] John R. Neill, Baum's original illustrator, depicts it as a decadent dandy, replete with Elizabethan ruff collar, tuxedo, waist sash, straw boater, and an Oscar Wilde shock of hair. Troped as queer, all that Wheelers can do is roll, or *stroll*—there is something of the flaneur about them, or the bicycle riding gay-blades of turn-of-the-century photographs and illustrations. Lots of toothy bark but no bite. Fey aliens.

If the iron giant is more working machine than robot and Tik-tok more thinking robot than human being, the Wheeler is more unproductive human than productive machine. The gadgetry that supplements it turns it into a drone, a piece of rolling kitsch, a commodity out for a stroll, a futurist turned into a belligerent fop. In Baum, a human gadget is a machine that performs no labor, a person on the way to becoming an object. With its dangerously ambiguous gender, the Wheeler collapses the categories "that reason has considered essentially distinct, creating a spectacle of impossible fusions." A wheeled human is less "real" than a robot with a metal mind.[27]

But real, actual people are *literally* turned into objects in the Kingdom of the Nomes. King Roquat rules a vast subterranean mining operation the purpose of which is to produce precisely the sorts of useless but pricey objects that grease the wheels of commodity culture: gems, jewels, and precious metals, which his Nome slaves hide in the earth for humans to extract and exploit. Roquat has a magic belt that allows him to turn people "into articles of ornament and bric-a-brac" that he "scatters around the various rooms of [his] apartments."[28] Most recently, he has turned the queen of Ev and her ten children into such tchotchkes, and he invites Dorothy and company, who have come to him expressly to beg the royal family's liberation, to play a dangerous game in an attempt to free them: "You shall go alone and unattended into my palace and examine carefully all that the rooms contain. Then you shall have permission to touch eleven different objects, pronouncing at the time the word 'Ev,' and if any one of them, or more than one, proves to be the transformation of the Queen of Ev or any of her ten children, then they will instantly be restored to their true form and may leave my palace and my kingdom in your company, without any objection whatever."[29] The king has only one dreadful condition: "If none of the eleven objects you touch proves to be the transformation of any of the royal family of Ev, then, instead of freeing them, you will yourself become enchanted, and transformed into an article of bric-a-brac or an ornament."[30]

A person thus becomes a thing when she enters the Nome Kingdom, the metaphysical world of the commodity fetish, false value and kitsch, objectified and alienated labor: an overstuffed nineteenth-century living room, full of plush and velvet, an arcade:

> [Ozma] found herself in a splendid hall that was more beautiful and grand than anything she had ever beheld. The ceilings were composed of great arches that rose far above her head, and all the walls and floors were of polished marble exquisitely tinted in many colors. Thick velvet carpets were on the floor and heavy silken draperies covered the arches leading to the various rooms of the palace. The furniture was made of rare old woods richly cared and covered with delicate satins. . . . Upon the mantels, and on many shelves and brackets and tables, were clustered ornaments of every description, seemingly made out of all sorts of metals, glass, china, stones and marbles. There were vases, and figures of men and animals, and graven platters and bowls, and mosaics of precious gems and many other things.[31]

How do you de-thing a person turned into an object? With an *egg*.

Billina the hen, it turns out, is the only member of the party, including Tik-tok, who is not finally turned into an ornament; she falls asleep under Roquat's throne and overhears him telling his royal steward how he effects his transformations through the agency of his magic belt. But she also learns that eggs are considered poisonous by Nomes. In a series of complicated plot twists, Billina frees all of the prisoners; the Scarecrow terrorizes the Nome king with two of the hen's eggs; and Dorothy steals the king's magic belt, which she uses to transform members of his attacking army themselves into eggs, inducing widespread panic in his soldiers. Magic and fairy tale, for sure—but more interesting are the thematic implications for sci-fi, for while the robot cannot defeat the Nome king or otherwise combat the mortifying effects of species alienation, the egg can: in the contest between inorganic machine and organic ovum, the latter wins. Corny, sure: but there is a pastoral moral in Baum's tale that translates handily into outer space and other sci-fi settings, where flesh and blood forever confront machine worlds or pumped up industrial extraterrestrials. If Goldberg uses a gadget to decrown an egg, Baum uses an egg to decrown a . . . gadget?—anyway, that infernal power that converts human beings into gadgets, ornaments, toys, kitsch: wrong life, lived wrongly. Baum's robot and egg foreshadow similar themes in science fiction, where sentient life and its thing-opposite lock in constant struggle.

One last trope in *Ozma* that will resonate thematically as sci-fi unfurls down the century: the parasitic head and its dumb appendage, the acephalic body, the old mind/body problem, although this is as much a brain/body problem, or a whatever-a-head-might-be/body problem. In the structural center of Baum's novel, we enter a palace with a circular room full of mirrors where we meet the languid Princess Langwidere. She is the conceited owner of thirty beautiful heads that she can take off and put on at will, and she spends all but the ten minutes of each day that she devotes to affairs of state admiring herself with her different heads in her mirrors. As useless as any Wheeler, Langwidere is much more dangerous—she demands Dorothy's head for her collection and, upon being refused, imprisons the girl, who only Ozma of Oz can rescue. The gender dynamics are worth remarking on here. All of the principle movers and shakers in Baum's novel are female: Dorothy, Ozma, Glinda the Good Witch, Billina the hen—even Jinjur, the suffragette, who in an earlier Oz book assembles an army of women and drives the Scarecrow from the Emerald City, makes an appearance. The male characters are either buffoons, like the soldiers in Ozma's small army; or grotesque gnomes; or they are made out of straw, tin, iron, or wood. No prince in shining armor here, but a feisty hen named Bill and a princess who was a little boy who turned out to be a girl.

Langwidere with her narcissistic heads, however, is a real menace. She is a kind of perverse praying mantis, a female who decapitates other females to feed her insatiable appetite for her own replicated image in a glass, which she literally sees everywhere she looks. A multiplied woman, she is fickle and self-absorbed, the ultimate consumer of beauty, a stereotype of feminine vanity and a fetishist of the gaze, locked in her own self-amplifying arcade.[32] Like one of Benjamin's mannequins, tailor's dummies, or dolls, "the true fairies of the arcades,"[33] she is a gatekeeper to the Nome kingdom and its ruler's cabinet of petrified curiosities. She is herself a piece of objectified kitsch, but unlike Roquat's human bric-a-brac, Langwidere is sensate and predatory, a cold image of commodity collapsed in upon itself and splintering into a subject constructed as a labyrinth of reflections.

KALDANES AND KEPHALES

Two other *caput-tantum* extraterrestrials appear around the same time as Langwidere in *Ozma of Oz*: the kephales in *The Nyctalope on Mars* and the kaldanes from Edgar Rice Burroughs's *The Chessmen of Mars*.[34] The former are based squarely on H. G. Wells's Martians, who during their invasion of Earth feed on humans via pipettes. De La Hire describes how this works back on their home planet:

> The three Martians were upright, their body-heads sustained by eight tentacles set directly on the ground. If front of each of them, a bizarre creature, half-humanoid and half-birdlike, bipedal and naked, was sitting, its short arms hanging down by its side. These creatures, white in color, with visibly soft and plump flesh devoid of musculature, were laying their heads forwards. At a certain point of each of their necks,

> beneath the ear, a thin trickle of blood emerged from a short appendage. Each Martian was collecting this blood in a sort of pipette held and manipulated by one of its tentacle-hands.[35]

The Martians, which the Nyctalope and his companions christen kephale after the Greek word for "head," then insert their pipettes into their cartilaginous beaks and drink, after which they close their eyes and remain motionless, each "taking on the appearance of an immense mushroom."[36] In spite of the fact that their humanoid birdlike lunch-buckets have language—at one point, Saint-Clair carries on rudimentary conversation with several of them—the Nyctalope ultimately declares them "inferior humans" and "resign[s] himself to making no attempt to elevate the biped livestock from the state of social inferiority in which the kephales maintained them. The life of Martian intelligence rendered the slavery and animality of the bipeds indispensable."[37] And the lumpen, too, shall serve their purpose.

Another nasty Martian race are the kaldanes from Burroughs's *The Chessmen of Mars*. Like all of the native species of Barsoom, these arachnoids are oviparous, although with a difference: unlike the other races of the planet, the kaldanes have no sex, with the exception of their king, who a kaldane named Ghek explains "is bi-sexual. He produces many eggs from which we, the workers and the warriors, are hatched; and one in every thousand eggs is another king egg, from which a king is hatched."[38] The reigning king kills off most of his potential rival royal offspring, saving only a handful, one of whom will replace him in the event that he dies. The kaldane egg is a kind of perversion of the life-force ovum that so successfully brings down the Nome kingdom in *Ozma*: it produces a *swarm*, a mass of creatures functionally indistinguishable from one another, parasitic, organic machines that might as well be things like the electrical men envisioned by Marinetti. Ghek explains that he and every other kaldane from the same swarm are exactly identical. They are as difficult to parse as the blank face of a robot: "The creatures seemed totally lacking in emotion, or, at least, the capacity to express it. It was impossible to judge what impression the story made upon them, or even if they heard it. Their protruding eyes simply stared and occasionally the muscles of their mouths opened and closed."[39]

Like the kephales, the kaldanes are caput-tantum, large heads with "six short, spiderlike legs and two stout chelae which [grow] in front of its legs and strongly resemble those of an earthly lobster."[40] Ninety percent brain, they feature protruding eyes, slits for a nose, and a "sphincter-like muscle" for a mouth and are lungless, with only the most rudimentary of vital organs. They also live off a different race of their fellow Martians, the rykors, headless humanoids whom they eat. But the main purpose of the rykor is to act as the body to the kaldane head. Ghek explains: "'Do you see this thing?' and he extended what appeared to be a bundle of tentacles from the posterior of his head. 'There is an aperture just back of the rykor's mouth and directly over the upper end of his spinal column. Into this aperture I insert my tentacles and seize the spinal cord. Immediately I control every muscle of the rykor's body—it becomes my own, just as you direct the movement of the muscles of your body. I feel what the rykor would feel if he had a head and brain."[41] The kaldanes and the rykors, we are told, coevolved over the millennia, and this evolution is ongoing: Burroughs's Barsoom is a dying planet, its atmosphere and water slowly disappearing, and ultimately the rykors will die out and the kaldanes will migrate deeply underground, where Ghek tells us that they will eventually "develop into the super-thing—just brain. The incubus of legs and chelae and vital organs will be removed. The future kaldane will be nothing but a great brain. Deaf, dumb, and blind it will lie sealed in its buried vault far beneath the surface of Barsoom—just a great, wonderful beautiful brain with nothing to distract it from eternal thought."[42] Burroughs shows us one possible outcome of Marinetti's futurist man who "will reduce his heart to its true distributive function. The heart must in some way become a kind of stomach for the brain, which will methodically empty and fill so that the spirit can go into action."[43] Instead of a better aviator, however, such a being will become a better mole, a spirit of dark intelligence, closed in on itself, its one thought filling immensity forever.

Whether or not this kephalic utopia will ever come about is never decided in *Chessmen of Mars*, but one kaldane at any rate becomes disillusioned with the whole scenario. Appointed guard over Tara of Helium—daughter of John Carter, warlord of Mars—who has been captured by the kaldanes, Ghek becomes enchanted by her singing: "The girl marveled at the effect her voice had upon the creature. Somewhere in that enormous brain there was a chord that was touched by melody. It was the sole link between herself and brain when detached from the rykor."[44] Ghek winds up saving Tara from the lascivious kaldane king, who intends to use his rykor to rape her, and eventually, Ghek becomes a citizen of Helium, her family's city. Tara's singing gives rise to a series of reflections in Ghek's mind:

> Recently something had awakened within him the existence of which he had never before even dreamed. Had the influence of the strange captive woman aught to do with this unrest and dissatisfaction? He did not know. He missed the soothing influence of the noise she called singing. Could it be that there were other things more desirable than cold logic and undefiled brain power? Was well balanced imperfection more to be sought after then, than the high development of a single characteristic? He thought of the great, ultimate brain toward which all kal-

> danes were striving. It would be deaf, and dumb, and blind. A thousand beautiful strangers might sing and dance about it, but it could derive no pleasure from the singing or the dancing since it would possess no perceptive faculties. Already had the kaldanes shut themselves off from most of the gratifications of the senses. Ghek wondered if much was to be gained by denying themselves still further, and with the thought came a question as to the whole fabric of their theory. After all perhaps the girl was right; what purpose could a great brain serve sealed in the bowels of the earth?[45]

As Ghek later puts it, "I cannot laugh nor smile, and yet within me is a sense of contentment when this woman sings—a sense that seems to open before me wondrous vistas of beauty and unguessed pleasure that far transcend the cold joys of a perfectly functioning brain."[46]

Hence a redemptive role for the arts, and especially music—and especially *lyric*—in the life of the alien mind. The cold kaldanes represent an extreme state of disembodiment; the rykors an extreme state of extremity—the condition of being nothing *but* extremities. In *Chessmen of Mars*, it is song that awakens the one to the other, lyric that ties the knot between brain and body. The Achilles heel to the perfectly functioning brain, poetry links kaldane to rykor in a fully humanizing synthesis of flesh and mind.

CYLINDERS AND OVA

What would it mean to read Mina Loy's poetry as science fiction? Loy is undoubtedly one of the great futurist poets, but along with Khlebnikov and Marinetti (and Baum and even Edgar Rice Burroughs), she does not classify easily as a writer of sci-fi. Again, arid taxonomy planet. Loy does however use certain science fiction tropes, and she does evince a sci-fi sensibility, if I may be so nebulous, and her work does point to what will become science fiction poetry and poetics down the line. Like her fellow futurists, she writes a prescience fiction poetry, prescient in its futuristic *ostranenie*, peopled with automatons and pitched through a warped kind of technorhetoric. Her lunar Baedeker might get us no farther than the moon, but it is a giant step for womankind: I take Loy as the first modern science fiction poet in English and her "Human Cylinders" as the first true sci-fi poem.

"Human Cylinders" (1915) is itself a marvelous spinning cylinder of a poem, three convoluted sentences torqued around forty-five tightly wound lines. A takedown of futurism in futurist manner and style, this frustrated love song to a human robot is set in an atmosphere of enervating dust/dusk and ends with a Big Bang (and begins with a little one). How do you make love—or even *speak*—to an automaton?

The human cylinders
Revolving in the enervating dust
That wraps each closer in the mystery
Of singularity
Among the litter of a sunless afternoon
Having eaten without tasting
Talked without   communion
And at least two of us
Loved a very little
Without seeking
To know if our two miseries
In the lucid rush-together of automatons
Could form one opulent well-being[47]

In "Multiplied Man and the Reign of the Machine," Marinetti calls for "energetic beings" who "have no sweet mistress to visit in the evening, but each morning they love to check meticulously the perfect working of their factories"; such a man "will methodically learn to destroy in himself all the sorrows of the heart, daily lacerating his affections and infinitely distracting his sex with swift, casual contacts with women."[48] How much fun can it be to hang out with a MACHO creep like this?[49] Eating without tasting and talking without communicating with one of these brown dwarves might lead to robotic sex—"the lucid rush-together of automatons," or the "impact of lighted bodies / knocking sparks off each other / In chaos," as Loy puts it in another futurist love song[50]—but cannot consummate in anything like opulent well-being or even interesting pillow talk:

Simplifications of men
In the enervating dusk
Your indistinctness
Serves me the core of the kernel of you
When in the frenzied reaching-out of intellect to intellect
Leaning brow to brow   communicative
Over the abyss of the potential
Concordance of respiration
Shames
Absence of corresponding between the verbal sensory
And reciprocity
Of conception and expression
Where each extrudes beyond the tangible
One thin pale trail of speculation
From among us we have sent out

Into the enervating dusk
One little whining beast
Whose longing
Is to slink back to antediluvian burrow
And one plastic tentacle of intuition
To quiver among the stars[51]

Futurist men are indistinct simplifications, hollow cylinders whose empty talk leads to the end of empathetic communication and any chance of reciprocal interchange, not just between the sexes but in the dynamics of thinking and speaking altogether, in the mutual interdependence of conception and expression: what one thinks and how one says it and all the ways in which those two basic cognitive functions operate independently or in concert with one another. All we are left with is an attenuated trail of speculation and a quivering tentacle of intuition—a sort of Martian-inflected sensitivity, to be sure—but not much to go on if the goal is the stars.

Outer space is thus used by Loy in this poem as a stage or a background for treating issues of human communication, imagination, and expression, as pitched through the question of the futurist robot, that weird slave whose head and body are so profoundly dissociated. Only the twisted gadgetry of the poem—its abrupt enjambments, ungainly vocabulary, strained conceits, mid-line gaps, and overriding sense of breakdown and collapse—can estrange this already strange condition to the extent that we can sense it palpably, in our ears as it were. The contraption rattles and catches, whines and slinks, and ultimately leads to apocalypse:

The impartiality of the absolute
Routs   the polemic
Or which of us
Would not
Receiving the holy-ghost
Catch it   and caging
Lose it
Or in the problematic
Destroy the Universe
With a solution[52]

In a problematic ending to a gnarly poem, the gender polemic at its base is nixed by the neutrality of cosmic indifference to all things human. We probably would not want to figure the whole thing out anyway, because, as William Blake puts it, “He who binds to himself a joy, / Does the winged life destroy”[53]: it is in the grinding of the gears that we hear the music of Loy’s spheres, or at any rate, the cold humming of her native lunar sphere, where "Pocked with personification / the fossil virgin of the skies / waxes and wanes."[54] Loy's poem shows us the futurist motor idling, burning gas in a poetic rattletrap like one of Marinetti's Model Ts. Its all too human cylinders need reboring or this reciprocating engine revolving in the dust will shudder and seize up.

Loy's name for herself in her semiautobiographical long poem *Anglo-Mongrels and the Rose* is Ova, eggs. As is true for Baum and Burroughs, the egg is a potent object for Loy—a symbol of futurist femininity, for woman in her childbearing capacity. The newborn baby, Loy says, is a "Stir of incipient life / Precipitating into me / The contents of the universe"—that is, into a communion with the cosmos that is the diametrical opposite of the "antediluvian burrow" that speculation longs to slink back to after the vacuous encounter between human cylinders.[55] In an astonishing description of parturition—"Parturition" (1914)—Loy writes what her editor Roger Conover calls "the putative first poem ever written about the physical experience of childbirth from the parturient woman's point of view,"[56] an experience that precipitates not only an absorption "Into / The was—is—ever—shall—be / Of cosmic reproductivity" but a full-blown crisis of the self and a dive into the subconscious:

> Relaxation
> Negation of myself as a unit
>   Vacuum interlude
> I should have been emptied of life
> Giving life
> For consciousness in crisis   races
> Through the subliminal deposits of evolutionary processes
> Have I not
> Somewhere
> Scrutinized
> A dead white feathered moth
> Laying eggs?[57]

Note how this poem deploys several of the futurist strategies espoused by Marinetti, although with a difference: free use of gerunds (rather than infinitives and compound nouns); relatively few adjectives, adverbs, and conjunctions; remote and extensive chains of analogies; and the negation of the self as a unit—although this latter is probably not exactly the sort of negation that Marinetti had in mind. Instead of evaporating into the machinery of a human robot, the "I" in Loy dissolves into a very fleshy, warm, moist, human body that contracts and dilates into a "congested cosmos of agony" and becomes "Identical / With infinite Maternity."[58] Loy winds down this section of the poem to the image of a dead moth laying eggs, a dramatically apt if jarring analogy for the exhausted mother in the pangs of childbirth. The poem also uses expressive typography: Conover claims that "Parturition" is "the first poem in English to use collage as a texturing device."[59]

In the same sentence, Conover calls "Parturition" "a significant event in the history of modern poetry as well as the literature of modern sexuality," but I would l add to the list of Loy's firsts (the first poet to treat childbirth, the first to use collage) a third item: Loy writes the first prescience fiction poetry, a poetry given over to the themes and issues of the futuristic worlds that slowly round into view during the first two decades of the twentieth century. In her poetry, fantasy and science fuse in a futurism staged in the primal settings of sci-fi. In the ongoing battle between cylinder and egg, metal and ova, we witness the cosmic struggle between life and its opposite that will galvanize the science fiction of the future.

2

Inner Worlds

Surrealism, William Burroughs, Ted Greenwald

> Some amusing fire-damp jobs are in preparation while, heads lowered, the smart set are leaving on a journey to the center of the earth.
>
> —André Breton and Philippe Soupault, *The Magnetic Fields*

Loy's races through the subliminal deposits of evolutionary processes will act as the entry point into our next topic: the influence of surrealism on science fiction poetry and poetics, and particularly surrealism's interests in the unconscious and dream, automatism and the uncanny. These migrate into the third space of science fiction, underground in the Earth's core (or, alternatively, twenty thousand leagues under the sea). The proceeding chapter explores the upward vertical axis of the sci-fi crystal as figured by outer space in *Lesabéndio* and by Mars with the Nyctalope and in the works of the futurists, E. R. Burroughs, Wells, and Loy; and the horizontal spatial axis as figured by Baum's lost island of Ev. We now drop down the lower vertical axis of the crystal, toward the Earth's center, where what we find more often than not are vestiges of the past, not traces of the present or the future (what would be the *future* of the center of the Earth?). This is the chthonic realm where things are buried, forgotten, sublimated, archetypal: drawing on both psychology and geology, the Earth's core figures as both the prehistoric past and the unconscious. As Carl Freedman puts it in his essay "Science Fiction and Critical Theory," "the 'theoretical fictions' of Freud, such as the description of drives in *Beyond the Pleasure Principle,* are in a real sense Sci-fi."[1] We now turn to the dynamics of that sense.

We have in fact already visited such a subterranean realm, in the Nome kingdom in *Ozma of Oz.* The Princess Langwidere and the brainless giant automaton that guards the entrance to the mines are apt figures for both the buried drives of the psyche and the fairy tale worlds of the past: gnomes and princesses and giants belong to folk tale and legend, and when we enter Roquat's halls, we encounter pure enchantment and magic, dream states of irrational transformation. The original title of Benjamin's *Passagen Werk* was "Pariser Passagen: Eine dialektische Feerie" ("Parisian passages: A dialectical fairy tale"), and it "burgeoned under the influence of Surrealism," according to his translators.[2] I have already suggested that the Nome king's apartments are arcade-like in their hodgepodge collection of bric-a-brac. Benjamin describes the Parisian arcades as "fairy grottoes" and "fairy palaces,"[3] and as quarries, catacombs, and caverns that lead into the antediluvian strata of lost capitalist eras: "As the rocks of the Miocene or Eocene in places bear the imprint of monstrous creatures from those ages, so today arcades dot the metropolitan landscape like caves containing the fossil remains of a vanished monster: the consumer of the pre-imperial era of capitalism, the last dinosaur of Europe. On the walls of these caverns their immemorial flora, the commodity, luxuriates and enters, like cancerous tissue, into the most irregular combinations."[4] Benjamin quotes from Louis Aragon's *Le Paysan de Paris* to the effect that the arcades are "human aquariums" whose distinctive light is "a glaucous gleam, seemingly filtered through deep water," following this with commentary on a similar description by Friedrich Gerstäcker of a Berlin street, "the sides of the houses in some spots almost overgrown with shells and seaweed." He continues, "If a work of literature, an imaginative composition, could arise from repressed economic contents in the consciousness of a collective, as Freud says it can from sexual contents in an individual consciousness, then in the above description we would have before our eyes the consummate sublimation of the arcades, with their bric-a-brac growing rankly out of their showcases."[5] Dolls and tailor's dummies are "the true fairies of the arcades," and Benjamin associates them schematically with both surrealism and "fashion as parody of the (motley) cadaver"; Langwidere with her macabre collection of replaceable heads is just such a fashionista mannequin.[6] The science-fictional center of the Earth is troped as a space of powerful dialectical images, fantasies of both the personal and the collective past that roar into the present as the hobgoblins and cavemen of humankind's archaic childhoods.[7] This invites both surrealist pastiche and the irregular combinations of dream; a journey there will unearth a potent spectacle of impossible fusions.

FIELDS OF ATTRACTION

> One is tempted to wonder what kind of Science Fiction might have emerged from the inaugural surrealist phrase, "un homme coupé en deux par la fenêtre." Breton's passion for B movies and for the most garish and vulgar kinds of cultural junk and paraliterature is also most relevant here.
>
> —Fredric Jameson, *Archaeologies of the Future*

"Impossible fusions" suggests that this netherworld of buried drives and lost times derives a poetics: the sci-fi Earth's core has a characteristic literary style and technique, and both are markedly surrealist. Breton in the *Manifesto of Surrealism* argues for a poetics based on the mechanics of dream and its "marvelous" oneiric imagery: for him, Freud points the way to a wholly new and unprecedented literature with roots in psychoanalysis and Dada's aggressive attacks on Western aesthetics. The surrealist world is built of incongruous juxtapositions, disjunctive and abrupt breaks, and collisions and syntheses of incompatible objects and images, all leading to its primary techniques of collage and montage. Breton quotes a passage from Pierre Reverdy that he says he "pondered for a long time": "*The image is a pure creation of the mind. It cannot be born from a comparison but from a juxtaposition of two more or less distant realities. The more the relationship between these two juxtaposed realities is distant and true, the stronger the image will be—the greater its emotional power and poetic reality.*[8]

Breton immediately follows this passage with his dream image, mentioned by Jameson in the epigraph above, of a man cut in two by a window, which he says was rapidly followed at the time by a flood of images that came to him almost too quickly to grasp. This in turn leads to his notion of automatic writing: "Completely occupied as I still was with Freud at that time, and familiar as I was with his methods of examination which I had some slight occasion to use on some patients during the war, I resolved to obtain from myself what we were trying to obtain from them, namely, a monologue spoken as rapidly as possible without any intervention on the part of the critical faculties, a monologue consequently unencumbered by the slightest inhibition and which was, as closely as possible, akin to spoken thought."[9] Both montage and automatism appear in science fiction poetry and poetics down the line, and, while it cannot be claimed that the founding surrealists wrote science fiction (although members of the group were influenced by sci-fi), according to Arthur B. Evans, "the many correlations between sci-fi and Surrealism seem obvious. Sci-fi's sense of wonder, estranging novums, and space-time manipulations closely recall Surrealisms's iconic dreamscapes, non-mimetic referentialities, and speculations on the 'inner beyond.'"[10] I would add to Evans's list, along with automatic writing and montage, surrealism's antirealist and antinarrative stances and its critique of the author as rational creator in control. These latter "correlations" might not show up so much or so frequently in science fiction *fiction*, but they do feature prominently in science fiction poetry: like futurism, surrealism offers a prescience fiction poetics.

Breton goes on to describe his breakthrough collaboration with Philippe Soupault, which resulted in *The Magnetic Fields*, published in 1920. This was the first major piece of surrealist automatic writing and was the origin of the name, if not the term itself, of the movement: "SURREALISM, n. Psychic automatism in its pure state, by which one proposes to express—verbally, by means of the written word, or in any other manner—the actual functioning of thought. Dictated by the thought, in the absence of any control exercised by reason, exempt from any aesthetic or moral concern."[11] The ten sections of *The Magnetic Fields* were all written at different tempos, but otherwise, the criterion for composition for each was the same: "None of [the text's] words, phrases or sentences, once having found their way to paper through the authors' intermediary, were to be in any way altered or improved," a technique leading, according to David Gascoyne, to a source for poetry "sought in an id no longer subservient to a super-ego" and a discipline "of vigilantly resisting the temptation to interrupt the stream of consciousness."[12] A surrealist, then, is a kind of organic automaton, a writing robot, a consciousness in crisis given over to automaticity in the service of plunging into the underworld of the unconscious in order to record the censored languages of dream: Surrealist *ostranenie* is designed to bring us deeper into our selves, nearer to what it means to be authentically human. The strange, it turns out, is the all too familiar: that which is closest to our inner selves is, given the dynamics of repression, the most forgotten.

This sense of the familiarly strange or the strangely familiar is of course the provenance of the uncanny, which Freud tells us is "that class of the terrifying which leads back to something long known to us, once very familiar"—it is "nothing new or foreign, but something familiar and old—established in the mind that has been estranged only by the process of repression."[13] While the feeling of uncanniness involves anything "that ought to have remained hidden and secret, and yet comes to the light," it is also triggered by "wax-work figures, artificial dolls, and automatons," which create "doubts whether an animate being is really alive; or conversely, whether a lifeless object might not be in fact animate."[14] It can also be caused by circumstances in which one feels that "automatic, mechanical processes are at work, concealed beneath the ordinary appearance of animation."[15] Finally, uncanny feelings can be stimulated by odd coincidences that "force upon us the idea of something fateful and unescapable where otherwise we should have spoken of 'chance' only" and by "dismembered limbs, a severed head, a hand cut off at the wrist, feet which dance by themselves."[16] This latter aspect of the uncanny becomes formalized in surrealist procedure, as described by Paul Nougé: "The method itself consists in isolating the object by breaking off its ties with the rest of the world in a more or less brutal or in a more or less insidious manner. We may cut off a hand and place it on the table, or we may paint the image of a cut-off hand on the wall. We may isolate by using a frame or by using a knife, but even more by a deformation, or a modification, in the subject of an object—a woman without a head, a hand of glass."[17]

Baum's Langwidere clearly exemplifies the uncanny, as do Burroughs's kaldanes and de La Hire's kephales: both surrealism and science fiction rely on such uncanny grotesqueries to produce their most cognitively estranging effects. Tik-tok and his nonsentient giant metal cousin trace the arc of what the roboticist Masahito Mori calls "the uncanny valley," that point at which a robot becomes creepy to human sensibilities because "an inanimate object becomes too much like an animate one."[18] Tik-tok does not live, but he gets as close to living as a machine can, and the infrathin gap makes him weird. The surrealist writing robot goes the other way: automatic writing suggests that "automatic, mechanical processes are at work, concealed beneath the ordinary appearance of animation"—but at work in the human, not in the machine. The Freudian drives are in a very real sense sci-fi or at any rate motivate the journey to the magnetic fields.

It is to this latter text that I now turn. I do not want to argue that *Magnetic Fields* is science fiction. For one thing, it is not fiction at all; the text is resolutely antinarrative, comprised of brief and exceedingly quixotic vignettes: it reads more like a Rimbaudian prose poem than anything else. I do propose however that we can read it as a prescience fiction poem; like Loy's "Human Cylinders," which antedates *Magnetic Fields* by several years, Breton and Soupault's somnambulistic collaboration prefigures themes, tropes, and methods that later sci-fi poetry will put into play. The question of genre here is not trivial; again, Frye classifies science fiction as a form of romance, but his designation is not designed to be limiting or final. In what itself is something of an uncanny coincidence, Frye uses the figure of the magnetic field to explain the dynamics of genre, as Joseph Adamson, quoting from Michael Dolzani's introduction to Frye's *Notebooks on Romance*, points out:

> Frye is not terribly interested in the definition of literary genres or categories, because definitions imply an essentialist view of literature that he does not share. "Romance" is not an essence or exactly delimited area but a context: that is, a set of expectations for the imagination of either the writer or the reader. Some of the fun and creativity of any literary form comes from the possibility of playing either with or against the expectations of the context; it can be even more creative to play with and against the conventions at the same time.[19]

Adamson continues, "As Frye himself put it, the context provided by such definitions is 'something like a magnetic field, not a farmer's field with a fence around it.'"[20]

As itself part of a generic magnetic field, then, *Magnetic Fields* may be said to *attract* a science fiction poetics reading: "contexts" like surrealist automatic writing and science fiction poetry mutually magnetize and constellate around one another. Part of the fun and force of literary criticism can also come from the possibility of playing either with or against the expectations of context: that is, from reading a text through the lens of a different genre. If we knock down the farmer's fence around the magnetic field, what Deleuzian frontiers might we discover?[21]

"Eclipses," the third entry in *Magnetic Fields*, begins with "a hole of unknown depth" and ends with "a journey to the center of the earth"[22]—the whole thing figuratively takes place underground in an infernal world of blood and milk in a "circus of leaps" that also opens and closes the text, although at the end "in place of the ring-master you notice a beautiful lioness" and "elephants with women's heads and flying lions."[23] Surrealist beasts run the show. The first paragraph lays out the scene: "The color of the fabulous salvations darkened until the slightest death-rattle; calm of the relative sighs. Despite the smell of milk and coagulated blood the circus of leaps is full of melancholy seconds. A little further, however, there is a hole of unknown depth that attracts the gaze of all of us, it is an organ of repeated joys. Simplicities of the ancient moons, you are masterly mysteries for our eyes injected with common places." This is a world of "mountains of sands and fossils," a "metallic valley" that is "the headland of our original sins" where "the whole troop of repulsed desires turn pale and lose an amount of turbid blood" and "monstrous theories of nightmares were dancing away out of sight discontinuously." The entrance to this eroticized space is itself an organ of repeated joys: we are deep in the sexualized id here, figured as a mother's body that is at the same time a Bosch-like landscape of war and trauma in whose "aimless lanes . . . the great mortal sins condemned to forgiveness are born." Archetypal and allegorical, the Earth's core "is a large landscape that is disappearing"; that is, it fades and changes even as we look at it, after the shifting manner of dream.[24]

As does the prose of *Magnetic Fields*. Gnomic hybrid phrases ("senseless bicycles," "the color of the fabulous salvations," "the donkey's carcass on the song of the dying"[25]) driven by relentless non sequitur torque the strangeness, although usually we can visualize the objects and events that we are being shown. Even something like a futurist appears at one point: "Of all supposable navigators, the one with his chest formed like a port pleases me most."[26] But "sweating vertebrate superior cathedrals" are more difficult to imagine, and "stiff stem of Suzanne uselessness especially village of flavors with a lobster church" strains meaning making to the limit.[27] But then why would the language of the id not slip toward the other-sense of dream? Project oneiric logic into syntax and you end up with a lobster church in a village of flavors or even the stiff stem of Suzanne uselessness. The smart set on their journey to the center of the Earth "have been told about buried suns," and "like you, they will go to sleep tonight in the breath of this optical bouquet which is a fond misuse."[28]

UNCANNY MOTHERS

An "optical bouquet which is a fond misuse" is an excellent way to describe surrealist writing in texts like "Eclipses," where bizarre fusions created out of fragments of syntax merge into radically disjunctive new orders. Automatic writing as practiced by Breton and Soupault allegedly gives authors access to a poetics based on the dynamics of dream or at any rate unseats the ego in its role of creative writer in order to produce an uncanny text in which one feels that automatic, mechanical processes are at work, concealed beneath the ordinary appearance of animation. How this informs science fiction poetry and poetics down the line is the subject of the rest of this chapter, but first I would like to take another brief excursion to the Earth's core, where we find both a buried sun and "rocks of the Miocene or Eocene bearing the imprint of monstrous creatures from those ages"—in fact, not just imprints, but the monstrous creatures themselves. Edgar Rice Burroughs's Pellucidar is perhaps the most finely discriminated fictional world at the center of the Earth, which it turns out is a hollow sphere with a stationary sun at its center, a kind of concave version of the Earth in which evolution has played out along different lines than it did on its surface. *At the Earth's Core*, published serially in *All Story-Weekly* in 1914, six years before *Magnetic Fields* appeared, is the first of seven novels that takes place in Pellucidar and illustrates in a popular and pulp science-fictional vein several of the tropes that I examine, including buried pasts, historical and psychological, and the sense of the uncanny. As an example of the "garish and vulgar kinds of cultural junk and paraliterature" that Jameson tells us Breton was enamored of, *At the Earth's Core* is relevant here. And while Burroughs in no way employs anything resembling surrealist techniques of disjuncture or fragmentation, Pellucidar is a kind of montage in its primitively filmic blending of different periods in the Earth's history and various phases of its biologic life. Burroughs's version of the sci-fi center of the Earth shares key features with Breton and Soupault's surrealist underworld.

Several geologic epochs coexist in Pellucidar, where dinosaurs and saber-toothed tigers compete for space along with "races" ostensibly representing various "stages" of humanity, the lower of which include arboreal ape-like humanoids who build tree houses and the Sagoths, simioids who at one point capture David Innes, the protagonist of the novel:

> Our guards, whom I already have described as gorilla-like men, were rather lighter in build than a gorilla, but even so they were indeed mighty creatures. Their arms and legs were proportioned more in conformity with human standards, but their entire bodies were covered with shaggy, brown hair, and their faces were quite as brutal as those of the few stuffed specimens of the gorilla which I had seen in the museums at home.

> Their only redeeming feature lay in the development of the head above and back of the ears. In this respect they were not one whit less human than we.[29]

These creatures are topped however by a "copper-colored" race of island dwellers, and finally by the Gilaks, "a noble-appearing race with well-formed heads and perfect physiques: The men were heavily bearded, tall and muscular; the women, smaller and more gracefully molded, with great masses of raven hair caught into loose knots upon their heads. The features of both sexes were well proportioned—there was not a face among them that would have been called even plain if judged by earthly standards."[30]

Burroughs here falls all too predictably into the "ascent of man" scenario envisioned by vulgar Darwinists at the turn of the century; along with the accompanying schematics of the period's racial and ethnic stratifications, this makes for some of the most unsavory reading in his novel, and both appear consistently throughout his oeuvre. Science fiction in the service of racialist essentialism: the naked arboreal ape-like creatures "were to all appearances strikingly similar in aspect to the Negro of Africa," their rudimentary language consisting of gibbering and chattering; the gorilla men wear loin cloths and tunics and speak a simple, pared-down language.[31] Ja the islander is "of a coppery red not unlike that of our own North American Indian, nor were his features dissimilar to theirs. He had the aquiline nose found among many of the higher tribes, the prominent cheek bones, and black hair and eyes, but his mouth and lips were better molded," and he is articulate.[32] The Gilaks, Innes says, "were fashioned along the same lines as ourselves—there was nothing grotesque or horrible about them as about the other creatures in this strange, weird world"; they are fully developed (read: White) human beings.[33] In Pellucidar, then, we find compacted traces of all of evolution, or at any rate its progression from the Triassic to the present, organized as a hierarchy of ranked lifeforms. Because the stationary sun at the Earth's core never rises or sets, there is no time there: all of the phases of evolution are simultaneously and eternally present at the center of the Earth.

The word *uncanny* appears six times in the novel, once to describe "the weird and uncanny aspect of the seascapes of Pellucidar," the surface of which, because it is literally the inside of a sphere, curves upward: "Behind us lay the broad inland sea, curving upward in the horizonless distance to merge into the blue of the sky, so that for all the world it looked as though the sea lapped back to arch completely over us and disappear beyond the distant mountains at our backs."[34] The other five times the word appears it is used to describe "the hideous and uncanny Mahars," truly the weirdest creatures in Pellucidar and "the heads—the brains—of the inner world"[35]:

> The all-powerful Mahars of Pellucidar are great reptiles, some six or eight feet in length, with long narrow heads and great round eyes. Their beak-like mouths are lined with sharp, white fangs, and the backs of their huge, lizard bodies are serrated into bony ridges from their necks to the end of their long tails. Their feet are equipped with three webbed toes, while from the fore feet membranous wings, which are attached to their bodies just in front of the hind legs, protrude at an angle of 45 degrees toward the rear, ending in sharp points several feet above their bodies.[36]

These giant living fossil rhamphorhynchi of the Middle Olitic "have no ears, not any spoken language. Among themselves they communicate by means of what . . . must be a sixth sense which is cognizant of a fourth dimension": the language of the Mahars etherealizes into pure telepathy.[37] They are also a race consisting exclusively of females:

> Once the males were all-powerful, but ages ago the females, little by little, assumed the mastery. For other ages no noticeable change took place in the race of Mahars. It continued to progress under the intelligent and beneficent rule of the ladies. Science took vast strides. This was especially true of the sciences which we know as biology and eugenics. Finally a certain female scientist announced the fact that she had discovered a method whereby eggs might be fertilized by chemical means after they were laid—all true reptiles, you know, are hatched from eggs.
>
> What happened? Immediately the necessity for males ceased to exist—the race was no longer dependent upon them.[38]

The undisputed rulers of inner Earth, the Mahars oversee a vast empire of underground cities; the Sagoths are their lackeys and make up their formidable army, while the other races of Pellucidar they use for slaves and servants.

And for *food*: Innes witnesses what he calls "the uncanny method of the Mahars" when it comes to dining. Prisoners are first fatted and then taken to a large temple, the lower floor of which "was an enormous tank of clear water in which numerous hideous Mahars swam lazily up and down. Artificial islands of granite rock dotted this artificial sea, and upon several of them I saw men and women like myself." What happens next is truly uncanny: individual Mahars swim slowly up to the marooned prisoners, select one, and then hypnotize him or her in a telepathic trance. Innes secretly watches the queen of the Mahars; it is worth quoting the passage at some length to get the twisted weirdness of the event:

> The queen fixed her gaze upon a plump young maiden. Her victim tried to turn away, hiding her face in her hands and kneeling behind a woman;

but the reptile, with unblinking eyes, stared on with such fixity that I could have sworn her vision penetrated the woman, and the girl's arms to reach at last the very center of her brain.

Slowly the reptile's head commenced to move to and fro, but the eyes never ceased to bore toward the frightened girl, and then the victim responded. She turned wide, fear-haunted eyes toward the Mahar queen, slowly she rose to her feet, and then as though dragged by some unseen power she moved as one in a trance straight toward the reptile, her glassy eyes fixed upon those of her captor. To the water's edge she came, nor did she even pause, but stepped into the shallows beside the little island. On she moved toward the Mahar, who now slowly retreated as though leading her victim on. The water rose to the girl's knees, and still she advanced, chained by that clammy eye. Now the water was at her waist; now her armpits. . . .

The Mahar sank now till only the long upper bill and eyes were exposed above the surface of the water, and the girl had advanced until the end of that repulsive beak was but an inch or two from her face, her horror-filled eyes riveted upon those of the reptile.

Now the water passed above the girl's mouth and nose—her eyes and forehead all that showed—yet still she walked on after the retreating Mahar. The queen's head slowly disappeared beneath the surface and after it went the eyes of her victim—only a slow ripple widened toward the shores to mark where the two vanished.

For a time all was silence within the temple. The slaves were motionless in terror. The Mahars watched the surface of the water for the reappearance of their queen, and presently at one end of the tank her head rose slowly into view. She was backing toward the surface, her eyes fixed before her as they had been when she dragged the helpless girl to her doom.

And then to my utter amazement I saw the forehead and eyes of the maiden come slowly out of the depths, following the gaze of the reptile just as when she had disappeared beneath the surface. On and on came the girl until she stood in water that reached barely to her knees, and though she had been beneath the surface sufficient time to have drowned her thrice over there was no indication, other than her dripping hair and glistening body, that she had been submerged at all.

Again and again the queen led the girl into the depths and out again, until the uncanny weirdness of the thing got on my nerves so that I could have leaped into the tank to the child's rescue had I not taken a firm hold of myself.

> Once they were below much longer than usual, and when they came to the surface I was horrified to see that one of the girl's arms was gone—gnawed completely off at the shoulder—but the poor thing gave no indication of realizing pain, only the horror in her set eyes seemed intensified.
>
> The next time they appeared the other arm was gone, and then the breasts, and then a part of the face—it was awful. The poor creatures on the islands awaiting their fate tried to cover their eyes with their hands to hide the fearful sight, but now I saw that they too were under the hypnotic spell of the reptiles, so that they could only crouch in terror with their eyes fixed upon the terrible thing that was transpiring before them.
>
> Finally the queen was under much longer than ever before, and when she rose she came alone and swam sleepily toward her bowlder. The moment she mounted it seemed to be the signal for the other Mahars to enter the tank, and then commenced, upon a larger scale, a repetition of the uncanny performance through which the queen had led her victim.[39]

In a textbook example of what Freud means by the uncanny, this passage shows us the dark fable at the heart of the core of the Earth, a sci-fi version of the dynamics of the unconscious played out in a cracked mirror of evolution. The hypnotic power that the Mahar queen exerts over the plump young maiden certainly suggests automatic, mechanical processes at work: the latter's unescapable fate leads to her gradual dismemberment while she is still living, her body losing its organs to the appetite of a devouring mother who communicates, purely on an instinctual level, the death drive in the service of a wicked anima. This is about the power of the archetypal mother in the primal waters of the id, a power that should have remained hidden but is brought to light by the males—David Innes and Burroughs himself—secretly witnessing the phantasmagorical violence at the heart of patriarchal consciousness. As in *Magnetic Fields* and Baum's Ev, the center of the Earth in Burroughs is a paranoid place of terror where sexual politics play out in mythic registers and the uncanny materializes in dismembered bodies and bodiless heads, human beings turned into automatons, fodder, things.

"THE OLD SPLINTERED PINK CARNIVAL 1917"

Another book that takes place in a "tortured metal Oz" whose "cities are controlled by the Elders who are heads in bottles" is William Burroughs's *Nova Express*, a volume in the so-called Cut-Up Trilogy. Nominated for the Nebula Award in 1965, *Nova Express* is science fiction on steroids, and it aggressively demonstrates many of the themes and formal strategies that I examine.[40] As the self-acknowledged heir of the Dadaists and surrealists—"the old splintered pink carnival 1917"[41]—Burroughs uses avant-garde techniques of collage, cut up, appropriation, sampling, juxtaposition, and general repurposing to create a multifaceted mash-up of a text mobilized by intense imagery and grammar based on the disjunctive visual dynamics of dreaming.[42] While it primarily takes place in outer space settings like the Crab Nebula and Venus, *Nova Express* is also an underground text, although the underground here has migrated from the Earth's core to a political "underground made up of adventurers who intend to outthink and displace the present heads" who not only rule the Crab Nebula but are locked with our band of adventurers in a cosmic struggle for control and domination that plays out in galactic, psychological, and technological registers that interpenetrate and overlap with one another.[43] *Where* exactly this "novel" takes place is a good question: the profoundly hybrid nature of its colliding and shifting settings and literary modalities makes for kaleidoscopically disoriented reading.

In *Nova Express*, every science fiction trope is exaggerated, enhanced, and literally driven into the structures and textures of the writing itself in order to produce a work that operates like a complicated gadget that performs in its machinations the very operations and events that it describes.[44] Burroughs abolishes or at any rate seriously refashions narrative. As Oliver Harris says, "there's no more 'plot' progression than there is 'character' development" in the text,[45] which works less like a novel and more like a comic book, whose irregularly gridded cells shatter narrative into a surface of excited vignettes in a collage of sharply angled views and agitated perspectives—and less like a comic book than a highly managed prose poem: in fact, in an interview, Burroughs cites Rimbaud's "poetic images" when explaining the cut-up method.[46] With neither plot progression nor character development, *Nova Express* might better be thought of as one of Frye's magnetic fields, an attractor inviting approaches from multiple genres—it can be read as a novel, a poem, a literary comic book, a dream sequence, a hallucination—or maybe it is best understood as a "textual war machine and homemade spaceship built for time travel," as Harris puts it.[47]

At issue in Burroughs's paranoid vision are the nature of information and the questions of who controls it and to what ends. Information is delivered through "image," and the ongoing struggle between the Nova Police and the Nova Mob—the good guys and the bad guys, roughly speaking—over control of image making is the subject of the bulk of the book. Image making occurs in a myriad of media formats—films and movies, television, radio, tape recordings, newspapers, and magazines like *Time* and *Life*—but it also operates on the "colorless sheets" of flesh, on and in the human body itself. Information is transdimensional and migrates through time, space, solids, fluids, bodies, minds—in short, everything and anything—and this contributes to the multiplexed and kaleidoscopic effect of the text. Burroughs's controlling metaphor for the dynamics of image is junk, heroin, along with morphine and mescaline: "Since junk *is* image the effects of junk can easily be produced and concentrated in a sound and image track."[48] Images deliver information like drugs deliver hallucinations, and whoever is pushing the images controls the information: "As we have seen image *is* junk—The hallucinogen drugs shift the scanning pattern of 'reality' so that we see a different 'reality'—'Reality' is simply a more or less constant scanning pattern—The scanning pattern we accept as 'reality' has been imposed by the controlling power on this planet, a power primarily oriented towards total control—In order to retain control they have moved to monopolize and deactivate the hallucinogen drugs by effecting noxious alterations on a molecular level."[49]

There are four ways of combating the reality-scanning patterns of the controlling powers: first, by "cut[ting] the control lines of word and image laid down by the nova mob" and interfering with their media platforms;[50] second, by taking over and assuming control of the platforms themselves in order to transmit alternative images and hence an alternative reality; third, by "not answering the machine" but instead "shutting it off," that is, by practicing noncompliance and silence in the face of media onslaught.[51] The fourth is Plan D, which "called for Total Exposure. Wise up all the marks everywhere. Show them the rigged wheel of Life-Time-Fortune. Storm the Reality Studio. And retake the universe": that is, write *Nova Express*.[52] Burroughs equates these acts of sabotage with the effects of apomorphine, a dopamine agonist used to neutralize the effects of hallucinogens: "Apomorphine combats parasite invasion by stimulating the regulatory centers to normalize metabolism. A powerful variation of this drug could deactivate all verbal units and blanket the earth in silence, disconnecting the entire heat syndrome."[53]

The book divides into two thematic halves: the first four chapters describe the ongoing war between the Nova Police and the Nova Mob, locked in cosmic struggle for control of the image-making powers that determine reality; the second four concern the "Biologic Courts," an intergalactic agency that regulates and adjudicates complaints and crimes in Burroughs's supremely dysfunctional universe. A myriad of characters roils through the text, where conspiratorial Nova criminals with noir-ish mobster names like "Sammy the Butcher" and "Green Tony" battle with their counterparts working in and around the Nova police, notably Inspector Lee, whose "program of total austerity and total resistance," involving "the judicious use of apomorphine and silence," opens and closes the book; and Agent K9, who we first encounter "in combat with the alien mind screen. . . . K9 moved back into the combat area—Standing now in the Chinese youth sent the resistance message jolting clicking tilting through the pinball machine—Enemy plans exploded in a burst of rapid calculations—Clicking in punch cards of redirected orders crackling shortwave static—Bleeeeeeeeeeeeeep—Sound of thinking metal—'Calling partisans of all nations—Word falling—Photo falling—Break through in the Grey Room'—Pinball led streets—Free doorways—Shift coordinate points—."[54] This passage illustrates the transmedial nature of information, here floating through pinball machines, computer-programming punch cards, and shortwave radio, and the disconnected phrases of the resistance message from "the sound of thinking metal"—"Word falling—Photo falling—Break through in the Grey Room"—are repeated many times throughout the text. Burroughs glosses this recurring passage in an interview:

> INTERVIEWER: Incidentally, one image in Nova Express keeps coming back to me and I don't quite understand it: the gray room, "breaking through to the gray room."
> BURROUGHS: I see that as very much like the photographic darkroom where the reality photographs are actually produced. Implicit in *Nova Express* is a theory that what we call reality is actually a movie. It's a film, what I call a biologic film. What has happened is that the underground and also the nova police have made a breakthrough past the guards and gotten into the darkroom where the films are processed, where they're in a position to expose negatives and prevent events from occurring. . . . For nova police, read technology, if you wish.[55]

A number of such battles between various Nova agents and a changing cast of aliens appear in the book. For instance, K9 encounters Insect People and Vegetable People, along with "The Elders who are heads in bottles," on the Brass and Copper Streets of the planet Minraud in "Crab Nebula," the critical and pivotal fourth chapter of *Nova Express*. Not only is this section literally the center of the book, but here we witness the key battles in the war and hear of Burroughs's three techniques for countering the image making of the Nova criminals—photomontage, tape splicing, and his own invention, the fold in. The scene opens with the

> Controller of The Crab Nebula on a slag heap of smoldering metal under the white hot sky channel[ling] all his pain into control thinking—He is protected by heat and crab guards and the brains armed now with The Blazing Photo from Hiroshima and Nagasaki—The brains under his control are encased in a vast structure of steel and crystal spinning thought patterns that control whole galaxies thousand years ahead on a chessboard of virus screen and juxtaposition formulae—
>
> So the Insect People Of Minraud formed an alliance with the Virus Power Of The Vegetable People to occupy planet earth—[56]

Blazing photos from Hiroshima and Nagasaki appear several times in the text; they are among the principal images used when the "Leaders turn on image rays to flood the world with replicas" and create the chaotic conditions that give them power.[57] Earlier we hear that audio recordings work the same way:

> The basic nova mechanism is very simple:: Always create as many insoluble conflicts as possible and always aggravate existing conflicts—. . . . Like this:: Take two opposed pressure groups—Record the most violent and threatening statements of group one with regard to group two and play back to group two—Record the answer and take it back to group one—Back and forth between opposed pressure groups—This process is known as "feed back"—You can see it operating in any bar room quarrel—In any quarrel for that matter—Manipulated on a global scale feed back nuclear war and nova—These conflicts are deliberately created and aggravated by nova criminals—[58]

Through the strategic and aggressive broadcasting of images, recordings, and texts, the Nova Mob choreographs the chaos that permits the Brains of the Crab Nebula to "hatch cosmologies of telepathic misdirection—Mind screen movies overlapping make recordings ahead and leave before thinking was recorded."[59]

In "Crab Nebula," we discover that Agent K9 has a special role to play in the war; he "was with the Biologic Police assigned to bring the Dwarf Plague under control by disconnecting the dwarfs from Central Control Station: The Insect Brain of Minraud enclosed in a crystal cylinder from which run the cold wires to an array of calculating machines feeding instructions to The Death Dwarf In The Street." He meets up with the dwarfs in a local café:

> Biologic Agent K9 called for his check and picked up supersonic imitation blats of The Death Dwarfs . . . — . . . He ordered another coffee and monitored the café—A whole table of them imitating word forms and spitting back at supersonic speed—Several patrons rolled on the floor in switch fits—These noxious dwarfs can spit out a whole newspaper in ten seconds imitating your words after and slinking in suggestion insults—That is the entry gimmick of The Death Dwarfs: supersonic imitation and playback so you think it is your own voice—(do you own a voice?) they invade The Right Centers which are The Speech Centers and they are in the right—[60]

In an earlier version of either the same scene or one that is uncannily similar, "when K9 entered the café he felt the colorless smell of The Vegetable People closing round him"; in both cases he fights agents of the Nova Mob in what turns out to be a café version of the Grey Room.[61] The question is, how to neutralize the "colorless sheets between you and what you see taste touch smell eat" that the Vegetable People generate and the noxious newspapers that the Death Dwarfs spit out, "imitating your words after and slinking in suggestion insults."

"The counter move" for dealing with the Vegetable People, Burroughs tells us

> is very simple—This is machine strategy and the machine can be redirected —Record for ten minutes on a tape recorder—Now run the tape back without playing and cut in other words at random—Where you have cut in and re-recorded words are wiped off the tape and new words in their place—you have turned time back ten minutes and wiped electromagnetic word patterns off the tape and substituted other patterns—You can do the same with mind tape after working with the tape recorder—(This takes some experimentation)—The old mind tapes can be wiped clean—Magnetic word dust falling from old patterns—Word falling—Photo falling—[62]

In other words, the way to induce a "break through in the Grey Room," "where the reality photographs [and tapes, and newspapers, and your mind, etc.] are actually produced," is to use the very cut-up and splicing techniques that Burroughs employs in composing *Nova Express*. When K9's attempt to release a "Silence Virus" to still the Death Dwarfs as they "yacked through the streets imitating words and gestures of everyone in sight" is thwarted by

> political leaders [who] projected stern noble image from control towers," K9 shrugged and put in a call for Technicians—"The error in enemy strategy is now obvious—It is machine strategy and the machine can be redirected. . . .
>
> The operation is very technical—Look at photomontage—It makes a statement in flexible picture language—Let us call the statement made by a given photomontage X—We can use X words X colors X odors X images and so forth to define the various aspects of X—Now we feed X into the calculating machine and X scans out related colors, juxtapositions, affect-charmed images and so forth we can attenuate or concentrate X by taking out or adding elements and feeding back into the machine factors we wish to concentrate—A Technician learns to think and write in association blocks which can then be manipulated according to the laws of association and juxtaposition—Our technicians learn to read newspapers and magazines for juxtaposition statements rather than alleged content—[63]

Photomontage is the pictorial equivalent of cutting and splicing audio tape; in both cases, surrealist juxtapositions are created, in effect disabling the logic of "reality" by interrupting the continuities and integrity of the scanning patterns of images and sounds that make it up: "materials from purge trials and concentration camps and reports from Nagasaki and Hiroshima" are cut and pasted in order to "construct another system working on quite different principals [*sic*]" from those of the Insect Leader Brains.[64] The consequences are dramatic:

> "Green Tony squealed and I'm off for Galaxy X—"
>
> "The whole mob squealed—Now we can move in for some definitive arrests Set arrest machinery in operation—Cover all agents and associations with juxtaposition formulae—Put out scanning patterns through coordinate points of the earth for Mr. and Mrs. D—Top Nova Criminals—Through mind screens of the earth covering coordinate points blocking D out of a hand a mouth a cold sore—Silver antibiotic handcuffs fitting D virus filters and—Lock—Click—We have made the arrest— . . .
>
> "That did it—Release Silence Virus—Blanket Area—"
>
> "Thinking in association blocks instead of words enables the operator to process data with the speed of light on the association line—Certain alterations are of course essential—"[65]

In between the twin accounts of K9's victorious battles with the Vegetable People and the Death Dwarfs, in what is structurally the exact center of *Nova Express*, is a short section titled "A Bad Move": "Could give no other information than wind walking in a rubbish heap to the sky—Solid shadow turned off the white film of noon heat—Exploded deep in the alley tortured metal Oz—Look anywhere, Dead hand—Phosphorescent bones—Cold Spring afterbirth of that hospital—Twinges of amputation—Bread knife in the heart paid taxi boys—If I knew I'd be glad to look anyplace—No good myself—Clom Friday."[66] Harris in his note to "A Bad Move" tells us that "shortly before submitting the March 1962 MS, Burroughs mailed [Bryan] Gysin a two-page typescript, illustrating his new 'fold-in' method, that overlaps this section and includes its specified literary source texts"[67]: thus a textbook example of K9's strategy of dismembering and reassembling image into new juxtapositions, recursively appearing as the original source of precisely these means of proceeding, the text itself working as a time machine of its own inception. In *Nova Express*, time, form, and content fuse and mutually inform one another to make a sci-fi gadget, an ensemble of parts and gears that perform in their machinations the very occasions they describe.

The tone of the text shifts perceptibly in the second half of the book, beginning with the chapter "From a Land of Grass without Mirrors." The war between the Nova Mob and the Nova Police appears to be over; handcuffs have been fitted to the wrists of conspirators, and the writing at times becomes almost bucolic: "Moments I could describe that were his eyes in the countries of the world—Left you the sick dawn bodies—Fading smiles—in other flesh—For now—Such gives no shelter—Shifted the visiting address—The wind at noon—walks beside you? Piece of a toy revolver there in nettles of the alley . . . over the empty broken streets a red white and blue kite."[68] An uneasy peace and a sense of restored law and order appear in the text, as we leave scenes of combat and enter the provenance of the Biologic Courts, which we first hear mentioned after the discussion of the basic Nova mechanism ("Always create as many insoluble conflicts as possible and always aggravate existing conflicts"): "Now you may well ask whether we can straighten out this mess to the satisfaction of any life forms involved and my answer is this—Your earth case must be processed by the Biologic Courts."[69] The scene opens with "corridors and patios and porticos of The Biologic Courts—Swarming with terminal life forms desperately seeking extension of canceled premissos and residence certificates."[70] Insect People of Minraud mingle peacefully with Heavy Metal People from Uranus, Green People, humans, and myriad other life forms, all seeking the resolution of "insoluble and existing conflicts." A sense of justice, fairness, and solidarity pervades the proceedings: "The judge, many light years away from possibility of corruption, grey and calm with infallible authority reads the brief— . . . —'My God what a mess'—he said at last—'Quiet all of you—You all understand I hope what is meant by biologic mediation—This means that the mediating life forms must simultaneously lay aside all defenses and all weapons—it comes to the same thing and all connection with retrospective controllers under space conditions merge into a single being which may or may not be successful—.'"[71] The Nova system is in a postconflict period in which war crimes are adjudicated and claims against former occupiers are settled as the court "brings action from unspeakable indignities and negligence demanding biologic lawyers who never hustle a form."[72]

In "A Horrible Case," we learn how the Biologic Courts arrive at juridical decisions. Burroughs gives us "the classic case presented to first year [law] students," called "The Oxygen Impasse":

> Life Form A arrives on alien planet from a crippled space craft—Life Form A breathes "oxygen"—There is no "oxygen" in the atmosphere of alien planet but by invading and occupying Life Form B native to alien planet they can convert the "oxygen" they need from the blood stream of Life Form B—The Occupying Life Form A directs all the behavior and energies of Host Life Form B into channels calculated to elicit the

> highest yield of oxygen—Health and interest of the host is disregarded—Development of the host to space state is arrested since such development would deprive the invaders by necessity of their "oxygen" supply—For many years Life Form A remains invisible to Life Form B by a simple operation scanning out areas of perception where another life form can be seen—However an emergency a shocking emergency quite unlooked-for has arisen—Life Form B *sees* Life Form A—(Watching you have they thought debarred) and brings action in The Biologic Courts alleging unspeakable indignities, mental and physical cruelty, deterioration of mind body and soul over thousands of years, demanding summary removal of the alien parasite— . . . —"So what else could we do under the circumstances? The life form we invaded was totally alien and detestable to us.—We do not have what they call 'emotions'—soft spots in there host marked for invasion and manipulation—"[73]

How to solve this devilishly complicated case? Which life form gets access to the oxygen that after all is a primary biologic necessity and presumably a fundamental right for any living organism? Who gets to live, and who deserves to thrive?: "The Oxygen Impasse is a basic statement in the algebra of absolute need—'Oxygen' interchangeable factor representing primary biologic need of a given life form—From this statement the students prepare briefs—sift cut and rearrange so they can view the case from varied angles and mediums."[74] Thus in order to get a fresh perspective on the case, the students begin by cutting up the text of "The Oxygen Impasse" and sifting it into new combinations, as in "so where to first years students of Biologic Law Circumstances?—Life Form A was totally alien crippled space craft—Do not have what they call 'emotion's oxygen' in the atmosphere."[75] This only gets the case so far, however, and leads to a next impasse: "In short the plea of need offered by Life Form A is inadequate—To prepare a case would be new essay to investigate the original conditions and biologic history of Life Form A on location—A Biologic Counselor must know his client and be 'trained in the body-prison contradictions of biologic law'—It will not be easy for Life Form A to find a counselor willing to handle 'this horrible case.'"[76]

Where to find such a Biologic Counselor, one who we learn would be destroyed immediately "on location" by the alien conditions on Life Form A's planet? Burroughs's answer is ingenious: "Biologic Counselors must be writers that is only writers can qualify since the function of a counselor is to *create* facts that will tend to open biologic potentials for his client—One of the great early counselors was Franz Kafka and his briefs are still standard—The student first writes his own brief then folds his pages down the middle and lays it on pages of Kafka relevant to the case in hand—." This is precisely what happens;

in what follows, Burroughs copies a passage from *The Trial* that concerns the lack of oxygen in the courtroom offices in which Kafka's K finds himself: "'I fancy,' said the man who was stylishly dressed, 'that the gentleman's faintness is due to the atmosphere here—You see it's only here that this gentleman feels upset, not in other places—' Accustomed as they were to the office air felt ill in the relatively fresh air that came up from the stairway—."[77]

This in turn is followed by a passage describing the juridical procedures that get triggered when an impasse in a case is reached and it can no longer be followed or solved. Hence in order to solve a difficult case in the Biologic Court, the Biologic Counselor finds a literary precedent of the same ilk ("oxygen" and "impasse" are key words) and folds into it the legal brief at hand: in the present case, the passage from *The Trial* is folded in with "The Oxygen Impasse" and sections of "Crab Nebula" that describe the battles between K9 and the Nova creatures of Minraud:

> **BRIEF FOR THE FIRST HEARING / / CASE OF LIFE FORM A**
>
> "I fancy," said the man who was on alien planet, "that crippled faintness is due to the 'oxygen'—There is no 'oxygen' this gentleman feels but by invading and occupying 'the office air' they can convert the 'oxygen' up from the stairway of Life Form B. . . ."
>
> "I fancy," said the man, "that this gentleman feels white hot blue skies—Haste he had already so?"
>
> Even so there is a devious underground either outright or partial misdirection—The office air are heads in bottles—Beyond all doubt intend to outthink and replace the advocate—A client revolution—For how could he keep fallen heads to help him?—Metal shimmering heat from the stage where further assistance melts at noon into remote inaccessible courts—[78]

Burroughs thus has three texts collide in order to forge a new perspective on "The Horrible Case" regarding the legality of the parasitism of Life Form A on Life Form B. What the court concludes is both bracing and salutary:

> Clearly this a difficult case to defend particularly considering avowed intention of the accused to use the counselor as a diving suit back to their medium where counselor would be destroyed by alien conditions—There is however one phrase in the brief on which a defense can be constructed—"They sometimes mutate to breathe here"—That is if a successful mutation of Life Form A can be called in as witness—Clearly the whole defense must be based on possibility of mutation and the less said about "absolute biologic need" to maintain a detrimental parasitic exis-

> tence at the total expense of Form B the better chance of a compromise verdict suspended pending mutation proceedings—[79]

"Thinking in association blocks" of fold-in montage, then, causes the court to arrive at the enlightened conclusion that the only way to reach a "compromise verdict" is the *possibility of mutation*—that is, using textual mutation leads the court to change its own guiding principle of "absolute biologic need" in favor of the fundamental fact of and right to *change*. The court comes down on the side of juridical flexibility and metamorphosis, on the principle that justice operates best when it can shift and reorient according to the particular circumstances that it encounters instead of rigidly applying petrified and unbending rules. As William Blake puts it, "One law for the lion and the ox is oppression": the law needs to accommodate itself to the world, not the other way around. The Biologic Court ultimately decides that mutability is its guiding principle: life mutates, hence justice must do so.

And so must writing: cut up and fold in are the textual equivalents of the ongoing mutation of the law, since "only writers can qualify [as Biologic Counselors] since the function of a counselor is to *create* facts that will tend to open biologic potentials for his client." Central to Burroughs's notion of information is the creative word: whoever or whatever controls language articulates the very structure and image of reality: "What scared you all into time? Into body? Into shit? I will tell you: '*the word*.' Alien Word '*the*.' '*The*' *word* of Alien Enemy imprisons '*thee*' in Time. In Body. In Shit. Prisoner, come out. The great skies are open."[80] *Nova Express* is explicitly designed to liberate perception by creating new facts through its compositional procedures of splicing and juxtaposing.

I cannot pretend to account in any comprehensive manner for the richness and complexity of Burroughs's text; both its content and its form, wedded in a synthesis of ongoing possibility and constant detour, proscribe any such ambition. I have followed a particular fractured thread through a maze of fractured threads. In doing so, I have not only remained faithful to the spirit of the book, but I have read it as a science fiction poem, or at any rate as a text with a sci-fi poetics that reads more like a modernist poem than it does a novel. If "'reality' is simply a more or less constant scanning pattern," then presumably we can *scan* it, and likewise we can scan *Nova Express*, itself a reality-scanning pattern. For instance, the book's constant collaging and folding in of text causes something like refrains to appear: the phrases in passages like "Shift linguals—Free doorways—Cut word lines—Photo falling—Word falling—Break through in the Grey Room" recur constantly and provide a kind of ongoing rhythm whose beats are distributed at key points throughout the text. Specific scenes reappear, often with different casts of characters: "I was traveling with The Intolerable Kid on The Nova Lark"; "I was traveling with Limestone John on The Carbonic Caper"; "I was traveling with Merit John on The Carbonic Caper"; "I was traveling with Merit Inc. checking store attendants for larceny with a crew of 'shoppers'"); again, this has to do with the constant cutting and splicing and folding of text, which suggests time travel and makes the book's multiple overlapping spatial simultaneities appear.[81] The sci-fi axes of space (metaphor) and time (metonymy) collapse into one another but also shatter and replicate into a rhizometric and entropic mess predicated on crystalline structures of repetition, mirroring, faceting, and interference. The ludic and kitsch aspects of science fiction are represented by what Harris calls "the book's stream of literary fragments, sampled narratives, shifts in point of view, clips from B-movies and subliminal single frames of current events";[82] I would add to this list references and tropes derived from noir detective fiction, comic books, gay porn, and pulp Westerns.[83] Burroughs adds one more: "The carny world was the one I exactly intended to create—a kind of midwestern, small-town, cracker-barrel, pratfall type of folklore, very much my own background." All of it is laced together by Burroughs's crackery Beat idioms: "By God before I give an inch the whole fucking shit house goes up in chunks."[84]

Finally, there is the lineation of the text, its Dickinson-esque use of dashes between phrases to provide another kind of scansion, a rhythm based on phrase and clause that echoes the dynamics of line break and enjambement. Presented as lines, the bucolic passage I cited earlier shows how the prose of the text works as a kind of excellent free verse:

> Moments I could describe that were his eyes in the countries of the world—
> Left you the sick dawn bodies—
> Fading smiles—in other flesh—
> For now—
> Such gives no shelter—
> Shifted the visiting address—
> The wind at noon—walks beside you?—
> Piece of a toy revolver there in nettles of the alley . . .
> over the empty broken streets a red white and blue kite.

The ghost iambics of *The Waste Land* can be heard here, and the isolation and stacking of fragmentary phrases model the jagged parataxis of modernist poetry. Jakobson defines the poetic function as "the set towards the message as such, focus on the message for its own sake":[85] What better description of both the form and the content of Burroughs's book, which is all about *message* and the networks and semantics that deliver it? *Nova Express* may be a failed science fiction novel, but it is a great science fiction poem.[86]

"UNZIP SUIT SUBPARTICLE"

I want to end this chapter with a brief look at another instance of the poetic legacy of surrealist automatic writing. The poet Ted Greenwald talks about his poetry as "a kind of science fiction": "I prefer dealing with items that are still charged with meaning and in fact are open to the change that happens over time in meanings. In other words, if I don't know exactly what a poem means when I write it I'm somehow writing a kind of science fiction, because the poem . . . will eventually make sense on a more than just, say, shape level or form level as time goes by and I'll start to understand it more."[87] Here then we have the sense of science fiction as willfully blind experiment, a writing explicitly for the future: like Breton and Soupault, Greenwald writes without knowing what his poem "means," hoping that the change over time in the meanings of the poem's words will eventually lead to his understanding. This is close to Deleuze's sense of science fiction as writing that occurs on the frontiers of knowledge where we write of "those things which we don't know, or know badly."[88] A text like Greenwald's *You Bet!*, from 1978, should be considered a kind of science fiction poetry according to both his and Deleuze's definitions:

> unzip suit subparticle
> Too nice getting
> Into attractive and
> Distracting light through it
>
> Being a long wait for you
> Discovering what you
> Meant when you
> Asked me here tonight
>
> Feel where's my child
> Take on authority through
> The author of your woes
> Only yourself to blame
>
> Dedicated to no one and
> Nothing leaves me be
> Strung out through,
> From where I know you?
>
> Some quiet some
> Swim point only condition
> Direction from modern
> Some day you'll understand[89]

Greenwald claims that he wrote the 350 quatrains of *You Bet!* in one sitting, hence the text as automatic, improvisational, and experimental. "Unzip suit subparticle" already evokes sci-fi, and in the fifth stanza's final two lines—"Direction from modern / Some day you'll understand"—we read a compact statement of Greenwald's future-oriented poetics.

The writing has a distinctly surrealist cast to it, especially on the level of image, but also in its syntax, where Greenwald employs a sophisticated and convoluted present perfect progressive tense in order to suggest an ongoing garbling of temporalities: When did/does the "being a long wait for you" occur? Is the speaker still waiting? "Discovering what you / Meant when you / Asked me here tonight": Will this insight into a past motivation for the staging of a present event be resolved in some future? When will the discovering end? Where exactly *is* "from where I know you?" Is that a temporal marker? Greenwald not only writes with items that "are open to the change that happens over time in meanings," he composes a prose that in its very syntax instantiates that change: a poetry comprised of snapshots of ongoing time traveling through densely nested temporal dimensions that warp and twist and blend into one another.

While *You Bet!* is neither cut up nor fold in, it displays a fully *motivated* "kind of science fiction," where the genre's main drives—exploration, discovery of strange new realities, experiment, the stress testing of materials under the pressure of estrangement, temporal and spatial distortion—are curated by the poet in the very instant of writing the poem's lines. This takes us to a sci-fi poetics where all pretense of narrative, character, plot, and theme dissolve into the momentary moves from phrase to phrase and word to word, themselves trace and evidence of the writing as literal activity, a speculative pressing on the borders of what is known and what is knowable.

3

Riding the Tachyon Showers

Ed Dorn's Gunslinger

> The Whole Set is Sinking
> And theyre still talkin œcology
> Without even blinking
>
> —Edward Dorn, *Gunslinger*

> INTERVIEWER: You've said your next book will be about the American West and a gunfighter.
>
> BURROUGHS: Yes, I've thought about this for years and I have hundreds of pages of notes on the whole concept of the gunfighter. The gun duel was a sort of Zen contest, a real spiritual contest like Zen swordsmanship.[1]

By his own account, William Burroughs had for years collected notes for a full-fledged Western, and while he never got around to writing it, Ed Dorn did: his long sci-fi poem *Gunslinger* is precisely about "the whole concept of the [Zen] gunfighter."[2] We now turn to the entangled worlds of the Western and science fiction. Sci-fi emerges from the Western like a surrealist sphinx moth from a chrysalis, ready to take wing and light out for the high desert stars.

We see this ongoing metamorphosis in any number of texts from the first decade of the twentieth century and up to the late 1930s. The "sci-fi Western" appears during this time, and in the American context, science fiction gradually transmutes into its own distinct generic shape and form; indeed, we might say that the sci-fi Western evolves into the Western sci-fi. This chapter looks at relevant works from 1912, 1934, and 1975, each of which plays science fiction through tropes of the Western. The setting of these texts is the American West itself, the grand landscapes that act at once as theatrical backdrops and as the natural environment against and in which their literary scenarios appear. These settings can be likened to the false fronts of the ramshackle buildings found in classic Western towns: "False fronts / my Gunslinger said make / the people mortal / and give their business / an inward cast. They cause culture."[3] Larger than life, false fronts signpost desire and distance and hence carry the inward cast and the outward projection of myth. The "culture" of the Western sci-fi originates in the cracker barrel of the general store out in front of the huge cardboard buttes of Monument Valley.

All three of my Western sci-fi's concern themselves at base with issues of natural resources and energy exploration and extraction. The West as it appears in these works is a vast ecology, a giant sandbox of precious metals, oil, natural gas, and fresh air, all ripe for exploitation. The West is simultaneously "the country of our consciousness" and "old dinosaur country / a record full of sudden changes" and, as such, it is a text where time and space are fully legible, if you only know how to read them.[4] Aliens and indigenes wander here, but who exactly is local and who is not are real questions, as these roles and identities shift and switch given colonial appropriation and the vagaries of property relations. Edgar Rice Burroughs's *A Princess of Mars*; the film serial *The Phantom Empire*, directed by Otto Brower and B. Reeves Eason; and Dorn's *Gunslinger* all play out in a science-fictionalized West marked by contest and conflict over who controls what resources: in *Gunslinger*, it is oil and gas, radium in *Phantom Empire*, and the planetary atmosphere itself in *Princess of Mars*. A novel, a film, and a long poem thus map the sci-fi crystal: with *Princess of Mars* we go up, into outer space; with *Phantom Empire* we go down, into the bowels of the Earth; with *Gunslinger* we traverse the state of New Mexico, rendered by Dorn as a Western "set" replete with cowpokes, hoodoos, stagecoaches, and a Mr. Ed–style talking horse. Each work breaks the generic bounds of the Western: stretch the borders of the west far enough either up, down, or laterally, and the sci-fi crystal appears as a categorical rupture. Even though the (Western) "Set is Sinking" in these works, they are still—and they are even *still*—"talking œcology."

APACHES ON THE PLANET OF PARADOXES

Princess of Mars begins as a straightforward Western but takes a sharp fork in the road—or into the air, as the case may be—two chapters in. The main protagonist of this first of twelve novels in Burroughs's Mars series is John Carter, a decommissioned Confederate officer who in 1866 discovers gold while mining in Arizona. Pursued by Apaches, he takes refuge in a cave, only to be paralyzed by a "slight vapor" that he takes to be poisonous gas. This leads to an out-of-body experience: terrified by the sounds of an invisible something-or-other moving around at the back of the cave, he mentally snaps his bonds only to find himself staring at his own body on the cave floor: "Unable longer to resist the temptation to escape this horrible place I leaped quickly through the opening into the starlight of a clear Arizona night. The crisp, fresh mountain air outside the cave acted as an immediate tonic and I felt new life and new courage coursing through me. Pausing upon the brink of the ledge I upbraided myself for what now seemed to me wholly unwarranted apprehension."[5]

What happens next will resonate in several ways through the entirety of the novel, hence I quote at some length:

> I decided to investigate, but first I lifted my head to fill my lungs with the pure, invigorating night air of the mountains. As I did so I saw stretching far below me the beautiful vista of rocky gorge, and level, cacti-studded flat, wrought by the moonlight into a miracle of soft splendor and wondrous enchantment.
>
> Few western wonders are more inspiring than the beauties of an Arizona moonlit landscape; the silvered mountains in the distance, the strange lights and shadows upon hog back and arroyo, and the grotesque details of the stiff, yet beautiful cacti form a picture at once enchanting and inspiring; as though one were catching for the first time a glimpse of some dead and forgotten world, so different is it from the aspect of any other spot upon our earth.
>
> As I stood thus meditating, I turned my gaze from the landscape to the heavens where the myriad stars formed a gorgeous and fitting canopy for the wonders of the earthly scene. My attention was quickly riveted by a large red star close to the distant horizon. As I gazed upon it I felt a spell of overpowering fascination—it was Mars, the god of war, and for me, the fighting man, it had always held the power of irresistible enchantment. As I gazed at it on that far-gone night it seemed to call across the unthinkable void, to lure me to it, to draw me as the lodestone attracts a particle of iron.
>
> My longing was beyond the power of opposition; I closed my eyes, stretched out my arms toward the god of my vocation and felt myself drawn with the suddenness of thought through the trackless immensity of space. There was an instant of extreme cold and utter darkness.[6]

Carter opens his eyes on the "dead and forgotten world"—or better the *dying* and *unknown* world—of Mars, or Barsoom in the local Martian parlance. In this passage, we see the Western hero literally projected into the outer space of science fiction, beamed from the Arizona desert to the surface of the red planet, which Burroughs calls a "world of paradoxes"; in fact, we see the West in its entirety broadcast there. The landscape Carter lands in is "strange and weird" like the "strange" and "grotesque" plateau country of the American Southwest, and even the region's weather is extended to the new setting: "It was midday, the sun was shining full upon me and the heat of it was rather intense upon my naked body, yet no greater than would have been true under similar conditions on an Arizona desert."[7]

The Southwest's Indigenous peoples appear on Mars as well or, at any rate, bizarre versions of them do: Carter is attacked and then taken in by a roving band of Tharks, members of the green warrior race of Barsoom: fifteen-foot-tall, olive-colored, four-armed bipeds with curved tusks, whose "eyes were set at the extreme sides of their heads a trifle above the center and protruded in such a manner that they could be directed either forward or back and also independently of each other." Of these "materialized nightmares," with their cup-shaped antennae and longitudinal nasal slits, seated astride massive eight-legged mounts and armed with forty-foot-long spears and rifles that shoot exploding radium bullets, Carter can only say, "I could not dissociate the people in my mind from those other warriors who, only the day before, had been pursuing me."[8] The Tharks even wear "gay-colored feathers and beautifully wrought leather trappings," and like Burroughs's Apaches, they delight in torturing their captives and mutilating their corpses.[9] They live like nomads in gigantic ancient ruined cities, reminiscent of the Anasazi and Mogollon pueblo ruins that dot Athabascan country. "They roamed an enormous tract of arid and semi-arid land between forty and eighty degrees south latitude, and bounded on the east and west by two large fertile tracts. Their headquarters lay in the southwest corner of this district, near the crossing of two of the so-called Martian canals" (the Gila River and the Rio Grande?). The American Southwest literally maps onto that part of Barsoom to which Carter so ardently beams.[10]

As do the racial dynamics of the country in whose Civil War Carter recently participated. The peoples of Barsoom are divided into a number of color-coded races—green, red, white, black, and yellow—locked in various grades of war in a never-ending struggle for the planet's ever-diminishing resources: its water, its food, and even its air. Burroughs rewrites the code: the green Tharks, as we have seen, resemble red Indians, while the red Martian race is equivalent to the white terrestrial race—Carter eventually marries a red Martian and becomes a Jed, a kind of emperor, of one of Barsoom's red cities. Members of the white Martian race, called Therns, wear blond wigs and are troped yellow in a kind of Orientalist fantasy of a far-away kingdom (actually queendom) of mystical priests; they are subservient to the warlike black pirates, described by Carter as handsome and blessed with "clear cut features," from one of Barsoom's moons. The yellow Martian race is known only in legend until Carter finds them out: its members sport beards and live at Mars's north pole in igloo-shaped structures (Eskimos? the Ainu?).

But more pertinent to the interests of the present chapter is the role of oxygen on the red planet and in the long passage I quote above. *Princess of*

Mars opens and closes with air: the fresh air that invigorates Carter when he first exits the cave and that inspires his awestruck vision of the moonlit Arizona vista, which leads directly to his visionary encounter with Mars in the night sky; and then the dying air of Barsoom, an increasingly arid world where oxygen has to be manufactured in a giant atmosphere factory manned by a single keeper, along with his one assistant, of the secret combination to opening the massive doors to the plant. At the end of the novel, both these characters die in suspicious circumstances, with the atmosphere factory inaccessibly shut and all life on Barsoom doomed to extinction. Carter it turns out knows the combination to the locking mechanism and races to open it, but he faints just as it opens. He wakes up back in the Arizona cave, ten years after he first beamed to Mars. The first thing he does is hasten out into the fresh air and onto eleven more books of adventure on Barsoom.

Air—oxygen, atmosphere—in *Princess of Mars* stands in for the invaluable but increasingly rare resources of the West and by extension of the Earth altogether. The trappings of the Western are all exaggerated on Barsoom, where Apaches inflate into gigantic green multilimbed warriors ranging over a land not just arid but desiccated, the seas and oceans long dried up, the famous canals in precarious condition and requiring constant surveillance and monitoring, and even the precious air in short supply. The amplifications and enhancement innate to science fiction are powerful tools for magnifying the dynamics of resource management in the West, the already gigantic scale of which balloons to fantastic proportions on Burroughs's Mars.

COWBOYS AT RADIUM RANCH

Phantom Empire also begins as a classic Western, replete with bucking broncos and a scene of gunslinging bandits chasing a stagecoach, but instead of projecting up into outer space, the film takes a downward turn into the Earth's core, or at any rate twenty-five thousand feet below its surface, where instead of the prehistoric world of Burrough's Pellucidar, we find the scientific city of Murania, a futuristic, super-technologically advanced civilization, presided over by Queen Tika and her Thunder Riders, horsemen who occasionally visit the surface dressed in capes and oxygen helmets. Tika and her advisors become aware of a plot by a band of unscrupulous scientists and entrepreneurs who want to mine for radium under Gene Autry's dude ranch, where every day at two o'clock the original Singing Cowboy and his Radio Riders broadcast a radio show featuring corny cowboy songs and an ongoing serial drama. Within the first seven minutes of *Phantom Empire*'s first episode, we discover that the stagecoach is a prop for the show. The bandits consist of Autry with a fake handlebar mustache and several members of his band, and the cargo of the coach is the band's instruments: the whole thing is staged for the guests at the ranch and provides a soundtrack for the broadcast. Autry and the Riders break into a comical song about Noah's ark, and then we watch a scene from the drama, staged like a movie, although not filmed but instead narrated by Autry into his giant microphone, and featuring a frontier woman cowering in the corner of a log cabin stage set while her husband heroically holds off a band of outlaws in a display of exaggerated melodrama. Autry then directs a technician to create the sound of the Thunder Riders by rattling a suspended sheet of metal.

In other words, we are not watching a Western, we are watching a "Western" or rather the making of a Western. Like Dorothy pulling back the curtain to reveal the real Oz, the movie gives us a peek behind the scenes of a scene. In a series of nested metadiscursive frames, we see a serial film of the making of a serial radio show based on a silent movie itself based on a melodrama. Another layer of framing is added when we watch Tika watching all this via a futuristic television from her underground palace. The West is no longer the frontier but has become the *set* for the *Western*, the landscape materializing in a dense interface of screens, radios, telephones, intercoms, cameras, scopes, lenses, and audio equipment. The settler's cabin has devolved into a dude ranch; the stagecoach has been replaced by automobiles; people fly across the sky in airplanes and descend into the Earth in futuristic elevators. Gridded and mapped by electronic media in an omnipresent mesh of technology, the Old West is clearly over, and the Western that so powerfully represented it is gradually morphing into an entirely different genre. The whole set is *literally* sinking, down into the lost world of Murania, where it will become a setting for the science fiction of the future.

All of this makes sense when we understand the dynamics of the period during which the serial was produced. It was shot in 1934 (released a year later), just seven years after the first feature length talkie (*The Jazz Singer* in 1927) and four years after the first full-sound serial appeared, 1930's *The Voice From the Sky*. Sound and voice were all the rage in 1934, which partially explains the Singing Cowboy and the embedded presence of radio in *Phantom Empire*. Movie audiences had never before *heard* the West, and the metal sheet thunder of the horses' hooves and Autry's plaintive warbling provided a proper soundtrack to accompany the false front scenarios of the generic Western. But more interesting is the fact that *The Voice From the Sky* was one of the first science fiction serials: sound and sci-fi serial films appeared at the same time. Westerns dominated the American serial film industry during its first three decades, during which a mere handful of silent sci-fi serials were produced; between 1930 and 1935, only two science fiction sound serials appeared while some twenty Westerns did so. After *Phantom Empire*, however, things changed:

Flash Gordon premiered in 1936 and *Buck Rogers* in 1939, while during 1945, three sci-fi serials and zero Westerns were produced. After World War II, science fiction and Western serials run pretty much neck and neck until the mid-1950s and the end of the serial altogether. *Phantom Empire* marks a transitional point between two genres in a moment of emergence of the one from the other.

An older media format appears in the film as well: Frankie, Autry's adolescent sidekick, a junior scientist with a secret laboratory in a barn loft, has been "reading books about a world underground"—most likely *At the Earth's Core* and other novels in the popular Pellucidar series (the latest of which at the time would have been 1930's *Tarzan at the Earth's Core*; the film serial *Tarzan the Fearless* aired in 1933). He also learns how to build his electronic "direction finder," a device with which he discovers the location of Murania, from a magazine. Clearly enthralled with the sci-fi worlds of Hugo Gernsbeck's scientific and pulp fiction periodicals, Frankie's magazines lead him away from the Western and down into the sci-fi center of the Earth in a dialectical spiral between the ranch and the city, the past and the future, and two ever-more distinct literary genres.

Murania is an odd collage of a place. The story goes that one hundred thousand years ago, during the last ice age, the original inhabitants of what is ostensibly New Mexico moved underground and built an Italian futurist city rivaling anything Antonio Sant'Elia could have designed.[11] Murania is inhabited by a race of white people who speak American English with a midwestern twang and who appear to be an amalgamation of different historical times and geographical places: Queen Tika sports an Elizabethan starched ruff and tiara; her courtiers and advisors wear costumes suggesting ancient Assyria, imperial China, and pharaonic Egypt; and her soldiers gad about in Roman garb and harness. It is all as if somebody had raided the costume shop of an opera company. They are served by a slave race of hilarious robots whose metal ears, noses, and tin cowboy hats serve no conceivable purpose; mute and rigid, these nonsentient automaton cowpokes provide for some of the funniest moments in the film as they stiffly haul about large objects and wield sledge hammers in the forges beneath the city. They guard Tika's realm in much the same way that the mechanical giant in *Ozma* guards the entrance to the Nome kingdom, by systematically waving broadswords up and down in front of entranceways, harmless drudge clocks.

Murania lends itself to any number of allegorical readings. For one, like all science fiction fantasies of the underground, it carries a sedimented timeline, although in this case not the collapsed evolutionary layers of Pellucidar. Murania instead comprises a compacted history of human culture, roughly from the period of the last glaciation to the present and on to the future but more narrowly focusing on "civilization," that is, on the "rise" of cities, kingdoms, empires, nations, and states, beginning with the ancient Near East and terminating in early modern England in a sort of accordioned westward march of civilization scenario. Inevitably, the trail ends under the American subcontinent and by extension deep in the American unconscious, where dreams of Manifest Destiny and modern technocratic supremacy blend seamlessly with *white* supremacy, that other staple of the sci-fi Western, traces of which we see in John Carter's Confederate roots. There are no Apaches—in fact, there are no Native Americans anywhere at all in the *Phantom Empire*: it turns out that the continent has always secretly been white, its original inhabitants having shifted underground well before the ancestors of the Amerindians crossed the Bering Strait. These latter peoples were not merely displaced by settlers but have been erased entirely from the historical record. What replaces Native presence in America is the spectral museum basement of European fantasies of culture and empire, transplanted into the very earth of its Great Southwest.

This vertical poetics of space has another dimension. Murania, as its name suggests, is powered by uranium, that baleful radioactive element that has been the cause of so much suffering—and wealth and power—in the West but especially in the Navajo and Western Pueblo lands of New Mexico and Arizona. Radio Ranch sits atop a huge deposit of uranium, and what initially disturbs the Muranians is their discovery of the nefarious plans hatched by Professor Beecham and his cronies to build a mine above their city in order to make a fortune extracting radium, used at the time primarily for illuminating glow-in-the-dark clock and watch dials, from their uranium deposits. The uranium market in the1930s was starting to take off due to American military interests: the horrible history of the atomic bomb in New Mexico was just beginning, and Beecham and his speculator friends were set to become millionaires. Something of the devastating effects of nuclear weapons ten years later (1945), in fact, is uncannily captured in the final episode of the series, as Murania is destroyed by a "disintegrating atom-smashing ray," designed by its own scientists, which gets out of control. The entire underground kingdom melts in front of your eyes in a jaw-dropping example of period special effects: the film appears to smear down the screen, its inhabitants and the city's dramatic architecture elongating fantastically as they drop into oblivion. Frankie's only comment on the catastrophe is that "it was worth it. I learned a lot of new scientific things"; Autry adds, "I'm afraid there isn't very much left of the city, but we'll probably find enough radium to make us all rich; it's under our ranch property." Property relations and resource extraction signal both the end of the past and the beginning of the future: somewhere between dude ranch and radio activity the Western is fading into cliches while science fiction explores ever weirder new worlds.

STAGECOACH, TIME MACHINE, SPACE CRAFT

I mean, there is no *way* to get rid of the cowboy. It's literally Star Wars.

—Edward Dorn, *Views*

I graduated in 1974 from Valley High School in Albuquerque, New Mexico. Our great pleasure that year was to drop acid and explore abandoned mines in the ghost towns near Magdalena and in the hills outside of Cerrillos and Mádrid. Our favorite spot though was a small mine just east of the village of Placitas, in the northern foothills of the Sandia Mountains. We would clamber down an ancient rickety ladder and then crawl on our bellies into the stygian gloom of what we called the Cone of Silence, a good-sized dome hewed out of the living rock at the end of a long narrow passage, where we would trip out in the profound darkness. My buddies Tom Coulter, Alfred Montoya, Goose McKenzie, and I spent many an hour watching the insides of our minds furl out in electric fireworks onto the intensely black canvas of the Cone.

Placitas at the time was a small adobe village; none of the rural suburban housing developments that presently sprawl west of town yet existed. It was famous for the Thunderbird Saloon, a low ramshackle hacienda that ran along the north side of the road that divides the town. Much beloved of bikers and used as a kind of community center by the locals, it burned to the ground in 1976. As Tony Hull puts it, "for those who lived in Placitas in the early Seventies, the Thunderbird was more than a bar, it was an institution without the pretension of being anything but itself."[12] Placitas was also at the time home to a number of poets, including Ed Dorn, who resided there for a brief period, and Robert Creeley, who owned a house in the village and lived there off and on during the 1970s. I had the good fortune to take several classes with him at the University of New Mexico. At the end of the semester, he would invite us all up to Placitas for drinks and food; I remember his wife, Penelope, setting out a huge bowl of fresh strawberries for everyone.

So when I read Ed Dorn's *Gunslinger*, I feel a sizable jolt of recognition, and it is not just the drugs and the hip-inflected southwestern landscape. After all, the cool bookstore in Albuquerque at the time, the Living Batch, was named after *Gunslinger*'s character I, who dies and is resurrected as "a living Batch" by being filled with a five-gallon can of pure LSD. I have already mentioned the mining towns—Placitas, Mádrid, and Cerrillos—through which the poem's stagecoach rambles, and I attended the Universe City in Albuquerque from 1974 to 1979. The philosophical currents there at the time were very much phenomenology and structuralism—Heidegger and Leví-Strauss, the two names of the Stoned Horse in *Gunslinger*—which we got in large doses, and with Creeley at the helm, the poetry buzz was all New American and Black Mountain. *Gunslinger* feels to me like an intimate roadmap of those days—Dorn says "this poem is like everyday life back then: it's a time trip"[13]—and while this does not necessarily qualify me to talk authoritatively about the book, it does provide a context and a location from which to begin.

Gunslinger likewise begins with a "map of locations," and below I trace that map and use it to organize the discussion that follows. In *Gunslinger,* we move along the horizontal pole of the sci-fi crystal, across its temporal and metonymical axis as opposed to its vertical and spatial axis, which we saw extend up into outer space in *Princess of Mars* and down into inner Earth in *Phantom Empire.* As the book's eponymous hero says, "Time is more fundamental than space":[14] Dorn calls his poem a *time trip,* a trip that unfolds in time—as all trips do! Of course, space also plays a major role for a Black Mountaineer like Dorn, for whom Olson's "I take SPACE to be the central fact to man born in America" is always crucial.[15] But *Gunslinger* is narrative, fictional, made up, linear, and plot driven in ways that Olson's work never was: Olson famously did not approve of the book, which is perhaps less an example of a projectivist poem than it is a poem about projectivism. The open field is present in *Gunslinger,* palpable in the huge empty stretches of the New Mexican landscape through which Slinger and his companions travel, but it is *inside* the poem, one of its objects, literally the stage for its coach. With his tightly wound, left justified, aggressively enjambed, columnar lines driving a phantasmal cast of characters across the set of a science-fictional Western, Dorn takes a step back from the projectivist field and the mandate of its *instanter* breath-based prosody and into the narratological temporality and orders of story. In a series of statements made about *Gunslinger,* he is careful to distance himself from projectivist poetics: "I never really could feel the faith in practicing what [Olson] thought of as breath. My line is never so radically long or short as his is, which is where the crucial point comes, the faith you have in the throw back from the end, and how the phrase is going to pick up again. I always mediated that. In that sense, I'm more conservative than he is."[16] Earlier, Dorn states: "I discovered had a much too turgid and complicated a line to be of use for this kind of work. This kind of statement, no matter how uneasy and difficult the content may get, calls for a fairly simple procedure. So the length of this line, as you can see, varies, from not quite short to very little beyond medium, pretty much throughout."[17]

Gunslinger is arti*fice* whereas *Maximus* is arti*fact*: the one an example of mediated construction, the other indexical testament to the immediacy of its own becoming. This is the "crucial point" that is embodied in line length and its throw back and pick up. We enter Dorn's poem via a different poetic of time and space, one not based in breath or body but instead designed as a "narrative [that is] essentially linguistic, because it starts with a series of standard settings, in cowboy times, with a coach in Billy the Kid country and it's on the border. . . . And it's just a series that moves along"—the way a sentence moves along, a vertical extension of contiguity and combination.[18] Less constellation than *vacation*, an ongoing account of a trip through a vacant space, *Gunslinger* is a moving locus reflecting upon a moving locus: "Again, it's drift. And there's locus, but the locus is where you're at and when you move, the locus moves."[19]

Where exactly does the locus move *from* and *to*? Tom Clark says that *Gunslinger* is "a text whose deepest engagement . . . is not with geography but ontology,"[20] but I would qualify that *Gunslinger* is a text that engages ontology *through* geography; the two cannot be separated, and in fact, this is one of the principle ideas—one of the riderless horses of instruction pulling Gunslinger's coach through the landscape—that motivates and mobilizes the poem. Like the Apaches who Dorn lionizes in *Recollections of Gran Apacheria*, whose ideas "come directly from their landform," *Gunslinger* is "wired to the desert,"[21] which is "the country of our consciousness" and through which "this group in which our brain is contained" moves: "The road along which we drive symbolizes // Symbolizes our thinking process."[22] Ontology, epistemology, and geography—that is, what *is*, how one *knows* it, and where it and one are *at*—make up the triad of Olson's human universe; separating these three from one another is the great error of Western metaphysics. I is located at the crossroads of this triad, and much of the first half of *Gunslinger* is a psychedelic comic-book treatise on how to keep I locked into what I sees as the source of what I knows and where I is. Pull these three "locations" apart and you get the sundered individual ego, the mortal small-s subject, terrified by its aloneness and alienated from the universe. During the course of the poem, I dies, resurrects, and becomes the secretary to Parmenides, the Eleatic philosopher who invented ontology and who advocates a kind of unified field theory of being while cautioning his readers not to ask too many Idiot Questions. This is also what I is told by both Gunslinger and his Bombed Horse, but it is equally the platform for the open field that Olson proposes in "Projective Verse" and the human universe envisioned in his essay of the same name. Dorn's *Gunslinger* proposes a redeemed I that, like the Thunderbird Saloon, is an institution without the pretension of being anything but itself, "an organ Ization / a pure containment" "I has shot past mortification / whispered the Slinger // I carries the Broken Code / the key to proprioception, / is it possible he has become the pure Come / of become."[23]

MAPS AND LEGENDS

> Landscape is not a poetic device. It is a material thing.
>
> —Ed Dorn, *Ed Dorn Live*

Gunslinger begins in southern New Mexico, in Mesilla, a small town that straddles the Rio Grande fifty miles north of the US border with Mexico at

Juarez, and it ends some five hundred miles away, just outside Cortez, Colorado, "in the very shadows of mesa verde."[24] The poem tracks the journey of the Gunslinger's metaphysical stagecoach as it travels due north up the Rio Grande to Albuquerque and then twenty miles beyond, at which point it leaves the river valley and heads east to Placitas, nestled in the northern foothills of the Sandia Mountains. From there, the coach tacks northeast and travels through the mining towns of Mádrid and Cerrillos, famous for its pre-Columbian turquoise and Spanish colonial silver mines. It then moves up Highway 14 to Santa Fe and stops at Kearny Avenue ("Phil Korny avenue") just north of the plaza, where one of the travelers in the coach has a rendezvous with his drug connection. We hear next of Farmington, in the far northwestern part of the state; presumably the coach takes Highway 84 from Santa Fe north to Abiquiu, Georgia O'Keefe country and the beginning of the Colorado Plateau ("We survey the Colorado plateau / There are no degrees of reality / in this handsome and singular mass, / or in the extravagant geometry / of its cliffs and pinnacles").[25] It then turns west at Chama, crosses the Jicarilla Apache reservation, and finally rolls on to Farmington, and beyond there to Shiprock, where it turns north and crosses the Colorado border on its way up to Cortez.

Why this close attention to the details of *Gunslinger*'s journey? I want to see Dorn's map of locations as part of what he at one point calls his "situational analysis," an analysis that is in equal parts historical, sociological, political, psychological, and geographical.[26] All of these "situations" are implicit in the map of Dorn's time trip poem with its mobile locus as it travels the length of New Mexico. The details of the journey locate us firmly in the landscape, a material thing rife with meaning and crucial to knowing what the poem is about.

Let me explain: first of all, the map maps exactly onto Gran Apacheria, the subject of Dorn's *Recollections of Gran Apacheria*, which was published just after *Gunslinger* and is a series of poems about the Apache Wars. In the poem "The Whole European Distinction," Dorn calls the wars "the longest continuous run / of external resistance" to US imperialism.[27] He tells us that the term was invented by the Spanish in colonial days to designate the area from central Texas to the Colorado River on the California/Arizona border and from northern Sonora in Mexico up to central Colorado. This is the ancestral homeland of the various bands of the Apache, and the coach travels directly up its spine; the Rio Grande historically divides the Eastern from the Western Apache (Dorn says he is particularly interested in the latter). We have already seen that for Dorn the Apache represent a deeply local sensibility, wired to the desert and literally in-formed by its landscapes. White people in this world are invaders from another genre, "always the conqueror waiting for the spaceship at the edge of the page," Dorn writes in "Reservations."[28] Traveling through sites of Indigenous resistance to this alien invasion, the stagecoach traces a sci-fi history straight up the western side of the middle of Apacheria, from Geronimo's Chiracahua lands southwest of Mesilla, which figured prominently in the Apache Wars (Fort Fillmore was built there in 1851 to protect the town), to the Jicarilla Apache reservation high in New Mexico's northwest quadrant.

There are plenty of reasons why *Gunslinger* should begin in Mesilla. The town marks the point of the Spanish Entrada into Nueva México, particularly the incursion in 1598 of the "Last Conquistador," Juan de Oñate, who became the province's first colonial governor and founder of its Catholic mission system. Oñate's party crossed the Rio Grande near present day El Paso and shortly thereafter traveled through the middle of where Mesilla now stands on its expedition north through what would become Albuquerque—precisely the route taken by *Gunslinger*'s stagecoach—and then on to the Tewa Pueblo villages above present-day Santa Fe. Mesilla also played an important role in the Anglo takeover of the New Mexico territory from Mexico after the Mexican-American War. It was the site of the signing in 1863 of the Treaty of Mesilla, which actualized the Gadsden Purchase, the acquisition by the United States of nearly thirty thousand square miles along its southern border. As a result, Mesilla became an important stop on two long-distance stagecoach routes—the El Camino Real, which reached from Chihuahua to Santa Fe, and the Butterfield stage route, which extended from San Antonio to San Diego. It makes sense that Gunslinger and his crew would begin their stagecoach journey there.

The timeline of the poem gets more complicated the further north *Gunslinger*'s coach travels: starting in the historical past, in "cowboy days," the narrative ends in the present, among the corporate mining operations of the 1970s Four Corners. Along the way, it draws a map tracing the history of New Mexico via the state's history of resource extraction. The smaller towns that are mentioned in the poem were all important historical mining centers: to wit, the earliest Spanish mining in New Mexico was for lead and turquoise in the Placitas and Cerrillos districts. Placitas was originally founded as Las Huertas in 1767, part of the San Antonio De Las Huertas land grant; the area around it is honeycombed with mines, some little more than shallow pits dating back to pre-Spanish times. Supposedly the location of the legendary Lost Mine of Montezuma, the village was deserted for nearly twenty years in the early nineteenth century due to Apache raids. Cerrillos was established in 1695, when the provincial governor appointed a mayor for El Real de los Cerrillos, making it the oldest western mining settlement on record. It was abandoned shortly thereafter, also because of Indian troubles (during the Reconquista of the Great Pueblo Revolt of 1680). The present town was originally established as a tent camp for miners in the late 1800s and was at one point seriously considered as a candidate for the capital of New Mexico Territory, but its mining operations peaked in the 1880s, and it remains a dusty byway to this day. Mádrid, located close by in the oldest coal mining region in the state, then took the resource reins; all coal production in the area was consolidated there in 1899, and it became a substantial settlement of some 2,500 souls. In *Gunslinger*'s day, it had become a ghost town where "the coach runs smartly now / by the torn rooves of this company town."[29] From Mádrid the stagecoach travels to present-day Farmington, a modern bustling mining and drilling town in the San Juan Basin, one of the largest reservoirs of oil and gas in the world, and as we have seen a major source of uranium. Autry's dude ranch and subterranean Murania are located somewhere around there.

The poem thus follows a map that simultaneously travels from south to north and from the sixteenth century into the twentieth. When Dorn has the stagecoach detour east to Placitas and then off to Mádrid and Cerrillos—towns that were not on any long-distance stagecoach lines and that you cannot actually get to from Placitas except by traveling on a long and treacherous dirt road over Sandia Peak, towering some six thousand feet above the village—he deliberately takes the coach out of the way of the direct line up the Rio Grande, the official stagecoach route from Mesilla to Santa Fe. As he does so, he explicitly points out "a certain destruction / the hills have been upended / they're no longer blended upon / the plates of their own dynamic principles" because "the miner has brought up / The madder from their graves."[30] In other words, we take a detour through mining country so that we can be shown the "civil scar" of resource extraction: "A superimposition, drawn up / like the ultimate property / of the ego, an invisible claim / to a scratchy indultum / from which smoke pours forth."[31] *Gunslinger*'s landscape is a material thing, in William Carlos Williams's phrase "one of the words of the poem."[32] It is the map of locations that Gunslinger would show us in the first stanza of *Gunslinger*. We are called on to *read* it.

Finally, Dorn's map covers the literary territory scoped out earlier in this chapter, that is, the area that stretches from John Carter's southern Arizona cave with its own Apache war up to the radium deposits of *Phantom Empire* in the Four Corners area. Mesilla as it turns out was briefly the capital of Confederate New Mexico, from 1861 to 1862; Carter could have been stationed there. And weirdly, Dorn claims that *Gunslinger* is partly based on early film serials: "The cast moves. It continues along the stage like a serial. I grew up on pre-TV serials, and the pre-TV continuity was serial. So this is a serial of very different time. This is a book."[33] Could Dorn be remembering *Phantom Empire*? *Gunslinger* even has its own singing cowboy, who periodically bursts into song, modeled, as are all singing cowboys, on Gene Autry; and the villain Robart (Howard Hughes)—who says things like "we're scientists, Al, Sometimes / we have to do Things we hate" and plans "a major invasion of the modality"—resembles *Phantom Empire*'s evil Dr. Beecham.[34] Both hail from the East and represent the big money powers in places like Boston and Chicago; both are intent on exploiting the mineral resources of the San Juan Basin; and both are thwarted by slick silver screen cowpoke heroes.

It's a genre thing, of course, and that's the point: these are all classic templates of the Western. But what about science fiction? Marjorie Perloff writes that Dorn's "West is not that of John Wayne or Gary Cooper; it is the plastic, gestural 'West' we encounter on TV, in comic strips, rock songs, drug argot and science fiction."[35] As it is in *Princess of Mars* and *Phantom Empire*, science fiction is symbiotically embedded in and entangled with the Western in *Gunslinger*; they both travel in the same coach, although in the time that it takes *Gunslinger*'s stagecoach to travel from Mesilla to Cortez, it morphs from a standard Western coach into a more complicated vehicle, one with a phone on the wall; at one point a Turing machine materializes inside it. By poem's end we are no longer in the Old West but very much in the new one, where mineral extraction has gone from a small hole scratched in the ground to a corporate operation; half way through the poem the Slinger says he has gotten "too inside oilrigs / and big assed gents from Corpus Christi."[36] The stagecoach travels through time as it travels through space: it is both a time machine and a spacecraft.

Thus, as Dorn says, there is no way to get rid of the cowboy; it's literally Star Wars. But what a strange cowboy Gunslinger is! "AN ILLUSTRIOUS TRAVELLER WHOSE EARTHNAME IS GUNSLINGER," he calls himself an "extraTerrestrial" whose "heart beats to another radio signal" as he jots in an "extragalactic notebook."[37] Before he leaves, he says, "I have grown to love your local star / But now niños, it is time for me to go inside / I must catch the timetrain / The parabolas are in sympathy . . . // I'll go along with the tachyon showers / Which are by definition faster than light / & faster than prime / I'll be home by suppertime."[38] This is the language of science fiction, not the Western. A filmic creature made of light, dust, and shadows, ensheathed in leather, whose arms can become a boom and stretch deeply into a crowd to pluck out a man by the neck or elongate to pierce the windows of the stagecoach on both sides, Gunslinger has about him something of Lesabéndio, or the Fantastic Four's Mr. Fantastic, the pliable Reed Richard: he is flexible and projective.[39] "The son of the sun," the Slinger travels via showers of subatomic particles. In *Gunslinger*, the reel becomes the real, and the character in the movie we watch is a visitor from the stars: "*The inside real / and the outsidereal*."[40]

In what follows, I organize my discussions of each of the poem's four books around a geographical location and a theme, based loosely on the schematics of the human universe that I sketched earlier. Book I is located in Mesilla and deals primarily with issues of epistemology. Book II plays out along the excursion up the banks of the Rio Grande and ends in Albuquerque; it treats questions of ontology. Book III takes place on the journey through the mining towns of Placitas, Mádrid, and Cerrillos, and winds up in Santa Fe; its theme is geography. Book IIII, set in the San Juan Basin country of the Colorado Plateau, focuses on geology. What happens here is the showdown between the human universe of the stagecoach and the forces of corporate resource extraction as exemplified by Robart, who is darkly portrayed in the poem's middle section, "The Cycle," which is both formally and structurally different from the rest of the books; I deal with it in sequence.

Throughout the discussion, I focus on *Gunslinger* as a piece of science fiction with the requisite generic themes, tropes, and issues. To my mind, the sci-fi features of *Gunslinger* are too often ignored or neglected; I situate them front and center. The science-fictional aspect of the poem allows Dorn to say things and deal with issues that he otherwise could not or would not. In every capacity, *Gunslinger* is crucial to science fiction poetry and poetics.

MESILLA: SYMPOSIUM IN THE SALOON

Mesilla, the crossroads of so much New Mexican history—the entrada point of the Spanish, the site of the Anglo takeover, the brief capital of the Confederacy, the center of the Apache Wars, the terminal of the stagecoach routes, the town where Billy the Kid was jailed and tried—has a saloon, or had a saloon back in cowboy days, a classic Western cantina with a swinging half-door; a gaudy madam named Lil; a long bas-relief bar of unruly, brawling cowboys; and pistols, card games, smoke, and tequila. Around "a table / obscure in the corner," Gunslinger, his Oblique Horse Heidegger/Leví-Strauss with "his stetson XX sorta cockwise / on his head," Lil, and I form a tableau vivant as they engage in a Symposium-style Platonic dialogue, replete with Socratic questions and answers: "What is the *principle* of what / you see," Gunslinger asks I, who, Agathon-like, "knew not the principle / of which he spoke."[41]

The principle of what you see is the epistemological issue that Book I bats around: as Gunslinger says, "In some parts of the Western world / men have mistakenly / called that phenomenology."[42] I is a bona fide Blakean Idiot Questioner, a Reasoner who irritates Lil, the Immobile Horse, and Gunslinger with his endless "Who What Where / What Where Who": Gunslinger chides him "because you are inattentive / and expect reason to Follow / as some future chain gang does / a well worn road."[43] I is "constructed of questions,"[44] and it is not just that he consistently gets the answers wrong; he gets the *questions* wrong—in fact, his inquisitiveness is wrong altogether. In a back-and-forth with Gunslinger, I asks "and may I enquire of you— / Enquire? he breathed / don't do *that* / Well then may I . . . / no I wouldn't do that Either."[45] Certainly do not beg permission: what sort of a stance toward reality would that entail?

The problem involves the circuits between seeing, knowing, interpreting, and understanding, and the speed with which they trigger and fuse:

> What does the foregoing mean?
> I asked. Mean?
> my Gunslinger laughed
> *Mean?*
> Questioner, you got some strange
> obsessions, you want to know
> what something *means* after you've
> seen it, after you've *been* there
> or were you *out* during
> That time? No.
> And you want some *reason.*
> How fast are you
> by the way?[46]

We are deep in Olson country here, in the instanter dynamics of the open field and the call to synthesize the perceptual and cognitive functions—partitioned off from one another in the Western mind since at least the days of the "generalizing" Greeks—in the service of reestablishing the fully integrated human universe of Olson's Maya, and Dorn's Apache, about whom Dorn patronizingly says "they had not invented Mind."[47] At any rate, they did not invent Plato and Aristotle and their divisive and hierarchical systems of logic and classification. Instead, Native people are thought to encounter reality head-on, with their senses alert in the immediacy of encounter, no categories or ideal forms between themselves and the fact of the matter of the occasion of what is actually present, literally in front of them: *wired to.* As the Turned On Horse puts it, "We'd all rather *be* here / than talk about it."[48]

I is given a great deal of advice in Book I: Do not describe. Do not mean. Do not enquire. Do not hasten to add. Do not be close. Do not ask permission. Do not get named. Do not become a reference or an institution. Do not question the difference between appearance and reality. Do not persist. Do not notice. Do not get bugged. Do not ask about Love. Do not rely on the copula: "*IS* is not the link . . . // it beats me how you mortals / can think something *is*," says Gunslinger in a deconstructive mood.[49] Do not use qualifiers like *more like*: "*More Like! /* how can distance / be more like," asks Martin the horse.[50] In other words, do not divide "appearance" from "Reality."[51] I begins more and more to "sound like the impact of a wet syllojsm," especially ".daeha sa kcab emas eht si I ecnis."[52]

What is this singular consciousness, cut in two by a mirror like Breton's man in the window? Can I never get out of his head, or is the problem that I is already so far out of it? "Where" exactly *is* I? With its deep doubts about its own substance and agency, the postmodern I materializes between Heidegger and Leví-Strauss, under the pressures of phenomenology and structuralism, the two grand inquisitors of the modern subject. Olson is hip to this when he criticizes "subjectism":

> It is now too late to be bothered with the latter. It has excellently done itself to death, even though we are all caught in its dying. What seems to me a more valid formulation for present use is "objectism" . . . the getting rid of the lyrical interference of the individual as ego, of the "subject" and his soul, that peculiar presumption by which Western man has interposed himself between what he is as a creature of nature (with certain instructions to carry out) and those other creations of nature which we may, with no derogation, call objects. For a man is himself an object.[53]

I has got to go—and he will in Book II. Meanwhile, it is not just being and time that I cannot wrap his head around, it is his own savage mind. I interrogates Claude the horse:

> Well what do you do I persisted.
> Don't persist.
> I study the savage mind.
> And what is that I asked.
> *That,* intoned Claude leaning over my shoulder
> is what you *have*
> in other words, you provide
> an instance
> you are purely animal
> sometimes purely plant
> but mostly you're just a
> classification, I mean it's conceivable
> but so many documents
> would have to be gone through
> and dimensions of such *variety*
> taken into account to realize what
> you are, that
> even if we confined ourselves
> to the societies for which
> the data are sufficiently full,
> accurate, and comparable
> among themselves

it could not be "done"
without the aid of machines.[54]

It is not what I *is* ("*IS* is not the link") but what I *has* that matters, and while I is surely purely an object (animal, plant) among other objects, I is mostly just a bunch of data, a syllojsm constructed of documents, one anthropological classification in a myriad of classifications. I has a savage mind, but it has been papered over by texts, facts, and figures—by what we know about I's society and what we can record about such various "dimensions" on our machines—in other words, by how we *describe* and *name* I. Gunslinger warns I of the peril:

Nevertheless,
it is dangerous to be named
and makes you mortal.
If you have a name
you can be sold
you can be sold
by that name leave, or come
you become, in short
a reference, or if bad luck
is large in your future
you might become an institution
which you will then mistake
for defense. I could
now place you
in a column from which
There is No Escape
and down which The Machine
will always recognize you.[55]

No one wants to become just another accident statistic. And nobody wants to be tracked and recognized by "The Machine," without the aid of which, says the Classical Horse, they cannot describe or name you. You are not your name: but if your name is I, then you are in a bit of a pickle: if I is not I, then who—or what—is I? Especially since I is the same back as ahead, always a reversible image of itself: " . . . you seem / constructed of questions, uh, / What's your name? // i , I answered. / That's a simple name. / Is it an initial? / No it is a single."[56]

Meanwhile, the power of describing is illustrated in the proprioceptive speed of Gunslinger's dazzling extragalactic gunplay. A cowpoke intolerant of allowing horses in saloons challenges Slinger to a showdown. Gunslinger's gun speaks:

the disputational .44
occurred in his hand and spun there
in that warp of relativity one sees
in the backward turning spokes
of a buckboard,

then came suddenly
to rest, the barrel utterly justified
with a line pointing
to the neighborhood of infinity.[57]

When Lil points out to Slinger that his gun is pointed away from his opponent, "out of town," he tells her not to worry: "This Stockholder will find / that his gun cannot speak / he'll find / that he has been Described." The latter's gun "coughed out some cheap powder, / and then changed its mind": "The total .44 / recurred in the Slinger's hand / and spun there / then came home like a sharp knock / and the intruder was described—/ a plain, unassorted white citizen."[58]

What a blow is there given! No way to live down that fatal description: plain, unassorted, white, *citizen*. After all, Gunslinger's pistol, like William Burroughs's weaponized media platforms, delivers bullets of "pure information"; nobody gets hurt, they are just disarmed. Gunslinger explains to I how it works:

A mathematician from Casper Wyoming
years ago taught me That
To eliminate the draw
permits an unmatchable Speed
a syzygy which hangs tight
just back of the curtain
of the reality theater
down the street,
speed is not necessarily fast.
Bullets are not necessarily specific.
When the act is
so self contained
and so dazzling in itself
the target then
can disappear
in the heated tension
which is an area between here
and formerly.[59]

Slinger's syzygy, hanging just behind the theater curtain of reality, is that self-contained act of the mind knowing *as* it sees, nothing interposed between perception and cognition; definition as much a part of the act as is sensation itself, as Olson puts it in "Human Universe"[60]: no infrathin layer between spatial "here" and temporal "formerly," which is the enormous space that Gunslinger and his horse traversed on their way to Mesilla. Intention and act, "discrimination (logos) and shout (tongue)," bullet and target become the same when a person, rid of the interference of the subject and his soul, acts like an object in a field of objects. Gunslinger is not magic, and *Gunslinger* is not fantasy. A work of science fiction, its hero is a traveler from the stars, an enhanced human being whose unearthly speed is an accelerated principle of epistemology. Gunslinger is not a wizard. He is a projectivist who operates at the speed of light.[61]

THE HUMAN GAUGE

We never knew anything much
about him did we. I
was the name he answered to,
and that was what he had
wanderin around inside him
askin so many questions
his eyes had already answered.[62]

Lil's concise statement about the matter of I summarizes the focus of book I, which is the *principle* of what I sees. The ego, that peculiar presumption that Western man has interposed between himself and other objects, fatally slows down and confuses response to the world with its endless stream of inquiry. Perception and cognition are disarticulated, while I's eyes literally give him the answers to questions he has not even thought to ask yet. As Lil puts it, "*We're at the Very beginning of logic / around here.*"[63]

Book II takes a different tack, both geographically and thematically: the stagecoach leaves Mesilla as "Our company thus moves collectively / along the River Rio Grande"—the moving locus begins to move—and the poem moves accordingly from epistemological questions of how I sees, to ontological questions of what "we concur To See / The Universe," or "the hallucination of the atmospheric realism" of "the stereoscopic world."[64] At issue here is "*materialism*, the result / of merely *real* speed," and we meet an astonishing new character: Everything, a kind of *Everyman* "Goods," who delivers a disquisition on ontology in what is rapidly becoming a "farflung passion play"—"Resume your Ontology, Everything," says Gunslinger, as if everything could ever do anything but.[65] If Book I concerns the metaphysician, Book II focuses on the Poet, who sings two long songs in a "fabulous accounting / of our coursing / the country of our consciousness": "The Coast of the Firmament," which is that space where tautologies are real—"When I say light I mean the light / Thats the light within the light"—and "Cool Liquid Comes," a paean to the dawn: "Cool liquid comes / the morning . . . sensing . . . / the morning sensing Inne / the blend of spatial hours / cool blending comes // Comes blending the arc / comes gripping urge timing."[66] This tentative, delicate hymn to the momentary sensing of brightening morning, which Gunslinger praises as "a spelling account / of this Zone" in a "rendering / of the Panorama," is the optic of Book II: the world present, *there*, as it appears and changes in the moment of its impinging upon our senses.[67] The characters spend the chapter discussing not the mind but "the parameters of reality."[68] Once we are proprioceptive, *what* is it that we see?

The Poet plays a special role in maintaining the freshness of the ongoing encounter with the world, determining what Olson describes as the "means of expression" proper to "a way which bears *in* instead of away, which meets head on what goes on each split second, a way which does not—in order to define—prevent, deter, distract, and so cease the act of, discovering"[69]: "In other words, the proposition here is that man at his peril breaks the full circuit of object, image, action at any point. The meeting edge of man and the world is also his cutting edge. If man is active, it is exactly here where experience comes in that it is delivered back, and if he stays fresh at the coming in he will be fresh at his going out."[70] This is precisely where the Poet—and Gunslinger—maintain their posts: at the doors of perception, the split-second cutting edges of sense, mind, and Everything else. The Poet is the pathfinder and cartographer of this zone: "The poet accompanies Lil / and guides her meanderings / over the civilian and pseudo-historical terrain / as if he had spent late hours / pouring over charts."[71] An "absolutist," he strums the Absolute, "the center of this terrific actualism," spelling an ongoing account of what is going on: "Cool Liquid, cool liquid distilled / of the scalar astral spirit / morning sensing congealing / our way, hours of spatial cooling / weighing the lark appealing."[72]

The Poet also plays a key part in resuscitating I, whose death and resurrection are at the center of Book II. Right after Everything—a "material question," not an "abstract" one[73]—shows up, I dies: as if the self, the subject, with its infernal doubts and internal divisions, cannot survive in the presence of a pure object—one of which, after all, it *is*. If the projectivist goal is to become an object in a field of objects, then the subject must pass. But to be replaced by what? Everything has a subtle drug, a perception-enhancing potion, that the Poet takes a whiff of:

> What subtle richness he whispered
> this would turn one into an allegory
> and after an inordinately long time
> he observed all eyes upon him
> and said I believe,
> not that it matters,
> this to be our solution
> the perceptual index

of Everythings batch
is High, to say the least.
What then, if we make I
a receptable of what
Everything has,
our gain will be twofold,
we will have the thing
we wish to keep
as the container of the solution
we wish to hold
a gauge in other words
in the form of man.
It is a derangement of considerable antiquity.[74]

The object is to see like an object. What does Everything have that we don't? Everything's five-gallon batch of LSD is pure: "Straight man. / 1000 percent, / nothin but molecules."[75] Everything has a very high *perceptual index*: "things" "perceive" *purely*, without any meddling from self or subject. If we can take the dead subject I and pour into him the perceptual index of the object, he will see with the speed of light: this is Rimbaud's derangement of the senses with a vengeance. Everything's batch of acid is pure information, just like Gunslinger's bullets, and the Poet is the primary dispenser thereof:

Only Time can reveal the immaterial
the poet said, rolling up
I's sleeve, at the same time
hanging the 5 gallon can spout down
from the ceiling of the coach
and adjusting the tubes.

I wont hold 5 gallons
Everything said as tho
he'd thot of a hitch.

I will the poet answered
we'll use his stomach too,
and elaborated,
All that I will hold
we will put into him.

That, observed the Slinger,
is where your race
puts its money.[76]

The Poet certainly will hold Everything's perceptual index—he is himself a subtle drug—and all that he will hold he will put into I: that's a poet's job, according to Gunslinger. When he does so, I becomes a living batch, a new sort of self, a Self, an object: "Your batch is now The batch / expropriation is accomplished / we stand before an original moment / in ontological history, the self, with one grab / has acquired a capital S, mark the date / the Gunslinger instructed, / we'll send a telegram to Parmenides."[77] When I shows up again, he has become the secretary to Parmenides, the first ontologist and the original philosopher of unified being. No more Idiot Questions. The subject has become the Subject: an object in a field of objects, its doors of perception cleansed and ready to receive the world and give it measure accordingly: *a gauge in the form of a man*. The self with its three disaggregated locations has become a single objectist "receptable," a *where it's at* that *has* and *is*: "Our company reassembled itself / and followed I with a triple impression— / for now they sought / to keep track of what they Had, / invested in where it Was, / and carried by where it's At."[78]

LITERATE PROJECTIVISTS IN OLD TOWN

Meanwhile, the stagecoach has arrived in Albuquerque, with its outskirts of "sheds / and huts of the suburbs," and even lawns! in the high desert: "these green plots / must be distress signals to God / that he might notice / their support of one of his minor proposals,"[79] no doubt to make the desert bloom. Also known in the poem as Universe City, Albuquerque is the only city of any size in the state (in 1970 it had a population of 370,000 people) and is home to the University of New Mexico. Here the travelers decoach in Old Town, the touristy plaza of the original Spanish settlement, a town square in the center of which sit a gazebo and an old cannon, flanked on one side by a handsome eighteenth-century adobe church and on the other three by rows of Western style false storefronts. While "The travelers drift easily / round the plaza, I / examines the jewellery of the native women," who sit on blankets and ply their wares under the porticoes of the eastern side of the plaza; the whole place "looks like a rundown movie lot / a population waiting around to become / White Extras."[80]

After a confrontation with a curious furious crowd of such extras and another showdown with an angry cowpoke, who Slinger's information gun describes into "an Old Rugged Statue / of the good old days"—truly the end of the Old Western—Book II deals with the weirdest of Dorn's science fiction objects: the Literate Projector, which, like *Phantom Empire*, is a new-sounding "kinda talkie," a "revolutionary medium / It's sure to turn everything around," says Everything: "Well, There's a Literate Projector, / which, when a 35 mm strip is put thru it / turns it into a Script / *Instantaneously!* / and projects that—the finished script / onto the white virgin screen / and theyre gonna run it / in Universe City tonight."[81] The projector "works best in University towns / and other natural centers of doubletalk": it "enables the user to fail insignificantly / and at the same time show up / behind a vocabulary of How It Is." Clearly this is Dorn's take on the literary culture of the university with its scholars and critics and the jargon of their endless explanations of how things are. A professor might very well be something like a Literate Projector, forever turning art into language: after all, "people who can't make films /. . . produce scripts" about them.[82] And indeed, the next new character to make an appearance is Dr. Jean Flamboyant, *Scientific American* in hand, flame of his Lyceum and author of the dissertation *The Tensile Strength of Last Winters Icicles*, "whats called a / post-ephemeral subject," he says, the object of which melted away before it could be read.[83] Forever an ABD Gradual Student, he never finished his degree. Talk about literate projection!

But Dorn might very well have another target in mind, for what is a projectivist poet other than *literally* a Literate Projector? Designed to be a revolutionary kinda talkie that will turn everything around *instantaneously* and give the poet "secrets objects share,"[84] projectivism is a practice that extends the sensed world into the breath of language, as Olson stated, "Breath is man's special qualification as animal. Sound is a dimension he has extended. Language is one of his proudest acts."[85] Olson's projectivist poet "comprehend[s] his own process as intact, from outside, by way of his skin, in, and by his own powers of conversion, out again. . . . It deserves this word, that it is the equal of its cause only when it proceeds unbroken from the threshold of a man through him and back out again, without loss of quality, to the external world from which it came. . . . Man at his peril breaks the full circuit of object, image, action at any point."[86] In this context, the projector's white virgin screen is the page, etched with the objects of the poet's mind as he has initially encountered them with his senses: his eye films the world and then his brain projects it back through his typewriter. The Literate Projector can be read as Dorn's sly and wry take on the New American poetry, which by 1970 had become increasingly accepted in the university; indeed, projectivist poets like Olson, Creeley, Denise Levertov, Robert Duncan, and Dorn himself all taught at—and their work was taught *in*—colleges and universities. Dorn distances his work from what he calls "academic regionalism," the earnest documentary aspects of poems like *Paterson* and *Maximus*.[87] Unlike Olson, Dorn is a cynic, who sees both the inherent romanticism of Olson's project and also the limits of its documentarian impulses.[88] A "kind of intellectual trick," the Literate Projector is a sci-fi writing machine that can turn world into word, but it also stands as a figure for the increasingly compromised "academic" poetics that *Gunslinger* sets out to challenge.[89]

A DAY IN THE LIFE OF THE MAN WHO GRABBED THE CRACK

> Howard Hughes is another category. He's more direct as a persona, although I'm increasingly not talking about him. . . . He's a great singular—in a strange way like a dinosaur.
>
> —Ed Dorn, "An Interview with Edward Dorn"

> This is old dinosaur country
>
> —Ed Dorn, *Gunslinger*

At the end of Book II, the Old Rugged Statue of the good old days is mistaken for "a Hughes disguise," and this leads directly to "The Cycle of Robart's Wallet," also called "the Cycle of Acquisition," a song about Howard Hughes (middle name Robart) sung by the Poet and comprised of seventy-nine quatrains (with a few exceptions), divided into three parts. Michael Davidson calls this section of *Gunslinger* "relentlessly obscure" and likens reading it to "decoding glyphs for which no Linear B is known."[90] The prose is punchy and jokey, gnarled and dense, riddled with non sequiturs and abrupt transitions; an aura of mad comic book pervades the writing, and the tightly wound stanzas twist with the torque of a drill bit, themselves suggesting cycles within the Cycle. The song traces Hughes's journey from Boston westward in a surreal train car, which is at once a portrait of his mind and "an echo of the psychological condition of the United States of America," according to Dorn.[91] The train runs along allegorical tracks, "All tied down with spikes These are the spines / Of the cold citizens made to run wheels upon," and is exceedingly difficult to visualize or distinguish "From the flak of Biodetail interference."[92] A "wheeléd apartment," its outside is "as blank as the loin of a Chester White" pig, and the interior is neither light nor dark; its "atmos / Is the medium of variable tubes of spectra."[93] At one point the car appears to fly over the North Pole, and when it shows up in Book IIII, it has transformed into a sixty-foot long wheeled chile relleno, a leaded "fixed head coupe" cattle car that carries a real cow—well "not exactly an ordinary cow," Dorn concedes.[94] It is staffed by "*living* Atlantes, a race of half-column half-man" androids with plaster heads who serve Rupert (Hughes's/Robart's name in "The Cycle") and "open and close the rear door / When Fear and Surrender"—two other allegorical henchmen—"come and go / on their unscheduled excursions."[95] Brainless yes-men, the Atlantes are masonry supports, plain unassorted white citizens who mindlessly mind the entrances and exits to the edifice of Hughes's empire. Rupert's main Atlante crony is Al, who dumps out the ashes of "a colossal clock / Which stood in the hallway / At the beginning of Organized History," spilling entropy into Hughes's grand car.[96]

The interior of the car is where the real crux of the matter appears; it has been admirably described by Davidson and others, and I will focus only on a few salient points.[97] The inside of the car is a congealed space that is at once psychological, political, geographic, and cosmic; in it, time bends—"This Grand Car with the Superior Interior / Moves with a basal shift So Large / It would be a dream to feel time curve / For no masses so locked serve straight time"—while the car itself travels by doppler shifting faster than the speed of light along Gunslinger's tachyon showers, as Rupert reminds Al, "You remember, when we was red-shifted / how sick I got / when I had that sharp focus view / of the Great Beyond / we were in motion ahead of the velocities / like the tachyon."[98] Like *Gunslinger*'s stagecoach, Rupert's car is a time machine and a spaceship, warping through the galaxy on its internal atmospheric tubes of spectra.

The furnishings of the car are run by "The Interior Decorator," or the I.D.: at once the official identity of its owner's outsized personality—the narcissistic, paranoid, ubercapitalist that was Howard Hughes—and at the same time the id, Rupert's unconscious with its barely repressed drives and appetites fully on display. Meanwhile, according to Davidson, the interior also represents "the nature of America,"[99] with *its* sundry drives and appetites. But it also suggests a geographical meaning, that is, the interior of the United States, the country that Rupert treats "as if it were a cloakroom," with its own decorator secretary of the interior.[100] The "uncentered locus" that is the car is also the geopolitical space of the cycle of acquisition, where things like real estate and property appear and change hands: at one point, Robart asks Surrender to "hand me that Panhandle," referring to the oil rich region of Oklahoma.[101]

What exactly is it that Robart/Hughes is so eager to acquire in "The Cycle"? The talk turns to acquiring *cracks*: "This is a pennsylvania crack, vertical vertical / Get me another, something up ahead / And I don't mean Indiana I know where that's at // Find me a crack from a society with no history // Find me a crack that ain't been surrendered in / Get me a crack from Way up ahead / All these cracks have already been You Know / Get me one from Around-the-Bend, somethin goin in."[102] Hughes it should be remembered acquired his great wealth via the Hughes Tool Company, his father's spectacularly successful business, which was initially built entirely on the two-cone rotary rock drill bit, invented by Howard Robard Hughes Sr. and patented in 1909. The bit revolutionized vertical mining and drilling in oil and natural gas production. In 1933, Hughes Tool engineers designed and patented the three-cone roller bit, which made an even bigger splash, and the company grew into a worldwide operation. The bit was used to drill virtually all of the oil produced in the glory days of wildcatting, and Howard Junior became the richest man in the world. By the 1960s, Hughes Tool had grown into one of the biggest oil tools manufacturers in the world, pumping out the latest, largest, and most automated equipment for foundries, forging, heat treating, and machining.

In other words, "The Man who grabbed the crack / And wrapped it around the Antho-space" is the godfather of fracking, the high-pressure injection of fluid into a vertical wellbore to create cracks in deep-rock formations so that natural gas and petroleum can flow more freely.[103] Hughes wants "vertical vertical" cracks in the West (not Pennsylvania or Indiana) from a society with no history (ostensibly like the Native lands of the Southwest). He is out to acquire mining and drilling leases in what he considers the vacant lands way up ahead and around the bend. In fact, "the crack we been waitin for," says Al, is "2 days minus 4 Corners" away, in the energy rich San Juan Basin:[104] Apacheria, Murania, dinosaur land, oil country.

WINTER IN THE UPENDED COUNTRY

It is winter in the high desert, "as the light snowe / casually attracted to the earth / drifting blew / thru the perfumery of the piñon clad hills,"[105] and the travelers in their stagecoach lift up into the northern foothills of the Sandia Mountains and roll through Placitas on their way into the mining country beyond and from thence "towards the land of the crazy Utes."[106] The mood in the coach is melancholy and fits the season—"snowe covers living things with quietude / Death rules over the visible"—as well as the ghostly countryside around the upended hills of Cerrillos and Mádrid.[107] Slinger senses "something Low this morning" in the Poet's demeanor, as the latter stares listlessly out the coach window: "In your eyes I see / the underground / like a miner with his lamp / turned around. . . . / The weather in the winter the poet nodded . . . / Hunts the land, and / all things there on."[108]

Gunslinger similarly feels confined and beset upon, too inside "big assed gents from Corpus Christi" and their oilrigs. It is as if the degraded and exploited landscape of New Mexico's mining country has migrated into the heads of the travelers as a winter of their discontent: their ideas, after all, like those of the Apache, "come directly from their landform." Wired to the Winterbook desert, this group in which our brain is contained registers uneasy feelings of dangers to come: someone out there is cracking and fracking the world, predatory Oil Smellers whose "prayers are now dripping / with hydrogen and carbon."[109] The road symbolizing our thinking has turned dark and cold. "Is this road not / 'on the road,'" Gunslinger queries.[110] He lifts a prayer to Jack Kerouac:

> OH Jack, the Slinger prayed
> I want you to feel
> and in your feeling move your bones
> for the want we now have of your access

in this time so little beyond you
as it dries tacked
on the warp of its own flat sedimentary . . . internalism. . . .
          It looks to me Jack
            like the Whole Set is Sinking
          And theyre still talkin œcology
          Without even Blinking[111]

Things have become sedimentary and internal in the dried-out, flattened, post-Beat world, a world where the Road only takes us deeper into ruin and ecological crisis. How can we still be talkin œcology at this late date? Without even blinking?

Gunslinger certainly does not blink while the coach rides through Mádrid, the deserted company town with its torn rooves and abandoned mineshafts; the very hills here have been knocked off their foundations: "Me sees / past the curtain / a certain destruction / the hills have been upended / theyre no longer blended upon / the plates of their own dynamic principles / could a lover have done this, hombre?" he asks the Poet.[112] The latter dares not say but responds with "The Poem Called Riding Throughe Mádrid," the structural center of Book III, literally its central event. The poem echoes Clint Eastwood's cowboy torch ballad "I Talk to the Trees" from the 1969 movie *Paint Your Wagon* ("I talk to the trees / But they don't listen to me / I talk to the stars / But they never hear me"), as the Poet tells us to "Talk with the Trees and / Speak into the Trees and / Get it on with the Trees . . . / Stand up in the Trees / They go straight to heaven / And they have heaved in waves / Their deposits in earth."[113] But this hippie vision is fatally disturbed, for the deposits are haunted: "The miner has brought up / The madder from their graves," and now ghosts and ghouls and Oil Smellers have been set loose upon the world. Slinger, quoting Plotinus, is reminded by the song that "the world soul / slumbers in matter," but it is hard to get into tree hugging when "quarrying starts us with amazed shock" and the landscape has been scraped and scarred into rubble.[114]

S'LLAB CODE

The next wrinkle in the plot occurs as the stagecoach is leaving Mádrid and is on its way to Cerrillos: the travelers receive an inscrutable Nightletter sent from I, who has become the secretary to Parmenides; and they first hear of Sllab, perhaps the most puzzling and complicated entity in *Gunslinger*. Sllab is pure science fiction—his genesis, according to Dorn, was the mysterious upright stone monolith in Stanley Kubrick's *2001: A Space Odyssey*.[115] A great deal of critical ink has been spilled on both Sllab and the Nightletter.[116] For the present purposes, I want to read these two enigmas through the twin lenses of geology and mining, an approach which as far as I know has not been taken before. Sllab is the Code of the Nightletter, "what's back of it," and in order to read the letter, we need to understand the Code.[117] To do so, I go to *Bean News*, where the "Sllab Outline Arrives," and on into Book IIII, where S'llab outline is filled out.

We do not learn much about Sllab in Book III. We only hear that he gets his information through a double trough antenna and that "he leases the data / to an activity called HooRay / which went right on down / to produce a group / with such a heavy assay / it was called Western Man / or, Imprudential Behavior."[118] This is cryptic at best, but suggests that Sllab is an agent of Western culture and perhaps the insurance industry with its Prudential Life and its "Get a Piece of the Rock" creed. This group, "a real flash in the pan," produced a hit song, the long title of which begins "LETS SPEND AN AFTERNOON ON THE MOON / DIGGIN IT UP WITH A SPOON."[119] Not much to go on here.

The antenna however is interesting and tethers Sllab simultaneously to outer space and to inner Earth. A double trough antenna has applications in radio astronomy as well as in ground-penetrating radar, where it is used to detect subsurface objects, changes in material properties, and voids and cracks in the Earth's mantle. If Robart's desire is to discover geothermal cracks and get a piece of the rock, S'llab antenna is crucial, and digging up the moon with a spoon looks to be all to the point—as is the flash in the (prospector's) pan and the group's "heavy assay" (compositional analysis of an ore, metal, or alloy): Sllab is *prospective*. In an editorial in *Bean News*, Sllab appears at one point to be transmitting from intergalactic space via "a late BNS [binary neutron star] signal" sent to Notsuoh (Houston), while the headline news is that at precisely 12:31 MST in Beenville, Colorado, "an unknown Quantity designated Sllab arrived preceeded by mass anvil noise and followed by debris from the astroid belt."[120] Here the clanking noise of industrial production and tool making precedes the appearance of Sllab, an extraterrestrial who trails stardust in his wake. We also learn from the editorial that "the physically real Sllab is *invisible to the naked eye*. . . . Dr. Flamboyant then paraphrased a famous Geologist who wants to go un-named, to the effect that S'llab mission could be the instruction of the local Mantle, well known to be cracked."[121] Sllab beams to the Earth from outer space, but his information is all about what is under its surface, the cracks in the layer of silicate rock between the Earth's crust and its outer core. A sci-fi entity from the astroid belt, Sllab is also a *geological* feature in *Gunslinger*, invisible but physically real.

I want to posit that Sllab can be taken as *slab*, the technical term referring to the subducting lower plate in plate tectonics: "The coupling of the flat slab to the upper plate is thought to change the style of deformation occurring on the upper plate's surface and form basement-cored uplifts like the Rocky Mountains," which run through the Western side of Colorado and end in the Sangre de Cristo range east of Santa Fe; Books III and IIII of *Gunslinger* play entirely within the area of the Southern Rockies.[122] The great ore, oil, and gas deposits of the San Juan Basin are the direct result of flat slab subduction and slab pull that occurred in the region during the collision of ancient tectonic plates. In other words, Sllab *instructs the local mantle*: slab is that subterranean force—physical yet invisible to the eye—that creates terrestrial cracks, rifts, and volcanic vents and tilts the subduction zones in the Earth's crust that signal and harbor the energy resources Robart so ardently desires.[123] At the end of Book IIII, we learn that Robart's agents "fucked really strong / with the subduction zone": I reports that "they seem to have done something / to the subduction zone / look over there at that cone / the way it's huffing and puffing," to which Gunslinger responds, "The immense inertia of the old order / buckles that chain of blue mountains / This is old dinosaur country / a record full of sudden changes."[124] The immense inertia of the old order is simultaneously tectonic Sllab pull and the dinosaur that is Hughes and his mountain-buckling mining as he drills for fossil fuel, the petroleum by-product supposedly of millennia of dead dinosaurs. *Gunslinger* ends in the slab subduction zone of La Lejanía: "the ancient / threadbare blanket of the floor / resting at the monuments to volcanic action / to the last peñasco, desprendimiento / de tierra, ash & lava / mojones superboa, paisaje magnífico / masculino, all thats left of the plumbing / dikes, flues, the tubes of frozen magma."[125] The strongest of the many forces driving tectonic plates, Sllab is the unfathomably powerful geological shearing force cracking the world. The wrinkle in the plot is the wrinkle in the plate.

LINGUATILT SURVEY SITE #1

The Nightletter is a document explicitly designed to give the coordinates of a time and a place—2 D[ay]s and 4 C[orner]s—and as such is a map of locations or, maybe better, a map of "RELATIVE DISLOCATIONS." It delineates a topography that is also a tomography, a hybrid map of a landscape that is simultaneously a cross-sectional scan of a body. The Nightletter after all is sent by I, the newly proprioceptive Self, the postmodern Apache whose senses and intellect are instant with the world. An object in an open field of objects, filled with the subtle drug of Everything, I's ideas come directly from the landform; his reciprocating mind is intimately wired to the desert, literally the country of his consciousness. "REPORT GX &c / the Public Version," as Gunslinger calls the Nightletter, figures the human being as a geological survey site and language as the tilt of slab subduction, words figured as mineral crystals, the body a mineshaft.

Let's work through the letter, which is divided into two parts.[126] In the first, "REPORT BGX," we are looking at a map of "QUAD III"—that is, Book III, the melancholy Winterbook centered in the upended mining country around Mádrid. In fact we are immediately directed to a "DEEP SECTION" of the Earth—a cross section of underground, no doubt made visible by S'llab double trough antenna—that is at the same time an "EMISSION POSITION," an image of some point in a body, made by x-ray. The letter is diagnosing a disease that is both geophysical and biological. I then issues a set of directions: we are told to clear past hours, present time, and alien plantations—to wipe the temporal slate clean—and then to "REVERSE SENSE EE GEE ROWS B TO Z": which must mean that only Row A is left as was. We are at the beginning of logic here, at some point of origin. "DECADE 7" pinpoints the 1970s, the present decade, the original moment in ontological history when the self acquires a capital S. This is followed by the alarming phrase "NATION 23 TERMINAL DISPOSABILITY," suggesting that the nation is terminal to the corporate mining interests that render it disposable. More instructions follow, which I separate out and lineate for clarity:

> SKIP SIMPLE NULLIFICATION
> NO
> HIT STOP
> HIT PROCESS

These are "STRICTLY FRONTBRAIN DEXTROROTARY EQUATIONS" that take us away from simple nullification to a more complicated response: what we get instead is a "SPECULATION SIMULATOR" that "NAILS" the "FOLLOWING PROBATE ON PROGRESSIVE WHOOPEE CURVE," or something like that, depending how one parses the grammar of the clause; at any rate, a healthy dose of skepticism about the legality of property succession, who owns what and why they get it. What this leads to is "ACTUAL NUMBERS—IRREVERSABLE PREFIX LINE" versus "LITERAL NUMBERS—FLATRAP INFORMATION TEETOTTER"—a step toward the actual concrete (1, 2, 3) and away from literal abstraction (a, b, c).[127] We are getting closer to the measurable real here. The "WORKING RESULT: IDENTICAL BUILT-IN 'NOOSE' EFFECTS," predicted in an earlier report: "REPT. GX + -2."[128]

The second part of the letter is somewhat easier to parse: "WE ANTICIPATE ABSOLUTE LINGUATILT SURVEY SITE #1" in order to "EFFECT RELATIVE DISLOCATION" in a "PARALLEL SURVEY" that "ASSURES COLLOQUIAL LOCKS HOLD AGAINST ANY METHOD APPLIED OUTSIDE TIME." Colloquial locks and coaloquial rocks are both found at parallel survey site #1, a surrealistic mixture of language and stones. Dorn tells us that in *Gunslinger* he tried "to include the greater precision of the vernacular. The quicker, harder, more inexorable precision of the vernacular": the colloquial, it turns out, is as hard as a lock.[129] We next read "ALL PRESENT SCHEMA KNOWN CONFORM LOCAL STRANDS: SET BIOLINES AT GROSS BODY MOTIONS," which Grant Jenkins argues is I's characterization of proprioception itself:[130] here the body is set to its own motions and rooted in locality. Another colon, then "RADICAL CONFORMATION CURVED TO SURVIVE SPLITTING .78 INTERIOR VECTORS AT 'WATCH IT!' We now appear to be at a molecular level, where radicals conform by curving in order to avoid splitting, after which point the vocabulary turns crystallographic. We are deep inside a mineralogical linguistics here, where "LINGUATILT PROVIDES TONAL EQUIVALENT FOR HABIT": a crystal's tilt boundaries and interior vectors determine its *habit*, the technical term for its characteristic shape, just as the tilt of language determines tonal equivalents for our own human habits.[131] It is like the sounds coming from an old 78 RPM record. A more tightly integrated metaphorical figure is difficult to imagine. It goes on: tilting also refers to the tilting slabs of continental drift: what we are cautioned with "WATCH IT!" above is "FREQUENCY # 4 : COMPENSATE STIMULATED DRIFT CONTINENTAL SLAVES": Sllab still slaves away in the Code. We finally get the message: "EXPECT MATERIALIZATION AT PRECISELY 4 CORNERS," where Book IIII plays out: in the handsome and singular mass of the Colorado Plateau and the San Juan Basin, "the old altar of fire," "now a worn and bitter fugue by Chaos."[132] This is where Robart plans his "major invasion of the modality."[133]

SHOWDOWN AT THE REDUIT

The Nightletter thus changes the course of the poem: Gunslinger and his companions receive confirmation from it that Robart's destination is not or is no longer Las Vegas. Instead, they learn that he intends to "materialize" AT PRECISELY 4 CORNERS; in fact, as the Poet puts it earlier, Robart's "crosshair" is "37° North / 109° West / more or less," exactly the coordinates of the Four Corners.[134] It is here that the showdown must take place, because "*Vegas*," as Lil puts it, "*is a* vast *decoy*," intended to divert the stagecoach from Robart's real target, the resource riches of the Basin: "This is San Juan reaching / still sagrado and not consagrado . . . // This is the quantus / laid as bare as it can be laid / It doesnt do to enter it / its scale is revelátory."[135] Riffing on the Revelations of St. John, Dorn tropes the Basin, sacred but not (yet) consecrated, as the site of the apocalypse. The dragon is coming: "This is a discreet rumor / Till quarrying starts us with amazed shock / hooked claws, wrinkled scale / This is a dragon flock / There won't be a defense of anything / All is Kaput." "Creeping Craters!" gasps the Poet.[136] The issue, as we have seen, is "the civil scar" of property, "so cosmetic, one can't see it": Robart's phantom superimposition, the ultimate property line of his ego, his invisible claim from which refinery smoke pours forth. As Robart tells Al, the goal is "to hold the property lines": the crack they've been waiting to grab is just up ahead, around the bend, "not far / from Farmington and other interferences."[137]

Book IIII is the longest book of *Gunslinger* and is divided into two parts.

The first begins with a scene inside Robart's grand car as he and his crew travel west through Colorado. They are preparing for their invasion of the modality. Robart's list of items they will need for the onslaught is itself revelátory: "Gums & resins, brimstone / naptha and the other bitumens / and uh more salt petre & sulphur / benzol & potassium, dont forget / the ducks grease / and pass me that dish of Radio poo / you got there by your elbow / and oh yes, one gross / CO2 pellets / a battery of HeNe lazers / one mobile Rulz Field Beam."[138] Add "a ton of Traen Oil" and "short time fuses" and you have a recipe for blowing one hell of a big hole: it is clear that Robarts is going a-mining. His ground troops, comprised of Oil Smellers, Mogollones, and Single Spacers, are all affiliated with industrial mining and resource extraction. The Mogollones "are the new machinists / Masters of the wedge inclined plane screw"[139]—think the Hughes triple cone rotary rock drill bit. Like the Muranian Thunder Riders, they breathe through octane tanks because they cannot abide surface air. The Single Spacers are geothermal berserkers who "stream in like a horde / of chromeplated ball bearings" and whose weapons include bags of bolts and Black & Decker high-speed drills. Crackers from Hardass Tennessee, they are the ones responsible for fracking with the subduction zone.[140]

Meanwhile, Gunslinger and his intrepid crew are on Apache time in the Café Sahagún—named after the Spanish colonial compiler of the Florentine Codex, and thus the rescuer of Nahuatal language and culture—in the Colorado town of Cortez—named after the conquistador conqueror of the Aztecs, and thus the destroyer of Nahuatal language and culture—where they are getting ready for the arrival of their nemesis: "Robart will be trying to cut / our ion source, Said the Slinger," and the travelers are wary of being caught unprepared.[141] They get in trouble when I gives Gunslinger a bag full of "all the known species of Cant": "And then he threw it on top of the coach / but, because the Zlinger undereckoned / the stupidity of the dead weight / the bag flew on West / with a systematic bias toward las esquinas / some miles away, where it evidently / came to ground a few seconds later / when an oppressive nugatory roar / was heard from that quarter / and there rose up a powerful / fountain of blobs, each one consisting / of forty-two U. S. gallons of highsulphur crude."[142] The oil industry around las 4 Esquinas, no big surprise, is the product of sanctimonious cant, hypocrisy, stupidity, and greed; the Oil Smellers immediately catch the scent of the bubbling crude, and the stagecoach lights out for the "nightmare limits" of Cortez and the safety of Mesa Verde.

It is upon this mesa that the Pleiad, Dorn's magnificent seven—the Gunslinger, Lil, the Stoned Horse, the Poet, Everything, I, and Dr. Flamboyant—prepare their defensive position for the final showdown with Robart's dragon flock: "I've just been up on the mesa / preparing the reduit, we can start up / anytime," reports Flamboyant.[143] The reduit on the top of the mesa commands a sweeping view "along the axes of upheaval" of the San Juan Basin,[144] but "Is that all you see / the Horse asked in his hammock / from this our reduit"? "Nay, mein Pferdehändler," says the Poet, who describes a surreal landscape of Hollow Men: "Shape without form / shade without colour," oil "xeiks" set to marry "those dumb ones / the ones with hands like chainsaws, while" "from down at the bottom / comes the Product, Robarts Mogollones."[145] Meanwhile "from the north the Single Spacers / have breached the pass the Poet cast / peering through his telescope."[146] The enemy is closing in, and the first thing it does is shake up the subduction zone: "look over there at that cone / the way it's huffing and puffing," I tells Lil.[147]

The Basin becomes a surreal sci-fi battleground, a cross between *Star Wars* and John Huston's *Stagecoach*: "What's it like down there on the flat / Bill, the poet asked // It's like Brutalidad, quarks / zippin right out of the main manifold / it's the tamale finale / screamin zucchini impaled on the pinnacles / all the hysteria of a fake disaster set."[148] For the moment, the travelers are safe in their mesa top redoubt, although things look dire: then all of a sudden Robart drives up in his chester white special chile relleno! His voice crackles over the radio; tension builds; but upon confronting Gunslinger's forces arrayed against him, Robart realizes that he cannot win. He tells Al to "*send for the Hydralicx / we're in a fracture / We gotta get as big as we can / as fast as we can, that's the game plan*": all he needs to frack the fracture is waterworks, but in the high desert he does not have a prayer for rain.[149] He redshifts away on his not exactly ordinary cow straight for the border and on to Chile (relleno?).

"Wellwellwell, the doctor raved / it looks like the Magma Source was saved,"[150] in a rhyming tetrameter couplet that sews everything up and takes us back to the crack prize in *Gunslinger*—the frozen magma of the San Juan Basin, no doubt consagrado now that it is safely out of the hands of the Oil Smellers and their boss. For the time being, the Four Corners are quiet, saved by the human universe of the stagecoach with its precious cargo: the proprioceptive I, sans soul, sans ego, filled with the perceptual index of Everything. The movie is over, and as Gunslinger takes off on the tachyon showers, we watch the Western fade once again into the outer space of science fiction, maybe this time for good: "Goodbye to Everything / waved the Zlinger thru the dust veil . . . // Adió por eternidad, Lindas / Hasta La Vista!"[151] Of course, the Western sci-fi never finally rides off into the sunset, as the various *Westworlds*, *Star Wars*, and *Fireflys* testify—and even *Star Trek*, in one episode of which, as Clark Coolidge points out, "Shattner [*sic*] ends busting into a 'Western' set."[152] You really cannot ever get rid of the space cowboy. And we are still talking ecology with scarcely a blink.

4

Spilling Time, the Poetics of Entropy

Clark Coolidge, Evelyn Reilly, Bruce Andrews

> If time is spilled in a gravityless space
> And becomes equally distributed
> That is if an absolute symmetry occurs
> And inertia is total
> That's as heavy as shit in suspension can get
>
> —Ed Dorn, *Gunslinger*

When Dorn has Al the Atlante dump out the ashes of the "colossal clock / Which stood in the hallway / At the beginning of Organized History" into Robart's grand car,[1] spilling time into a gravity-less vacuum, he touches on one of the major tropes of postwar science fiction: entropy, the theoretical heat death of the universe and the catastrophic freezing of time and space into a crystalline condition of absolute symmetry and eternal stasis, Smithson's "ultimate future [in which] the whole universe will burn out and be transformed into an all-encompassing sameness." For Smithson, as it is for Dorn and Thomas Pynchon and many another writer of the period, this steady state acts as an analog for midcentury America, with the cookie-cutter homogeneity of its suburbs and strip malls and the bland conformity of its cultural and intellectual life.[2] J. G. Ballard is the science fiction writer perhaps most frequently associated with entropy, although many other sci-fi novels, short stories, and films deal with the issue to one extent or another. But what happens when entropy migrates into poetics? What does an entropic sci-fi poem look like? The first part of this chapter deals explicitly with entropy's crystallographic aspects as they play out formally and thematically in poetry, while the second examines the crystal's evil twin and constitutional opposite, the formless and rhizometric Blob, as in Paul Thek's hyperopulent geometries. The last section discusses Bruce Andrews's recasting of Dante's *Paradiso*, arguing that in *Lip Service*, Andrews fuses the crystal and the Blob into a dialectical synthesis that addresses the issue of entropy and language. Writers I deal with in this chapter include Clark Coolidge, Smithson, Ballard, E. R. Burroughs, Evelyn Reilly, and Andrews, with glances at Dante and Chaucer.

QUARTZ ARTS

Coolidge is the best reader of Smithson, whose works he works over systematically in a series of remarkable texts composed during the 1960s, 1970s, and 1980s. Biographically and artistically, the two are cut from the same cloth. Born within a year of one another (1939 and 1938, respectively), both were avid amateur rockhounds as adolescents, and both shared a lifelong fascination with the natural sciences, especially geology, mineralogy, and crystallography, which they used as subject, material, and model for their respective arts. Both describe early formative encounters with museums of natural history, and both shared deep backgrounds in modernist and avant-garde art, film, music, and literature (William Carlos Williams in particular looms large for each). Both came of age as artists in the cultural ferment of the late 1950s and 1960s, and both evolved into minimalists whose interests extended into geology and land art during the 1970s. They are both considered among the most important and influential figures of their generation: Smithson as a postmodern visual artist and writer and Coolidge as a forerunner of Language poetry and other innovative writing of the last fifty years.

Both avid science fiction readers, they place sci-fi squarely at the center of their practice: in fact, among other novels and films, they cite the same obscure short story—Lewis Padgett's "Mimsy Were the Borogoves"—as key to their work. As we have already seen, for Smithson, the *ostranenie* of the Jabberwock's language points a way to the verbalized entropy of fourth-dimension solid-state hilarity; for Coolidge, the story's bizarre gadgets provide a model for a sci-fi poetics, the key term of which is *arrangement*. Coolidge begins his talk of the same name at Naropa's Jack Kerouac School of Disembodied Poetics by quoting a long passage from Padgett's story involving its weird toys and then explaining his interest in it:

> That story now comes back to me with all the feelings of great discovery and mystery and desire to do something with this [*picks up piece of chalk, a book, etc.*] . . . and this . . . and this. Where do I put it? What happens when I put it there? What does it do to *this*? How close is it? Does it repel me? Does it repel you? How much does it weigh down the table? Can I look through it? What do I see when I look through it, and another whole vector of stuff coming in visually? Anyway, it took years to begin to articulate that in a form of art.[3]

Coolidge follows this statement with a lengthy discussion of his fascination with crystals and other minerals, first in the context of seeing them arranged in exhibits in the natural history museum in Boston and then also as "the minerals themselves as an arrangement of molecules, the axes of a crystal."[4] He goes on to cite as an early influence Yves Tanguy, whose paintings have "these forms. Are they mineral, are they animal, are they about to move or are they frozen there since before time? Fantastic. They're placed. There's an arrangement."[5] Science fiction, crystallography, and surrealism are the first three entries in Coolidge's list of items (which goes on to include jazz, spelunking, and contemporary art) that go into the making of his poems.

In other words, if you project the sci-fi trope of defamiliarization via surrealist montage into words arranged after the pattern of a geomorphic crystal lattice structure, you might get something like a Clark Coolidge poem:

> bearer
>   dome milks
> addage
>   scow mime[6]

According to Coolidge, a poem like this is meant to operate like one of the "toys that came from another planet in the future"—like Paradine's "abacus," with the vaguely shocking angles of its wires in Padgett's "Mimsy Were the Borogoves."[7] Note that the poem is organized in planes, lines aligned and symmetrically indented, after the arrangements of axial facets in a crystal. It raises the "what happens when I" sorts of questions that Coolidge lists above: What happens when I put *milks* next to *dome*? Is this poem an adage? Why the extra "d"? Is that what is added in order to add to "adage"? Does the ear in b*ear*er hear an utterance here? Is that milky dome an udder? Is that a cow peeking out of *scow*? What surrealist beast is this udderance miming, in its very letters? And note the vectoral prosody: *mime* assonates with *dome*; *scow* points back to *milk*. This poem is dinghy; it shatters articulation into shards of ha-ha. Padgett's weird sci-fi gadget has plunged from outer space into the very textures of language here, its non-Euclidean crystalline machineries migrating into syntagm and alphabet. Try stringing a bead along a line; play with the toy; see what happens. Maybe, like Paradine's children, you'll vanish into another dimension.

The critical point here is that Coolidge's poetics derive from science fiction more than they do from science. It would perhaps be easy enough to compose a poetic "crystal" along the lines of Smithson's definition of "an abstract crystal as a solid bounded by symmetrically grouped surfaces, which have definite relationships to a set of imaginary lines called axes," as he puts it in "Entropy and the New Monuments."[8] This would be to treat the poem as an exercise in sheer form in a poetics derived from the geometries of crystallography.[9] But to design a poem as a dangerous toy from outer space is another issue. As a cognitively estranging object with sci-fi affect, bundled as it is with fictionalized tropes of entropy, energy drain, and Smithson's petrified landscapes of social and political inertia, the sci-fi crystal not only moves but is made to *move* its reader.[10]

This sociological aspect of entropy can be more readily seen in Coolidge's *Quartz Hearts*, written two years after "bearer / dome milks / addage / scow mime" was published (although the poem was most likely composed a few years earlier). Coolidge's writing in this work has shifted from the tiny crystal puzzles and larger gridded structures collected in *Space* and *Polaroid* toward what he calls "prosoid" works, texts in which he gradually introduces increasingly standard syntax and semantics with varying modicums of narrative integrity.[11] It is as if the crystals in *Space* have been linked by syntax into linguistic constellations capable of carrying larger ranges of meaning:

> Somewhat light. Left of the leather.
> The tongue on the rod of air instead of
> the key axis. Slowly the dusty room.
> Anything circular worse than unimaginable.
> A stair.[12]

Composed for the most part in this sort of lyric block, the one hundred poems in this collection—of varying lengths, each separated by a centered period—coalesce into a series of increasingly abstract and gnomic statements. The first third of the book is situated firmly in what appears to be a suburban setting, replete with backyards, fences, laundry lines, empty lots, and neighborhood blocks. Note that the block-shape of the poem formalizes the "block" of the neighborhood:

> The mud of the bulk of the back yard.
> Itch of wash. The sun through a board
> crack a splinter up it. Noise or
> rail yards behind white sheets. A nose
> turned in window. Lock it up and smell
> off the brass shine. Two steps by
> a cat. Air and hewn lots. The view
> across and the walk back home. Blocks.[13]

Nothing of moment happens in this neighborhood or inside its houses; the sense of stasis verges on catatonia. In a concatenation of attenuated glimpses, the text alternates between verbless free-standing noun phrases ("A stair," "The mud of the bulk of the back yard") and simple descriptions of the most banal and quotidian activities:

He walked up and knocked at the front.
His shoe was the same color as the step.

·

A black tree on a purple shoulder.
The sock hidden in the stump. Pliers
in a room beneath a wind across a valley.

·

There was a block on the door.
The handle turned out to be square.

·

We have blue water in our toilet.
I pass through the space between
it and the door to my room.

·

Black shoes and brown shoes. The cat snaps
her orange tail. Aqua water in the toilet
bowl flushed away. If the disc was certain
one could put it to the man. Lime kiln
avenue in a shower going away.[14]

Nothing moves, or moves very far, in this airless crystal land, delineated sheerly by objects set in places appearing at distances from one another. *Quartz Hearts* enacts what Smithson calls "the architecture of entropy" found in "the slurbs, urban sprawl, and the infinite number of housing developments of the postwar boom." He describes this malaise in "Spectral Suburbs" as

> a place where buildings seem to sink away from one's vision—buildings fall back into spiraling babels or limbos. Every site glides away toward absence. An immense negative entity of formlessness displaces the center which is the city and swamps the country. From the worn down mountains of North New Jersey to postcard skylines of Manhattan, the prodigious variety of "housing projects" radiate into a vaporized world of cubes. The landscape is effaced into sidereal expanses and contractions. . . . All the buildings expire along a horizon broken at intervals by vacant lots, luminous avenues, and modernistic perspectives. . . .

> Exterior space gives way to the total vacuity of time. Time as a concrete aspect of mind mixed with things is attenuated into ever greater distances, that leave one fixed in a certain spot.[15]

Coolidge echoes this at the end of his book: "Houses that look like cubes. Houses that / look like tubes. Nothing looks like / anything. Nothing looks like homes."[16]

Concurrently, a weird temporality appears in *Quartz Hearts*: "Time seemed to expand into a pin which holds this picture up"; "The time is later one inch away"; "Lots of time that professional knots"; "Of the plug it lots of time budges"; "Time standing as an eye."[17] Time is spatialized and fixed here; it crawls and knots and budges. The quartz heart of the clock is winding down and spilling into distant gravity-less vacuity. As in Smithson's essay "The Crystal Land," the landscape resolves into "tiny boxlike arrangements. . . . In fact, the entire landscape has a mineral presence. From the shiny chrome diners to glass windows of shopping centers, a sense of the crystalline prevails."[18] The inertia, Dorn would say, is total.

Part of what gives *Quartz Hearts* its punch is what Dorn calls the "absolute symmetry" of its tone, its blocks of motionless declaratives gliding toward absence. In such writing, in Smithson's words, "Reality dissolves into leaden and incessant lattices of solid diminution."[19] It is just this entropic dissolve that both Smithson and Coolidge derive from science fiction—the latter drawing it largely from the writings of J. G. Ballard. Coolidge deposes both Ballard and Smithson, and a host of other writers, in his next book.

PASSAGES, SEDIMENTS, DEPOSITS, SITES

In the middle of *Quartz Hearts,* the setting suddenly changes; we move from "The this and the that / the beyond the house" and the leaden incessant lattice of the neighborhood to several poems longer than any that had come before describing scenes from "on the road back east, 1973," as Coolidge tells us in the notes at the end of the book.[20] I select salient passages:

> What is seen, not known. Billerica highways.
> The beach in Nevada. Putting back the rusty disc
> to cover any strata that might be loose.
> Maps. Straights. Caves. I'll go out on a
> temperature mountain. Cent calls by the way.
> Vista cardboards. Subgum forks. The Seven Caves . . .
>
> ·
>
> I could use the map book that pages fall out.
> Pilaster under the sun. Gumbo till. The clock

comes around. The wind rises. Culpables.
Inroads. The seven caves. Noontime earth place . . .
Stalactical ooze. . . .

.

Reno's Mapes, Hotel, "where the
action is." Two chaps make an M. Scheelite
mine. Where diving white dots make jets.
White-face steers come out. Bristlecone pines
are oldest living things. Spessartite garnets
at the rate of a dozen per hour in better
places (Garnet Hill, Ely). Particles on the
freeway, sagebrush in colors. The way of the
worlds. Cliff Leemans Cave[21]

The setting is the American West—California, Utah, Colorado, "Dawn Arizona" —and the list of the "seven caves" that Coolidge includes in his notes—"Lehman Caves, Arches Utah, Black Canyon of the Gunnison, Onondaga Cave, Mammoth Cave, Grapevine Cave, Luray Caverns"—traces an itinerary traveling from Nevada east to Virginia.[22] Clearly the trip had an agenda. We move in *Quartz Hearts* from "a landscape that has a mineral presence" to a landscape that has a mineral presence.[23] And—while I do not want to push this reading too far—the bleak mood of the writing changes in the second half of the book. Coolidge largely leaves off his blunt descriptions of rooms and blocked blocks; the writing becomes more adventurous and abstract, for lack of a better term, and the book ends in a scene of determined writing:

I walked on the street and closed
the door. I passed trees (my height
and other). I passed another. Thinking
on changing one's mind. The glass of a
store side comes up. A fish on wooden board.
I don't go in the door's shut. Small rings
and catches are they brass. The grey feeling,
the air glasses, the walking down. I
don't sense I state.

A pebble next to a pencil.[24]

One gets the sense that the journey to the West was transformative for Coolidge, a move from the crystal world of the slurbs to the crystalline world of the caves, where one freshly encounters "What is seen, not known." The clock comes around and the wind rises: Dawn Arizona. Thinking on changing one's mind, one *states*, altogether. But this might be entirely too romantic of a reading.

At any rate, two of the long travelogue sections from *Quartz Hearts* appear almost verbatim in *Smithsonian Depositions*, Coolidge's long prose piece published a year later, suggesting a continuity with the themes and issues of the later work that only deepens as we read it. *Smithsonian Depositions* to my mind is one of the great neglected masterpieces of postwar American literature, a densely constellated kaleidoscope of a text that collages passages deriving from a myriad of sources, including geology textbooks; artists' writings; naturalist and mountaineering texts; books of anthropology and crystallography; *The International Motion Picture Almanac* list of movies produced in 1959; newspaper articles and reviews; chunks of writing from W. C. Williams, Jack Kerouac, and Bernadette Mayer; record album notes; discussions of film and maps; Coolidge's own writings; and selections from other peoples' letters, interviews, and memoirs—and works of science fiction, notably J. G. Ballard's "Cage of Sand," *The Crystal World*, and "Terminal Beach." And loads of writing from Robert Smithson, repurposed and often itself cut up.

Coolidge appends an index of these sources, listed in the sequence in which they appear in the text, to the end of the poem. Most of these materials he sifts into long prose poem paragraphs, many of which are comprised of passages from just two or three sources, often themselves built up from cut and spliced text. The formal conceit is text as *deposit*, as in mineral deposits: the found materials are layered upon one another after the manner of the geological sediments and strata visible in cliff sides and caves, both of which Coolidge describes as models for his writing in "Arrangement."[25] Smithson's writings involving quarries, which he became interested in and visited with Donald Judd, also appear in *Smithsonian Depositions*, along with passages from Judd's *Arts Magazine* reviews. In fact, Smithson's comments on Judd's work in his article "Donald Judd" from 1966 might stand as a description of Coolidge's project in *Smithsonian Depositions* and might very well be the source of its title: "Space in Judd's art seems to belong to an order of increasing hardness, not unlike geological formation. He has put space down in the form of deposits. Such deposits come from his mind rather than nature. Instead of bringing Christ down from the cross, the way the painters of the Renaissance, Baroque, and Mannerist periods did in their many versions of The Deposition, Judd has brought space down into an abstract world of mineral forms. He is involved in what could be called, 'The Deposition of Infinite Space.'"[26]

A good example of Coolidge's method appears on page thirty-six of *Smithsonian Depositions*. The long paragraph begins with a quotation from Smithson—"Double perspective is composed of 'hardpan'"—itself cut from a sentence in

Smithson's "A Sedimentation of the Mind"—"The earth surrounding this double perspective is composed of 'hardpan'"—which follows a description of Smithson's excursion to quarries in Pennsylvania with Judd, where he collected slate fragments for one of his nonsites.[27] This is followed by two other such sentences, and then a series of sentences and fragments derived from Joseph Le Conte's *Elements of Geology*: "The field geologist follows the strike up in the form of a cone or dome. Let it be borne in mind. The Giant throws up a column. The Giantess throws up a large column. The Beehive throws up a splendid column and plays until the water will cool" (the Giant, the Giantess, and the Beehive are all names of famous geysers). The paragraph ends with a series of quotations from Donald Judd's art writings—"The black is discrete, hard, and projects. There aren't any other colors or divisions. The surface bends to the mark. The bands are often adjacent"—which reads as if it could be describing a rock formation as readily as an artwork. This paragraph is immediately followed by a second that begins with a collage of fragments from "Discussion with Heizer, Oppenheim, Smithson" dealing with maps and photography and set next to a passage on pictographs and petroglyphs from Edward Abbey's *Desert Solitaire*.[28] A layered and sifted deposit of textual sediments, then—Smithson on earthworks and materials, maps, and photographic reproduction; Le Conte on geology; Judd on minimalist art; Abbey on the West and prehistoric geomarking, itself a kind of precursor to earthworks—making a kind of ideogram or a nonsite for Coolidge's range of preoccupations and method in *Smithsonian Depositions*. "The strata of the earth," Smithson writes in "The Wreck of Former Boundaries," "is a jumbled museum. Embedded in the sediment is a text that contains limits and boundaries which evade the rational order, and social structures which confine art."[29] Smithson goes on to call this condition "entropy." It can easily stand as a motto for Coolidge's text.

SELF-PORTRAIT IN A CONCAVE MIRROR

In 1978, Aram Saroyan classified Coolidge's work as "very spacey autobiography," and *Smithsonian Depositions* certainly reads that way, especially the first half of the text.[30] Beginning on page twelve with a passage from *The Secret Life of Salvador Dali* in which Dali describes hyperventilating and hallucinating "eggs of fire" as a child, it traces a kind of condensed bildungsroman, pitched partly through other peoples' writings. The Dali passage is followed by a description of a grade school classroom, seemingly in Coolidge's own hand, and is in turn followed by an account of visiting the natural history museum with an uncle and a trip to a caverns, possibly Secret Caverns in upstate New York; the passage appears to derive from a tourist brochure.[31] A few pages later, we read a long description of a "typical high school day," again ostensibly from

Coolidge's pen; this is followed by an account of a trip to "the raw and mighty West," culled partly from the purple prose of Clarence Mulford's *Hopalong Cassidy* and concluding with a few sentences from an interview with Smithson concerning nonsites.[32] This is followed in turn by the two road trip passages from *Quartz Hearts*.[33] In other words, the first half of *Smithsonian Depositions* chronologically documents Coolidge's early interests in natural history, geology, surrealism—and science fiction: passages from Arthur Conan Doyle's *The Lost World* and Ballard's "Cage of Sand" appear in this section, as well as the discussion of Captain Kirk in *Star Trek* where "Shattner [*sic*] ends busting into a 'Western' set."[34] It ends with the writing of *Quartz Hearts*.

The Smithson passage I mention is the third of three in the first half of *Smithsonian Depositions*; after the *Quartz Hearts* sections, quotations from Smithson's works multiply.[35] All of the texts Coolidge chooses derive from Smithson's writings on entropy and, along with several substantial quotes from Ballard, punctuate and frame *Smithsonian Depositions*, situating it in a sci-fi context that acts like one of Frye's generic magnetic fields. By focusing on two key passages from Ballard and the writing that immediately surrounds them, the science-fictional aspects of the text and the accompanying entropic, geological, and crystallographic conceits at the heart of Coolidge's work become clear.

The first Ballard section is a long paragraph spanning pages twenty-seven and twenty-eight comprised of two separate passages from *The Crystal World*, Ballard's novel about the heat death of the universe and the subsequent crystallization of time and space and ending with brief quotations from *Hopalong Cassidy* and Smithson's "Entropy and the New Monuments."[36]

> Just as a super-saturated solution will discharge itself into a crystalline mass, so the super-saturation of matter in our continuum leads to its appearance in a parallel spatial matrix. As more and more time "leaks" away, the process of super-saturation continues, the original atoms and molecules producing spatial replicas of themselves, substance without mass, in an attempt to increase their foot-hold upon existence. The process in theoretically without end, and it may be possible eventually for a single atom to produce an infinite number of duplicates of itself and so fill the entire universe, from which simultaneously all time has expired, an ultimate macrocosmic zero beyond the wildest dreams of Plato and Democritus. And I am convinced, Paul, that the sun itself has begun to effloresce. At sunset, when its disc is veiled by the crimson dust, it seems to be crossed by a distinctive latticework, a vast portcullis

> that will one day spread outwards to the planets and stars, halting them in their courses. Pete'll hold 'em with one leg in th'air if they happen to be takin a step when he sees 'em, he laughed.
>
> Sets hard titter against soft snickers.
> Puts hard guffaws onto soft giggles.[37]

At the center of Coolidge's book, then, we find a precise statement about entropy from one of the major writers of science fiction, rounded off with a sentence from a kitschy Western novel and a passage from Smithson's writing about the "'ha-ha crystal' concept" of entropic laughter that he derives from his reading of "Mimsy Were the Borogoves." *Smithsonian Depositions* literally pivots around this paragraph, which echoes and extends material from and to the paragraphs that immediately precede and follow it after the manner of the axial armatures and faceted vectors of crystal structures.

This middle section of the book is the kernel of the text-as-crystal-as-entropy conceit that mobilizes *Smithsonian Depositions*. The paragraph just before the Ballard section that I cite is a surreal alphabetized list of some twenty minerals: "As for Apatite, fraud is a matter of bones. Biotite peels from Biot's sheets. In a pinch, Feldspar may be used as field chalk. Garnet eats a granular pome," and so on.[38] The long paragraph before this one sews together passages from Alan Holden and Phylis Singer's *Crystal and Crystal Growing* concerning Polaroid film—"Polaroid contains crystals that behave like tourmaline"—with a passage comparing the dictionary to "a vastly supersaturated solution of languages, roots entangled along sunken axes, originations buried in the dawn of man," and finally on to a passage from Smithson's "A Sedimentation of the Mind":

> Words and rocks contain a language that follows a syntax of splits and ruptures. Look at any *word* long enough and you will see it open up into a series of faults, into a terrain of particles each containing its own void. This discomforting language of fragmentation offers no easy gestalt solution; the certainties of didactic discourse are hurled into the erosion of the poetic principle. Poetry being forever lost must submit to its own vacuity; it is somehow a product of exhaustion rather than creation. Poetry is always a dying language but never a dead language.[39]

Here then is a classic constellation of Coolidge's favorite preoccupations—crystallography; words construed as rocks and minerals; poetry, entropy, and the "erosion of the poetic principle"; and the dictionary as a crystalline latticework arrangement of language—but the ante has been upped: it turns out that photographs and films are also crystal objects, by virtue of the gelatin emulsion containing the microscopic silver halide crystals that coat film. Immediately after the crystal titters and guffaws ending the Ballard section, we find a long passage beginning with a cut-up description of the spatial dynamics of a planetarium and what is most likely a Zeiss projector: "Then the double-ended rattle insect dumbell shape starts to turn, list in 3-dimensions disorients tilting seats, speeding rotation overexposes retina lines."[40] This is followed with no break by a list of some three hundred movies produced in 1959 from the International Motion Picture Almanac: an alphabetical arrangement of crystal texts in a fusion of the mineral, museal, literary, bibliographic, filmic, and arts tropes that Coolidge deploys in *Smithsonian Depositions*.

The second Ballard passage appears shortly thereafter, preceded by a brief paragraph collaged entirely from "Entropy and the New Monuments": "The action is frozen into an array of plastic and neon, and enhanced by the sound of Muzak, faintly playing in the background. At a certain time of day you may also see a movie called The Petrified River. Some artists see an infinite amount of movies. The slippery bubbling ooze from the movie The Blob creeps into one's mind. Even more a mental conditioner than the movies, is the actual movie house. To spend time in a movie house is to make a 'hole' in one's life."[41] Just before the last sentence, Smithson's text says, "Time is compressed or stopped inside the movie house, and this in turn provides the viewer with an entropic condition." Itself a box "full of box-type fixtures like the soda-machine, the candy counter, and telephone booths," with a box office and a cube-shaped projection booth running crystalline film stock, the movie theater makes a multifaceted crystal complex and a trip to the cinema an experience in entropy.[42]

The next paragraph in *Smithsonian Depositions* shows us Ballard's own version of an entropic condition, as he describes it in "Terminal Beach":

> As he entered the first of the long aisles, Traven felt the sense of fatigue that had dogged him so many months begin to lift. With their geometric regularity and finish, the blocks seemed to occupy more than their own volumes of space, imposing on him a mood of absolute calm and order. There were two thousand of them, each a perfect cube 15 feet in height, regularly spaced at ten-yard intervals. These were arranged in a series of tracts, each composed of two hundred blocks, inclined to one another and to the direction of the blast.[43]

Smithson quotes a similar passage from *Terminal Beach*—"The system of megaliths now provided a complete substitute for those functions of [Traven's] mind which gave to it its sense of the sustained rational order of time and space": for Ballard, he writes, "the environment is coded into exact units of order, as well as being prior to all rational theory; hence it is prior to all explanatory naturalism, to physical science, psychology, and also to metaphysics."[44] A better description of an entropic sedimentation of the mind is hard to imagine. Nothing moves and thought stops in this petrified world of crystal blocks, boxes, and cubes.[45] The paragraph continues with a description of the landscape around San Francisco lifted from the pages of the *Papers of the California Historical Society* (vol. 1, iss. 1–2, [1887–88]) (unattributed in the poem's "Sources"): the ground there "seems hard, bare, dead and bleak": the trees are stiff and rigid, "dull and monotonous in color and ungraceful in form," the atmosphere colorless and toneless. Even the Bay Area, where Coolidge lived for several years starting in the late 1960s, is given over to entropy.[46]

LIGHTBULBS OVER PARADISE

Smithsonian Depositions is Coolidge's self-portrait in a concave mirror. Unlike John Ashbery's *Self Portrait in a Convex Mirror*, published five years earlier—where we see the world ostensibly reflected around the outer surface of the curve of Parmigianino's mirrored ball, stretched and elongated—we instead look from inside the inner surface of the ball, from the floor of a hidden cave world like E. R. Burroughs's Pellucidar, where the horizon stretches up in the distance and time is frozen around a stationary sun. Coolidge's craggy collage—blending science fiction, speleology, geology, crystallography, anthropology, surrealism, film, minimalist art, earthworks, and more—is a layered textual record of his reading and interests, a sedimentary time machine where "Tracks of times like a story pile down to the edge of what eyes can see."[47] The force of entropy—as it is derived from the writings of Smithson and Ballard, which he quotes, cites, and warps into the text as a dynamic part of its framing—is the thermodynamic mortar keeping the strata of *Smithsonian Depositions* in place.

I would be remiss however, not to point out the ludic and kitsch aspects of *Smithsonian Depositions*, its pitch toward the arcade with its jumbled constellations of dialectical images. Reading this work is something like perambulating through one of Benjamin's fairy grottoes, whose Miocene rocks bear the imprint of the texts of bygone ages and the fossil remains of the consumer, always the last dinosaur of an earlier age or better perhaps a used book store, full of tattered paperbacks, old geology catalogs, and postcards from decades ago, like the one that appears in the center of *Smithsonian Depositions*: "But there were too many books the eye blurs. Colors and shelves. Turning the head slanting the floor to pick out words on spines. People ask for titles the store hasn't in stock. Upstairs a half-floor, a loft of more books, and variant magazines in stacks. A phone-book of book titles titled Books In Print on a table marks a tiny gravity anomaly."[48]

If this is paradise, it is one that needs a lightbulb.[49] Here the commodity luxuriates and enters into the most irregular combinations and secret affinities—Hopalong Cassidy and cement pits full of snakes, plywood whales and the Great Hall of Dinosaurs, motels at the entrance to Bridal Cave and plastic exhibits of the Jurassic, Captain Kirk and ham radio manuals, Conan Doyle's Challenger's brain force and junior science comics, *The Petrified River* and muzak, pulp science fiction and Western cardboard vistas, and a stack of scratched jazz records—all set to erupt into the present from futures imagined in the past. Coolidge is hardly the author of this spacey autobiography—instead, he is its collector, its arranger constructing an alarm clock to rouse the kitsch of the previous decades to assembly. Somebody else wrote most of it. Someone else even has the last word: *Smithsonian Depositions* ends with a passage from *Triste Tropiques* in which Lévi-Strauss likens his own past to "strata displaced by the tremors on the crust of an ageing planet: Some insignificant detail belonging to the distant past may now stand out like a peak, while whole layers of my past have disappeared without a trace. Events without any apparent connection, and originating from incongruous periods and places, slide one over the other and suddenly crystallize into a sort of edifice which seems to have been constructed by an architect wiser than my personal history."[50]

CULTURE VATS

> The culture vats as they were emptied by the development of their horrid spawn.
>
> —Edgar Rice Burroughs, *Synthetic Men of Mars*

The literary geologist reading Coolidge's cave-wall edifice might find the most legible of its sedimented fossil layers, the stratum of crystal texts that best captures the zeitgeist of the period, to be the list of films from 1959. After all, what better captures the phantasmagoria of mid-twentieth-century American arcade culture than its sci-fi B-movies, with titles like *The Brain Machine, The Broken Star, Corridor of Mirrors, The Frozen Ghost, The Gamma People, The Giant Claw, King Dinosaur, Lost Boundaries, The Magnetic Monster, The Night the World Exploded, Partners in Time, The Snow Creature, The Space Children, Star in the Dust, Superman and the Mole Man, Throw a Saddle on a Star, Zombies on Broadway*?[51]

> *He came to this island to perfect a discovery he had been working on for years. It was the creation of human beings from human tissue. He had perfected a culture in which tissue grew continuously. The growth from a tiny particle of living tissue filled an entire room in his laboratory, but it was formless. His problem was to direct this growth. He experimented with various reptiles which reproduce certain parts of their bodies, such as toes, tails, and limbs, when they are cut off; and eventually he discovered the principle. This he has applied to the control of the growth of human tissue in a highly specialized culture. Seventy-five*

> *per cent of the buildings are devoted to the culture and growth of these horrid creatures.*[52]

While *The Blob* does not show up for an obvious reason in the *Motion Picture Almanac's* 1959 list—it was released in 1958—Coolidge as noted earlier does quote a sentence from Smithson's "Entropy and the New Monuments" mentioning it—"The slippery bubbling ooze from the movie The Blob creeps into one's mind"—recalling that iconic moment in the film when the Blob oozes out of the windows of the projection booth and drips into the movie theater below, inducing hysterical panic: film culture construed as parasitical entropic brain-eating medium.[53] We have seen that Smithson associates the Blob with the putrefactive finesse of Paul Thek, whose sculptures of bloody meat contained under chrome frameworks arrest the movement of blob-type matter, a primal nightmare that otherwise presumably would bubble out and ooze over the gallery floor, inducing hysterical panic.

> *In the center of the room was a huge tank about four feet high from which were emerging hideous monstrosities almost beyond the powers of human imagination to conceive; and surrounding the tank were a great number of warriors with their officers, rushing upon the terrible creatures, overpowering and binding them, or destroying them if they were too malformed to function successfully as fighting men. At least fifty per centum of them had to be thus destroyed—fearful caricatures of life that were neither beast nor man. One was only a great mass of living flesh with an eye somewhere and a single hand.*[54]

The structural opposite of the crystal, the Blob is equally an index of entropy, following Smithson's dichotomy between the "hyper-prosaism" of LeWitt's and Judd's crystal and lattice structures and the hyperopulent works of Thek and Kauffman, with the pale lustrous surface presence of their translucent plastics and solid goo. When the Blob migrates into poetry, a different poetics appears, one absorbing and absorbed by that creature's undifferentiated tissues and morphing shapelessness. The Blob is a mouthless mobile stomach of congealed digestive juices, an organ without a body whose insides have paradoxically become its outside, a liquid globule with a lustrous veneer like the hyaline surface of water. The Blob is not hungry: it *is* hunger, appetite as sheer presence, a shimmering lump of gastric acid converting everything it comes into contact with into an all-encompassing sameness.

> *A new race of deathless supermen emerged constantly from the culture tank which swarmed with writhing life like an enormous witch's pot. Noses, ears, eyes, mouths might be scattered indiscriminately anywhere over the surfaces of torso or limbs. These were all destroyed; only those*

> *were preserved which had two arms and legs and the facial features somewhere upon the head. The nose might be under an ear and the mouth above the eyes, but if they could function appearance was of no importance.*[55]

The key word for Smithson in describing such hyperopulence is *plastic*, referring both to the surfaceless blunt substance itself and to its ability to be shaped and formed. Plastic embodies plasticity: the word *plastic* is both noun and adjective—noun elementally *as* adjective, substance as finally nothing more than quality and function. Roland Barthes is the great metaphysician of plastic; in his essay of the same name, he points out that "despite having names of Greek shepherds (Polystyrene, Polyvinyl, Polyethylene)," plastic is "in essence the stuff of alchemy," its concern "the transmutation of matter": "So, more than a substance, plastic is the very idea of its infinite transformation: as its everyday name indicates, it is ubiquity made visible. . . . It is less a thing than the trace of a movement." Plastic "keeps a flocculent appearance, something opaque, creamy and curdled." Its destiny is to abolish the hierarchy of substances, replacing them with itself: "The whole world *can* be plasticized, and even life itself."[56]

> *Here was a single huge mass of animal tissue emerging from the vat and rolling out over the floor. Various internal and external human parts and organs grew out of it without any relation to other parts, a leg here, a hand there, a head somewhere else; and the heads were mouthing and screaming, which only added to the horror of the scene.*[57]

The Blob then is plastic rendered through science fiction as existential menace, a brainless monad of conversive predation out to liquidate the universe. You cannot see *in* the Blob, just as you cannot see "into" plastic, but you know that both are uniform throughout, densely packed and radically singular homogeneities. Neither the Blob nor plastic has essence; both are substance through and through, pure surface inflated into three dimensions. The question is not so much what is plastic, but *where* is plastic?

> *The sight that met my eyes as I looked out into the courtyard was absolutely appalling. The mass of living tissue had grown so rapidly in the forcing culture medium that it had completely filled the room, exerting such pressure in all directions that finally a window had given way; and the horrid mass was billowing out into the courtyard. "If it doesn't stop growing it will crowd every other living thing out. It grows and grows and feeds upon itself. It might even envelop the whole world. What is there to stop it?" By this time the entire floor of the courtyard was covered with the wriggling, jibbering mass; and more was oozing down from the broken window above.*[58]

Plastic is everywhere! As the filament, texture, and tissue of modern consumption, plastic filters into everything we make, do, consume, operate. We even pay with it. Plastic floats in our oceans and overflows our landfills, where it will outlast creation. It stuffs the bellies of fish and birds and all the rest of wildlife. Infinitely friable, it has disintegrated into microscopic pellets and dusts borne on the atmosphere and settled into soils; it circumambulates the globe as outer space junk and satellite. The *ne plus ultra* of trash, it is the very ends of garbage. The Blob has exploded into trillions of particles that are gradually blending into the fabric of life itself and filling up the dead zones in time and space. At the end of the movie, the citizens of the small terrorized American town immobilize the Blob by freezing it with fire extinguishers.[59] It is then airlifted to Antarctica, where presumably it will remain frozen for eternity: "Dave: I don't think it can be killed, / but at least we've got it stopped. // Steve: Yeah, as long as the Antarctic stays cold."[60] Given the pace at which Antarctica is currently thawing, the Blob might very well be set loose sooner than we think.

> *By all means make every preparation you can to escape if you are unable to stem the growth in No. 4 vat room. Eventually it will envelop the entire island if it is not checked. Theoretically, it might cover the entire surface, smothering all other forms of life. It is the original life principal that cannot die, but it must be controlled. Nature controlled it, but I have learned to my sorrow that man cannot. I interfered with the systematic functioning of Nature; and this, perhaps, is to be my punishment.*[61]

Dave and Steve's brief comments regarding the freezing of the Blob end the movie, but they are also the last lines—along with "John Carpenter's 1982 re-make / of the horror classic, 'The Thing' // in which an abhorrent force of plasticity imitates / and destroys almost any form of life it encounters"—in the penultimate poem of Evelyn Reilly's *Styrofoam*, her 2009 collection exploring the disastrous ecology of disposable thermoplastics.[62] These two extraterrestrial rhizomatic monsters operate as formal models and narrative schema for *Styrofoam*—and for Styrofoam itself, "which can be molded into almost anything" "in.magificent . unscrupulous . quantities," a "poly.fix.styx.fury.flurry. slurry / of extra-terrain garbage": "*The modern world being filled with untold substances /* (in our infinite plasticity prosperity plenitude."[63] Reilly calls her book "this apoplexy apocalypse incantation / this devastation deflection invocation / this reflex context perplex,"[64] and that is what it is: a sustained invective against the polluting of the planet and the trashing and poisoning of the world.

> *It was indescribable—a strange surging sound, unlike any other sound in the world, and blending with it were strange human voices mouthing unintelligibly. Even before I looked out, I knew then what it was; and as I stepped into the corridor I saw at my right and not far from the*

door a billowing mass of slimy, human tissue creeping gradually toward me. Protruding from it were unrelated fragments of human anatomy—a hand, an entire leg, a foot, a lung, a heart, and here and there a horribly mouthing head. The heads screamed at me, and a hand tried to reach forth and clutch me; but I was well without their reach.[65]

Styrofoam has attracted a respectable modicum of critical attention, especially as concerns Reilly's ethical and political sentiments and the science behind her book; I am interested here instead in drawing out the implications of the science fiction motivating her poetry.[66] Echoing Barthes, Reilly wryly underscores the literary and especially the classic patrimony of plastics, providing us with "A Key to the Families of Thermoplastics"—"Polyethylene, Most Ancient of the Crystalline Polymers"; "Polypropylene, also called Mother of Abundance"; "PVC, the prince of Commodity Plastics"—but rather than casting plastics as pastoral shepherds, she scripts them into divine and aristocratic registers. Plastic is a god and a king—or a Blob and a Thing, for "*Plastica*, when compounded / (pliant, pliable, formative, ductile / [is] capable of being deformed continuously without rupture."[67] Mythically, plastic situates somewhere between Ovid and Hesiod, or between Homer's Proteus and Ridley Scott's *Alien*: "THUS THE IMMORTALITY OF WHAT PERSISTS / BEYOND THE CYCLE OF GENERATION AND / CORRUPTION" (ZIZEK CORNUCOPIA, CIT / 'Lacan as a Viewer of *Alien*')."[68] Reilly delimits not only a poetry of ecology, but an ecology of poetry, as she cites Shakespeare, Ezra Pound, D. H. Lawrence, Wallace Stevens, Samuel Taylor Coleridge, Lord Byron, as well as Gertrude Stein, Herman Melville, and Elaine Scarry, among others. All of these authors provide the book with a dense web of allusions, what Reilly at one point describes as a "*net of nodes noded net of netted nodes*."[69]

What, I wondered, would be the end? Theoretically, it would never cease to grow and spread unless entirely destroyed. It would engulf cities; or failing to mount their walls, it would surround and isolate them, condemning their inhabitants to slow starvation. Eventually it would cover the entire surface of the planet, destroying all other life. Conceivably, it might grow and grow through all eternity devouring and living upon itself.[70]

In other words, *Styrofoam* works like a rhizome, each individual line alluding to, pointing at, and otherwise implicating every other line in the collection, in a proliferating folding and billowing of intravoluted reference.[71] The poems' shards of aggressively antilyrical fragments are blended and blurred into a literary tissue, which, while never resolving into systematic pattern, suggests an underlying *substance*, not unlike the identically homogeneous molecules that make up Styrofoam.[72] This effect is achieved partly by reference and echo and repetition but also by Reilly's idiosyncratic use of periods, which take the place of spaces between words; it is as if the centered dots separating the blocks of writing in Coolidge's work have migrated into the phrasal chain itself:

> the.terrain
>
> of polished visitation.ecstasy   the interlaced
>
> figures   abandonments and inter-
> spersements.of
>
> earth.clay.stone.foam.Floam®[73]

The effect is precisely one of interlaced figures interspersed in a textual density that instead of evoking the crystalline faceting of *Quartz Hearts* or Judd's transparent plexiglass boxes imagines the tensile surface blur of the Blob, the thick fibrous packing of meat, or the beaded slime of Floam®—and the World Wide Web, whose domain names are clearly also part of Reilly's floating target. *Styrofoam* arrows out to the larger monstrosities morphing along with the disaster of plastic: the Blob is the blog. And all of culture is implicated: the baroque folds of Saint Teresa's gown "among altered alters / at www.artnut.bernini/ecstasy.html" resemble nothing so much as a photograph of a pile of flotsam and garbage on a beach, Cupid and his dart replaced by a pelican and its beak.[74] The most apposite poem of all might very well be "Synonyms of Polystyrene," the airless solid block of the hundreds of designations for Styrofoam that ends Reilly's book. All of the Names of Blob are recorded here.

Reilly ends her "Key" with Gustave Doré's engraving of Dante and Virgil at the foot of the Mount of Purgatory, the poem terminating in a sight rhyme for plastic's ostensible immortality—like a zombie, plastic is a dead thing that will die forever:

> THUS THOSE STUCK BETWEEN THE DEAD
> AND THE LIVING (PURGATORY CORNUCOPIA)
>
> *Ye have seen so many / to whose desires repose / would have been giv'n*
> *That now but serve them for eternal grief (Canto III)*[75]

This passage serves several purposes. First of all, it brings Reilly's poem about thermoplastics back around full circle to its classical patrimony: cantos 1 to 3 in *Purgatorio* are a sustained meditation on classical culture, not on the purgatorial trials of winning Christian redemption. In the first canto, the poets meet the guardian of purgatory, Cato of Utica, who is a pagan and a suicide: a puzzling figure to encounter here since neither is supposed to be welcome outside of hell. The quotation taken from canto 3 is Virgil talking about the virtuous pagans back in *Inferno*'s limbo, untainted souls who are denied salvation because they either died before Christ's resurrection or otherwise had no access to Christian theology. And the souls that line the cliffs above Virgil and Dante are the excommunicates, sinless Christians whom the church cast out. What we have here, in other words, is less the penitential "space of the undead" than it is the space of an unredeemable innocence.[76] Plastic inhabits that vexed liminal condition that appears when a thing is fundamentally good—or, anyway, at least not bad (the Blob is not evil; it is just hungry)—but is neither worth saving nor is otherwise salvageable or subject to salvation.[77] Born degraded as the mere "trace of a movement," plastics, *The Blob*, *The Thing*, *Alien*, finally end up in the trash. They join the melancholic kitsch and castoff crap—the "LIVING HINGES / IV tubing, urine sample cups (YOUR NAME HERE) / vacuum flasks, automobile gas pedals and other / FAUX ODE MATERIALS"[78]—in the limbo of the dump and the arcade of the junk shop. Reilly's faux ode to plastic sings intimations of immortality of a sci-fi creature threatening to thaw out of the ice of Antarctica and bubble out of the local landfill.

> *If the building and the corridor filled with the mass, the great pressure that it would exert might conceivably break down even the massive door. Then those horrid heads would devour me; or, if the mass spread from the Island across the marshes, it would be impossible ever to retrieve my body even though it remained forever untouched.*[79]

THE SECRET OF THE OOZE

The Blorb:

> To show the possibilities of sense & meaning being constructed; to foreground the limits of the possible—& our possible lives; to create impossibility.
>
> —Bruce Andrews, blurb for "Im/Posssibilty: On the Production, Distribution, and Articulation of the Possible and Impossible," September 30 to October 1, 2016, University of Kiel, conference description

> The uses which are implicated might be sci fi—imagined possibilities of a future.
>
> —Bruce Andrews, *Paradise and Method*

I. *Primum Mobile*

Bodies threatened by a voracious goo are in a manner of speaking what Bruce Andrews's *Lip Service* is about. Andrews conceives of language as an all-devouring parasitic body embodying the Body; hence reading becomes a complicated, self-involved dance, "an experimental choreography of the sign." "Our bodies & the bodies of text are dancing a courtship dance called ethnomethodology": "A mutually enhancing facework behind two bodies—a reader's & a language's—with the text as referee, to discourage a fixing of positions. Limb distance. A self-measuring torso."[80] Language, via its vocabularies and structures, the strictures of its grammar and the nuances of its semantics, *measures* the body, and the human torso syntacticalizes itself accordingly—"the skin is a grammarian"[81]—more often than not into a linguistic straitjacket: word itself as predatory blob, digestive and absorptive. Another language is possible, however—an antiabsorptive, utopian, *abstract* language that foregrounds the limits of the possible instead of rehearsing the stresses of the conventional: what Andrews calls a "sci fi" language built to imagine possibilities of a future, along the lines of Deleuze's writing at the border that separates our knowledge from our ignorance and transforms the one into the other.[82] This is paradise, where poetry can organize "a situation, a meeting place, for the erotic life of words & phrases & . . . 'It'-centered—word-to-word fluidities. Ellipsis maneuvers. Suspicious of preset apparatuses of referential connections (and harm). The secret of the ooze? Unrepetitivistic."[83] To give shape to this erotic, unrepetitivistic language while at the same time destabilizing the scaffolding of hegemonic reference, Andrews ingeniously casts his oozy writing into the crystal-sphere constellations of Dante's Paradiso, itself a frozen outer space edifice dedicated to the inscribing of Utopia.[84]

~~vocable adjective amply bachelors~~
spoonlike ikon guesswork
gonadvertising like the adding together of zeros;
and *whose* cum thirst?—~~. . .~~
vocable adjective amply bachelors . . .
breath brands the ooze Venus 1[85]

The tension between a language in radical flux and a rigidly hierarchical formal structure—vocable ooze branded by the structuring breath of the poet—creates a dialectic in which the twin types of entropy—crystal and rhizome, constellation and mess—attract, repel, and careen into one another in an erotic ethnomethodological dance:

> Radical Language Writing rejects wholeness in the Text—in order to restore it to Language &, maybe later, to a transformed Reader.
>
> Implicating constellations, it encourages a constellational approach. It solicits a call for linking.
>
> The whole is a Network—a rhizome or spreading root system, instead of roots.[86]

II. *Fixed Stars*

The three texts I discuss in this chapter exemplify the three axial directions of the sci-fi crystal. *Smithsonian Depositions* orients down, toward the Earth's core, in caves and mineral strata, and concerns itself with sedimented histories and memories: generically, it maps onto the underworld, Inferno. *Styrofoam* spreads along the lateral axis; its concern is the present, the surface of the globe, its provenance lost worlds and Purgatory, where we presently work out our ecological sins and crimes. *Lip Service* projects upward, into outer space: modeled explicitly on Dante's Paradiso, it choreographs love, eros, the body, redemption, the music of the spheres, the ecstatic ongoing dance of writing at the edge of what we know. All three texts deal with entropy: as crystal stasis, as Blob-like predation, and as a language that synthesizes the two, like freezing the Blob into an arctic ice sculpture. To return to Smithson's scheme, if Coolidge's writing draws on crystal lattices and axial facets and Reilly's works through shiny globules and morphing plastics, then Andrews's text operates like Thek's sadistic geometry of meat contained under a pyramidal chrome framework, a spectacle of an impossible fusion broadcast to the outer edges of the galaxy, or into the body:

> Self-therapy for the butter
> murmur garment, this muscled pant of view—
> ribbed hilt heart beats like a hammer:
> heat bulk gated pulse quickened germ
> elusive chaste throbs
> hardy heat dalliance *steals away*
> bone-controlled parade:
> courteous deliberately loutish
> blood stood deep blue ploy blushing mask Venus 2[87]

The body here is imagined as a skeletal cage for palpitating viscera, a bone-controlled parade: the bloody valve of the heart convulsing behind the ribs, its pulse gated and spurting along the canals of the veins; chastity itself throbbing as blood blushes into the face—desire boiling under tremendous pressures, contractions, and restrictions. "Courteous deliberately loutish" might stand as an apt description for Andrews's procedures in *Lip Service*, its construction of a meeting place for the erotic lives of words and phrases that range along the arc of language from the sublime to the obscene.

III. *Saturn*

Scholastic Dilatio: Like Andrews, Chaucer treats the "impossible" several times in *The Canterbury Tales*, nowhere more forcefully than in "The Summoner's Tale," where the issue becomes a matter of diabolical complexity and metaphysical speculation. It is also the only time as far as I know where Chaucer speaks of "*an* inpossible": in other words, an impossible is a *thing*. The Summoner tells the story of a corrupt Parson, who bilks the inhabitants of a small town by promising them that he will intercede with God on their behalf if they give him chickens, foodstuffs, money, and so on, which he tells them he will share with others of the clergy while secretly intending to keep it all for himself. A local wag in the town figures out what is going on and decides to teach the Parson a lesson. He tells him that he, too, is a clergyman, and that he has an item of great value that he wants personally to give in to the hand of the Parson to share with his holy brethren. He tells the Parson that he is sitting on the object and that the Parson should feel about under him to find it. The Parson excitedly does so, at which point the fellow blows a gigantic fart into the palm of his hand:

> "Now well," quod he, "and somewhat shall I give
> Unto your holy convent while I live;
> And in thine hand thou shalt it have anon,
> On this condition, and other none,
> That thou depart it so, my dearè brother,
> That every friar have as much as other.
> This shalt thou swear on thy profession
> Withouten fraud or cavillation."
> "I swear it," quod the friar, "upon my faith."
> And therewithal his hand in his he layth;
> "Lo here my faith, in me shall be no lack."
> "Then put thine hand adown right by my back,"
> Saidè this man, "and gropè well behind,
> Beneath my buttock, therè thou shalt find
> A thing that I have hid in privity."
> "Ah," thought this friar, "that shall go with me."
> And down his hand he launcheth to the clift,
> In hopè for to finden there a gift.
> And when this sickè man felt this frere
> About his towel gropen there and here
> Amid his hand he let the friar a fart;
> There n'is no capel drawing in a cart,
> That might have let a fart of such a sound.[88]

The disgusted Parson goes to the lord of the town to complain, and this initiates a scholastic discussion of what the lord terms "an inpossible": for how can flatulence be divided and shared?

The lord sat still, as he were in a trance,
And in his heart he rollèd up and down,
How had this churl imagination
To showen such a problem to the frere?
"Never erst ere now ne heard I such mattér;
I trow the Devil put it in his mind.
In all ars metric shall there no man find
Before this day of such a question.
Who shouldè make a demonstration
That every man should have alike his part
As of a sound or savour of a fart?
O nicè, proudè churl, I shrew his face.
Lo, Sires," quod the lord, "with hardè grace,
Who ever heard of such a thing ere now?
To every man alikè ! Tell me how.
It is an inpossíble, it may not be.[89]

Chaucer is parodying what in the Middle Ages were called "insolubilia" or "sophismata": exercises in paradox and contradiction that were classified as impossibles. Originally derived from Aristotle's cataloguing of errors of deduction and reasoning in *Sophistical Refutations*, they became all the rage among learned academicians in the late thirteenth and early fourteenth centuries.[90] Interestingly, Aristotle closes *Poetics* with a discussion of the impossible, which he compares to the improbable. He gives both tragedy and epic poetry the permission to deal with the impossible, which, in fact, he privileges over the possible: as he puts it, "a convincing impossibility is preferable to an unconvincing possibility."[91] The question is, how plausible is an impossible? What is a convincing impossible? These conundrums suggest that poetics has been wrapped up with the issue of the impossible for a long time, and that the impossible might just be the great gas of philosophy.

And elevate perturbs
blood-spattered *repertorio*—banality at its bluepoint
to salute that obstacle jellied promontory
squiring eclipse, wolfing schizated flash
banners a need away, dread treasure, sweat perfected vanity:
that's what scares me to vomit cum-like paint Venus 3[92]

Like Dante and Chaucer, Andrews's tongue is vulgar, a slice of our own vernacular: good old English, premier language of conquest, crux of slavery and empire, fatal idiom of colonialism; is it possible to elevate this blood-spattered "*repertorio*"? It is a filthy speech of profanities and curses, dirty words and insults, crass terms for bodies, women, biological functions. (Think of the vile cruel mouth of our forty-fifth president.) Other languages of course do the same, but English is bigger, the lingua franca of a dying planet. It is a dread treasure for sure, a word hoard of fraught terms for predation and rape.

IV. *Jupiter*

I recently read a short story anthology entitled *Possible Worlds of Science Fiction*. Published in 1951, the introduction makes a great deal of the role that science fiction has historically played in anticipating developments in the sciences and technology—human flight, submarines, radio and television, genetic engineering, and so on—that were once deemed impossible. The next conquest, the editor claims, will be the moon: "The idea of flight into space has been marching from the realm of impossible fantasy toward that of actual achievement. Space travel is a definite probability, and in the near future, too."[93] This militant "march" from one realm to the next, from the fantastical impossible to the actual probable, is at stake in science fiction, philosophy, and poetics, where what is impossible is somehow rendered probable—or at any rate ponderable. As Deleuze puts it, the literary universe expands at the frontiers of our knowledge, where we imagine we have something to say.

Dreamish retreat
leaps only blemish tongue feast tears cut the sound
jism carnations falsify, brittle middle
cold searching—seams grew despondenter, you can close
your mouth or I'll put it back in: iron quell liason
membrane maidenhead lip gloss fully intact
ruins;
I'll pine away Venus 4[94]

In Andrews's dreamish retreat of paradisical writing, his bowery of bliss, the tongue is a blemish that cuts sound in a linguistic copulating that constantly verges on pornography in its pining for some impossible expression. The ongoing collisions of mouth, tongue, "jism," lip, membrane tumble and mix in the brittle crystal of the poem's faceted lines: erotic appetite caught in the whirling blades of a prosodic blender. One recalls Csicsery-Ronay's observation of "the enormous range of styles of incongruity-management used in the history of [science fiction], from outright satire and parody, comedy, pornography, and allusion, to near-surrealistic arbitrariness of imagery": a better description of *Lip Service* could scarcely be concocted.

V. *Mars*

Upon opening *Possible Worlds of Science Fiction*, I discovered that the anthology does not proceed chronologically or thematically but instead is organized by planet: the book is divided into two sections, "The Solar System" and "The Galaxy." The stories in the first section all take place on the known planets orbiting our sun and are organized according to their relative distances from it. The stories begin on Earth's moon, move on to Mars, then take place on Venus, next on a moon of Jupiter, then on Saturn and Uranus, and finally end up all the way out on Neptune. The stories in the second section occur among distant stars and galaxies. In other words, the anthology is modeled, consciously or not, on Dante's Paradiso, which chronicles Dante's celestial journey as he translates from the sphere of the moon to each of the known planetary spheres and then on past the Fixed Stars to the Primum Mobile. Ten spheres, rechristened by Andrews as

> Immersible—Unanswered—Escortention—Turnover—
> Boom Boom Bunny—Little Cutes—Decent
> Hug—Romeo—Bedminster—
> down flesh lathe
> in fist shape pressing fix
> raffle spurts on cranking tunes. Venus 5[95]

Dante knew Aristotle's *Poetics*, and he certainly conceives of paradise as an Aristotelian probable impossible: a utopia, literally a nowhere. We remember that in canto 4, Beatrice tells Dante that the scenes he witnesses in Paradiso are not actually *there*; the celestial spirits are putting on a show for him because human beings literally cannot sense the divine. Both Andrews and Dante understand poetry explicitly as a means for making an image of what it is impossible to make an image of, raffle spurts on cranking tunes.

VI. *Sun*

The Dantescan legacy is visible everywhere in science fiction poetry; for example, in these lines by Mike Allen, winner of the short poem category of the 2006 Rhysling Prize, granted annually to the best science fiction poem by Suzette Haden Elgin's Science Fiction Poetry Association, founded in 1978: "The Gate said 'Abandon All Hope.' // I thought I'd tossed all my hope away, / but when I stepped through the Gate, it still pinged. / One of the guards slithered out of its seat, / snarling as it drew forth a wand. / C'mere, it hissed, / it seems you're still holding out hope."[96] The poem goes on to relate the strip search of the narrator by the slithering guard, whose "crusted hide" is described as "a Venus landscape up close"; in spite of the creature's thoroughness, however, it cannot find the narrator's hope, and the poem ends with the latter's defiant statement: "I still have hope. I do. I'm not going to tell you where I hid it." These are classic science fiction moves: the genre's distant patrimony in medieval romance and epic, in this case Dante's Inferno with its motto over Hell Gate enjoining the damned to "Abandon all Hope"; the heroic human being at odds with a monstrous alienness, threatening human dignity and freedom; the marked pitch toward allegory, in a Pauline echo: with hope, safe, faith and love cannot be far behind. Science fiction here has devolved into a predictable assemblage of tropes, a Classics Comic book of lurid cartoons: this is less imagining the impossible than rehearsing the obvious. Allen's piece reads like a prose vignette; nothing in the narrative or theme calls for the formal gestures of poetry; apparently, "Strip Search" is classifiable as a poem purely by virtue of its broken lines. Should something not happen to science fiction when it appears in poetic form? Should the form of the poem not matter to the science fiction impulse, whatever it may be? It has to be more than John Carter of Mars in quatrains.

> Ah, compulsive unbosoming—
> can single people avoid love?—multiply sixteen
> candles in scandalese, but I doubt you will [you think all
> my attacks are feminist] vanity-adhesive
> phobia disappliance: you've got fetus on the breath—
> Oh no, not that manhandler! Venus 6[97]

VII. *Venus*

Like Dante and Mike Allen, Andrews also writes of hope and love, and he also confronts a monstrous alienness, threatening human dignity and freedom, this time figured not by a belligerent lizard with a wand but secreted by a monstrous language into the body politic itself. Deleuze's frontier of knowledge migrates into the registers of syntax, and this is where Andrews composes *Lip Service*, his recasting of Paradiso, itself arguably the first work of prescience fiction in the Western canon: not only does this last book of the *Divine Comedy* literally take place in outer space, but in its calendars of church doctors and hierarchical orders of angels, it systematically catalogs what was known, and knowable, in thirteenth-century Europe. The poem stages itself explicitly at the frontiers of knowledge, in fact moving beyond them as the poet imagines what is impossible to imagine via the angelic pageant presented to his all-too-human senses. Dante is a *space man*, floating like an astronaut through the airless planets, describing the landscape of Venus not as reptilian hide but as translucent sphere—a mirror world of interpenetrating sounds and lights. He creates an astonishingly complex figure of voices within voices whose "movements" paradoxically are measured not by the ear, but by the faculty of internal sight: "And as we see a spark within a flame, and as a voice within a voice is distinguished when one holds the note and another comes and goes, I saw within that light other lamps moving in a circle more and less swift according to the measure, I believe, of their internal sight."[98] This is Venus—and by extension love—in a nutshell, the moment when lover and beloved circle around and circulate through one another, becoming fire within fire and voices within voices—and, counterintuitively, lamps contained within light—all impossible figures of amorous circularity mobilized according to the particular measure of one's internal vision: How else do we move—or are we moved by—one another? This is about what—and how—a lover sees as she hears: as Dante puts it, "e come in voce voce si discerne": "as a voice within a voice is discerned."[99] Delicate stuff. Now observe how Andrews rewrites this same section of canto 8:

> And pap size voice
> voice visual victory
> painterly near like a luau pit metrically leering
> circle encloses zero[100]

Here, as in Dante, we encounter impossibles: we see sound—"voice visual, painterly near"—as the doubling in "voice / voice" (a precise rendering of Dante's "voce voce") works formally to render the vocal visual. And what is a metrical leer but the impossible conflation of what a poem sees and how it sounds—as if the face itself had a prosody or prosody a mouth: its mouth a luau pit, a crude hole for roasting pigs, shaped like a zero, a nothing enclosed by the circle that is its sign, in a graphemic parallel to lamps moving through the light that simultaneously surrounds and shines out of them. This is science fiction working in marvelously impossible registers of image, idea, and syntax.

VIII. *Mercury*

As Andrews puts it in *Paradise and Method*, both he and Dante write "where Paradise is translated as Love and as Language" with "the capitalized L's, of *Lip Service*, of meaning service and investigation and discovery."[101] Dante after all also pays poetic lip service to Love and Language, as well as to his poetic precursors Virgil and St. John. Andrews writes *Lip Service* as a language astronaut or a lingual spaceman—improvising at the edge of what he knows, broadcasting ooze through the crystal lattices of Dante's galaxy. As he puts it, "Words float, prepersonally. . . . Some of the former uses & users are talking back at us through the syllables. The uses which are implicated might be sci fi—imagined possibilities of a future."[102] Those users talking back at us through the syllables are postmodern versions of the voices within voices that Dante hears in the sphere of Venus—the syllables you use carry ghostly traces of their former speakers; when you speak, you speaks with all the yous who have ever spoken. Indeed, the uses of these talking syllables, as Andrews tells us, might well be science fiction: that is, ways to collectively imagine an impossible future. It is as if language itself were doing the talking, the impossibilities of science fiction appearing in grammar and syntax rather than in extraterrestrial reptiles and worn-out narratives of redemption.

> And genes this bored very spermatic megalovanity
> taking without, being taken lips are pre-registered
> silken serious mute for frozen vendetta
> tartophile wolf *coeur de lion*
> sober I reckon *degree* been seduced bark was heat Mr Centerfold
> rogue venom's spit & smear expectant ego illogic
> am a tit valve hog for you, the decapitated chicken
> desperately heating retail. Venus 8[103]

Lips are always preregistered in this seamy Paradiso, where language comes down to us genetically as a kind of aggressive beefcake logic, a megalovanity of ego torqued around a violent and obscene patriarchy whose venomous "spit & smear" broadcast in wolf calls and come-hither barks, in fantasies of tarts and tits and dead chicks.

IX. *Moon*

> Lip Service *is a dense, discontinuous but homogenous poem of almost four hundred pages divided into one hundred similar sections. Wherever the reading eye glances there is energetic syntactic displacement, subversion, shock, Althusserian analysis crumbled amid tossed street and media talk; nowhere is there any sense of even minimal continuity.*[104] *You don't have to look inside this language; it's there, splayed on the page and you apply your own tourniquet to its flows, its spatter and machine gun spray, paintball epiphanic phantasms aimed at your eyes and splicing there.*[105] *Andrews' text operates as both a critique and extension of the high modernist long poem, a kind of radical response to Ezra Pound's attempt 'to write paradise,' as Pound described the* Cantos *after they had irresolved into drafts and fragments.*[106] *If* Lip Service *is, like Dante's* Paradiso, *a portrayal of the Beloved then that portrayal of the Beloved is pretty horrific. The explicit sexual language, the events referred to (*"I took a shit in the bed"*) are horrible.*[107] *Indeed, to ignore* Lip Service *is to ignore feminine writing. To ignore Andrews's poetics of écriture féminine is to reinforce the marginalization, erasure, and silencing that feminism sought to stop. Despite all of the subtle analyses of the opacity and dissonance which other critics have offered, despite the endless wringing-of-hands over the 'difficulty' and 'offensive' language in Andrews's work, I wish to offer the much more cynical hypothesis that actually it is the gender of the writer himself which we find so difficult, so offensive, so impossible to swallow.*[108] *Additionally, one of the major targets of* Lip Service

> *is the mediation and commodification of sexuality that occurs in consumer culture, especially in advertising.* Lip Service *mounts its critique of that culture by inhabiting it—by demonstrating not only what makes it banal and manipulative, but also what makes it compelling.*[109] *As he derides the pieties of what passes for liberal well-meaning or good consciousness, Bruce Andrews has produced multiplying rhetorical worlds wherein image-making and language use—as potentials in the aesthetic sense—have rarely appeared so structurally ripped-through and so demanding of examination and argument—and it all hangs heavy as a limit-case in the precarious hegemonies from which he speaks as a US cultural producer. In his writing, silent omissions, performance anxiety and the acting-out of public identities in a mediated sphere repeatedly beg the desperate questions of sexual and social organization, and of cultural reproduction as rendered by the endowments of the yet to be known.*[110] Lip Service *believes in language's ability to mean because our uncertainty in language keeps us shifting from place to place, knocking into other subject positions and other meanings. In this way meaning and belief come to hold equivalent positions inside Andrews's poetics because both are the consequence of holding something up in its social condition in order to question and understand it.*[111]

A gymnastics of lick danger lilies up complaining
                                        inlay spike heeled loan hive without honey
                                        cantilevered in coma naughtied burdens—
improbably impasse arm
aloft as weeping index
                                        simonized as separates:
it's rubber, it's the brake.   Venus 9[112]

X. *Earth*

But *Lip Service*, I would argue, has further ambitions. By casting the matter of his poem into the formal and thematic modalities of Dante's *Paradiso*, Andrews writes a science fiction poem about the ways one makes meaning altogether. *Paradiso* is an allegory of the stages of human love—from its origin in pure reflection, imaged by the pearly sphere of the moon, to its apotheosis in the mystic rose of divine love, fully petalled out in the Primum Mobile. Comprised of the shreds and patches of stories—biblical, classical, mythical, historical—that were familiar to thirteenth-century Italy, the poem takes the metaphor of spiritual life as a cosmic journey and projects it into the meticulous details of Dante's impossible planets. Likewise, Andrews builds up *Lip Service* from the scraps of contemporary language he collected on cards from 1986 to 1988, which he then ethnomethodically sifted into the stained glass armatures of Dante's system. Andrews's poem is a kind of alien parasite: he sites his cites alongside (Latin "para") and within Dante's concentric spheres, in the process creating a text that treats not only twentieth-century American vernacular but also the gigantic transparent edifice of logocentric philosophy inherited by the West from the early modern period. It's like he vomits into a chandelier. Paradiso is an idealist allegory devoted to the imagination of alternative social and economic forms, and outer space is always where we find utopia: literally, a where that is not there, "no place," an impossible location from which we can begin writing. If, as Ezra Pound—who also tried to write paradise—said, we no longer read Dante to learn about the procession of the saints or to hear expositions about the nature of the moon but instead to *see poetic images*, Andrews returns us through his sci-fi language to Earth and to contemplation of the Thrones, Virtues, and Dominations controlling contemporary political, social, and psychosexual life—and to imagined impossible possibilities of a future.

> But failure surfeits
> supreme adverse circumcision arrears
> the inaccessible theoretical loss baitings abdicating pleasure
> to please by abdication, limit clasp fit
> of pique over *faux pas* blushed devices convene. . . .
> because the musically dethroned brain cannot survive
> without the oxygen nor the heart without semen Venus 10[113]

5

The Diploetics of AlienNations

Amiri Baraka, Sun Ra, Jazz, Sherwin Bitsui

the musically dethroned brain cannot survive
—Bruce Andrews, *Lip Service*

Another poet of the impossible is Sun Ra, for whom science fiction is both a time machine and a spaceship for exploring the outer cosmos while articulating an Astro Black mythology in a grand and granular synthesis of sound, word, dance, and far-out space outfits, all fused into the Arkestra, a potent spectacle of impossible sublations for sure.[1] But the stakes of the sci-fi impossible are different for writers and performers of color, and certainly for African Americans and Native Americans, who, as we have seen, are interpolated early on in science fiction as models for the alien, the savage, the other, the primitive, the in- or pre- or protohuman—or simply do not appear at all, erased even from their native landscapes, and certainly absent from the decks of intergalactic cruisers. All of this slowly changed over the course of the last several decades, but in spite of any ostensible progress that has been made, Afrofuturism and Indigenous sci-fi remain powerful venues for interrogating the ongoing traumas of national and global racism.

The trope of the alien has played a significant role in the disposal of people of color in the United States, where it carries a double valence that plays out differently according to particular historical circumstances. African Americans have always been treated as aliens to the body politic, initially as intractable and expendable slaves, involuntarily ripped from their homelands in forced migrations and kept as virtual prisoners, then begrudgingly resigned to ghettoes and other liminal social and political spaces. In the classic American imaginary, Black people are aliens brought from outside into what was already a "native" White space where they constantly threaten to compromise and contaminate White racial hegemony. Native Americans, on the other hand, have paradoxically and cynically been treated as aliens in their own ancestral lands: they were aliens in the sense of the local frontier indigenes—whether non-White humans or nonhumans altogether—encountered by settlers and explorers as they colonized strange new lands—or planets!—and were fated to be absorbed or even entirely liquidated according to the ineluctable dictates of one manifest destiny or the other. It has been pointed out that both Native and African Americans have, in a nontrivial sense, historically always been subjected *avant la lettre* to science-fictional forms and pressures, in their respective experiences as slaves and enemy Natives overrun by a belligerent alien race armed with unfamiliar technologies, subjected to biological and germ warfare and pandemics, penned in carceral spaces and on reservations, treated as human robots and sideshow specimens, and victimized in genocidal wars and massacres.[2] All of the tropes are there, sedimented in the historical record, a sllab of bedrock that migrates easily into science fiction.

Writing Native and African Americans into science fiction as aliens thus has the uncanny effect of doubling their alienness—of rendering them alien aliens, as it were: aliens projected into literature *as* aliens. Already estranged in an estranged land, people of color are estranged in sci-fi yet again, according to the formal principle of cognitive *ostranenie* basic to the genre. What happens when cognitive estrangement is itself estranged? The doubling produces a weird superimposition, a jarring or a shuddering in the image leading to intensified distortion and blurring: cognitive estrangement turns into cognitive *dissonance*, a dysynchronous and disharmonious conjunction of two elements that can be as much a formal feature of the way something sounds as how it appears or what it sees. The distortion deepens into the very textures of sound and word, body and mind, especially in Afrofuturist sci-fi, where the screw of cognitive strangeness is twisted several turns deeper.

This doubled alienation is a formal and even a structural element in Black science fiction poetry that produces what I call a *diploetics*—a poetics grounded in double vision (Lat. *diplopia*) that generates dissonant images and sounds premised on an aesthetics of fractured juxtaposition and grounded ultimately on *distortion*: from Late Latin *tortura*, from Latin *tortus*, past participle of *torquēre* to twist (hence *torture* and *torque*); akin to Old High German *drāhsil* (turner), Greek *atraktos* (spindle)—what is the Arkestra but an Atraktostra, a distortion machine, a twisting spindle of strangeness? In Black sci-fi poetry, science fiction tropes and modes are used as means to enhance cognitive estrangement and render it dissonant in a thematics premised on the internally shifted double as both figure and ground.

This strategy of estranged doubling maps (perhaps all too easily) onto W. E. B. Du Bois's notion of double consciousness, especially when it comes to Black science fiction, and the term comes up often in the critical literature. Du Bois himself wrote at least one science fiction short story, which has been treated as illustrating double consciousness in its Black protagonist, who, along with a single White woman, is the only inhabitant of New York City to survive a catastrophic brush with a rogue comet that dispenses poisonous gases over the city.[3] Following an imminent and potentially utopian moment of collapse in the racial distance between the two, the woman's father and fiancé return from sheltering in the countryside, and racial barriers and hierarchies immediately reestablish themselves.[4] Indeed, addressing and challenging such dystopian scenarios is fundamental to Afrofuturist science fiction, as explained by Lisa Yaszek:

> Afrofuturist artists fight these dystopic futures in two related ways. First, they use the vocabulary of science fiction to demonstrate how black alienation—what W. E. B. Du Bois called "double consciousness"—is exacerbated rather than alleviated by those visions of tomorrow that are disseminated by the futures industry. Second, they disrupt, challenge, and otherwise transform those futures with fantastic stories that, as Ruth Mayer puts it, "move seamlessly back and forth through time and space, between cultural traditions and geographic time zones"—and thus between blackness as a dystopic relic of the past and as a harbinger of a new and more promising alien future.[5]

Yaszek goes on in this passage to cite Kodwo Eshun, who elsewhere describes Afrofuturism's exacerbation of double consciousness as a kind of *multiplication*: "Afrofuturism's specificity lies in assembling conceptual approaches and countermemorial mediated practices in order to access triple consciousness, quadruple consciousness, previously inaccessible alienations."[6] When double consciousness is doubled under the pressures of sci-fi *ostranenie* in poetry, a formal fracturing and shattering appears that produces enhanced distortion in a diploetics predicated on the dysynchrony of doubled double vision and an amplified focus on *sound*. Sun Ra speaks in his poem "The Double Knowledge" and elsewhere of "the double space of dual change": driven by "a word of strange duplicity," such writing carries with it a "plane of duality comprehension requirement" that demands a heightened rigor of reading designed to deepen consciousness of what it means to be an "unknown-twin dimension-being."[7] Le Sony'r Ra sees—and hears!—in four dimensions, at least.[8]

DO ROBOTS SCREAM IN ELECTRIC SLEEP?: AMIRI BARAKA

The multiplied double consciousness of diploetics is powerfully illustrated in "An Agony. As Now," a poem published in 1964 by Sun Ra's fellow traveler and equally intrepid space man, Amiri Baraka (at that date still known as LeRoi Jones).[9] A savagely twisted portrait of a soul on fire, the poem is a variation of the Human Cylinder that moves from Italian to Afrofuturism while riffing on the sci-fi trope of the robot, the metallic man whose consciousness in this case is blown into excruciating registers of alienation and pain. Encased in white hot burning metal, the poem's speaker splinters into a bewildering shatter of voices, perspectives, points of view, memories, and versions of himself that are alternately nostalgic, self-loathing, terrified, and existential:

> I am inside someone
> who hates me. I look
> out from his eyes. Smell
> what fouled tunes come in
> to his breath. Love his
> wretched women.
>
> Slits in the metal, for sun. Where
> my eyes sit turning, at the cool air
> the glance of light, or hard flesh
> rubbed against me, a woman, a man,
> without shadow, or voice, or meaning.[10]

We are immediately confronted by an unsettling disconnect: What or who exactly is the I inside of? Himself? Some version of himself? Does his self hate himself? Or is it a matter of being trapped by the White world; is the sci-fi metal casing in which he finds himself an allegory for the racism surrounding him? His identification with this enigmatic "someone" is a matter of infrathin synesthesia: he looks through the slits of someone's eyes, synesthetically smells tunes on his breath, loves with his heart. Out of phase with his metallic host body, the speaker's senses and his sensibilities nevertheless align seamlessly with it. Either the speaker himself is without shadow, voice, or meaning, or the bearers of the equally hard bodies rubbing against him are. Baraka's words of strange duplicity strain to express a person profoundly at odds with himself as well as the world around him.

Things complicate immediately: the metal frame it turns out is flesh, and a "you," who might be the speaker's soul, is addressed:

> This is the enclosure (flesh,
> where innocence is a weapon. An
> Abstraction. Touch. (Not mine.
> Or yours, if you are the soul I had
> and abandoned when I was blind and had
> my enemies carry me as a dead man
> (if he is beautiful, or pitied.

In an agonized dialogue of self and soul, the speaker's voice ricochets back and forth like the shards of reflection in a nightmare house of mirrors, as images of *he*, *you*, and *I* multiply and refract: If the speaker is not his soul, then who or what is he? His soul has become wholly other, a spectral emanation, an abandoned second person—if indeed this "you" is even the soul he is talking to. Who exactly is being addressed here? You? Me? Us? The dissociation of sensibility is complete: touch itself has become as humanly abstract as Innocence, like a Blakean category weaponized into a strangled pathos, at once beautiful and pitiable. The speaker was blind, but now he can see—in Blake's racially charged parlance, the Little Black Boy has morphed into the Chimney Sweep—but what does he see? There are only two options in Experience: pain or pain: "It can be pain. (As now, as all his / flesh hurts me.) It can be that. Or / pain. As when she ran from me into / that forest." Like a demon's refrain, the phrase "Or pain" sutures this passage into a litany of hurt from hell. The stanza continues: "Or pain, the mind / silver spiraled whirled against the / sun, higher than even old men thought / God would be. Or pain."

Is there no way out of this infernal mental spiraling in circles of relentless, self-destructive negation? For the briefest moment, the poem suggests that there might be. Continuing the line above: "Or pain. And the other. The *yes. . . .* / The yes. You will, lost soul, say / 'beauty.' Beauty, practiced, as the tree. The / slow river. A white sun in its wet sentences. / Or, the cold men in their gale. Ecstasy. Flesh / or soul. The yes." The alternative to the refrain of fleshly pain is the affirmation of the lost soul's *yes*—its declaration of beauty, *practiced.* The warm sun *or* the cold men. The dichotomy is stark, but it ends up not being a choice: "Where the answer moves too quickly. / Where the God is a self, after all)"—that is, a self, not a soul that remains intractably lost. The poem returns to the burning thing in its furnace:

> Cold air blown through narrow blind eyes. Flesh,
> white hot metal. Glows as the day with its sun.
> It is a human love, I live inside. A bony skeleton
> you recognize as words or simple feeling.
>
> But it has no feeling. As the metal, is hot, it is not,
> given to love.
>
> It burns the thing
> inside it. And that thing
> screams.

"How you sound??" Baraka asks in an early essay on poetics.[11] Not so good, by all accounts. A scream is certainly a sound: if laughter is shattered articulation, a scream might be understood as articulated shatter, the actual real noise of distress, the sonic of terror, breakdown, anguish. A scream means deep and wrenching dissociation, a painful loss of alignment and synchronicity, the splitting of the self into mirrored multiples that only partially explode out of one another before they freeze, smeared in the very act of rupture. Caught forever in its moment of dying, the soul in hell never dies. And how in the name of heaven can it escape that defiling and disfigured shape the mirror of malicious eyes casts upon its eyes, until at last it thinks that shape must be its shape? "An Agony. As Now" illustrates—or better, embodies—the first of the two related "ways" that Yaszek discriminates as key to Afrofuturism's battle against dystopic futures: that is, the use of the vocabulary of science fiction in the service of exacerbating Black alienation. The second way, that of harbingering a new and promising alien future, is decidedly absent from Baraka's poem.

Robot), in Parenthesis

Baraka's speaker describes the bony skeleton inside of which he lives as alternately white hot metal or flesh, but *you,* he says, recognize it as words or feelings: that is, the poem itself embodies the speaker, in the emotionally wrought and patterned language of lyric. Since it is the hot bones of the writing that burn the man, let us examine the poem's kinetics: How is this skeleton articulated; how do its metallic gears and joints reticulate; what sort of collagenous spindle of estrangement does Baraka construct in this portrait of the bad dreaming of a tortured robot? The doubled shudder of Afrofuturist diploetics rides on the dynamics of the textures of its writing: the vagaries of its syntax, the abruptness of its cuts and swerves, the oddities of its punctuation, its ranges of tempo and tone and pitch. The scream can be parsed.

The aggressive energy of "An Agony. As Now" is transferred to the reader via several formal means and measures, all of which help mobilize the writing's strange duplicity, its shifting points of view and the ambiguities in its lines of address. The hard enjambments of its short lines coupled with stand-alone periodic clauses and phrases, headless predicates and stranded subjects, cut a tightly wound spiral of alternatives that makes for quick, fragmented, faceted reading: the poem seems to twist down into itself, as if we were cranking into the interior of the robot. "I am inside someone" is weird; "who hates me" is appalling: the urgency of the enjambed drop ends in a shock. The middle lines of the first stanza all end with cliffhanging verbals that similarly press to locate their objects: *look→, Smell→, come in→, Love his→*. It is the hitch of the eye in moving from the end of one line to the beginning of the next that jars the reading as the poem splinters down the page. Stanza 2 locates us firmly inside Baraka's iron carapace with a blunt noun phrase that reads like an itemized entry in an industrial catalog: "Slits in the metal, for sun." Boom. This line ends with ". Where"—another anxious dangle—followed by "my eyes sit turning, at the cool air," the end rhyme *Where/air* clinching the *verse,* the turn, as in Yeats's winding stair, although instead of being summoned to ascend, we are ushered down and in. Tightly patterned rhyme, assonance, and alliteration stitch the long fourth stanza into a dizzying aural pattern—*old / soul / slow / cold / soul / robes / blown / soul*—that resounds in the fragments that begin the fifth stanza: "*Cold* air *blown* through *narrow* eyes. Flesh, / white hot metal. *Glows* as the day with its sun" (italics mine). The bony skeleton, we learn, "is a human love, I live inside . . . // But it has no feeling. As the metal, is hot, it is not, / given to love." The rhyme *hot/not* pops, but how do the commas work here? The syncopated hesitation, the uncertainty of attribution and confusion about what is dependent on what, is brutal, pathetic. The shudder is palpable. How *do* you sound??

The other unusual punctuation that Baraka puts to good use in "An Agony. As Now" is the open parenthesis, a device pioneered and theorized by Charles Olson in "La Préface," from 1947. This poem deals with the Jewish Holocaust, and I want to suggest that "An Agony. As Now" can be read as a response to it and indeed to several other Olson texts: Baraka uses techniques that derive from Olson in order to write a poem about the *Black* Holocaust. Certainly the fiery furnace of Baraka's poem evokes the ovens of Buchenwald, and both poems end with an agonized cry: Baraka's scream and Olson's howl, derived from Blake's howling Babe in "The Mental Traveller." Baraka acknowledges his general debt to Olson in "How You Sound??," which was published alongside Olson's "Projective Verse" essay by Donald Allen in *The New American Poetry* in 1960: "For me, Lorca, Williams, Pound and Charles Olson have had the greatest influence."[12] In fact, it is precisely the issue of the *sound* of poetry that Baraka says he follows from Olson: "'Who knows what a poem ought to sound like?' Until it's thar. Says Charles Olson . . . & so I follow closely on that."[13] One of Baraka's earliest uses of the open parenthesis can be found in "From an Almanac (3)," published in his first book in 1961 and dedicated to Olson, and several poems in this collection also feature the midsentence slash, also pioneered by Olson, who describes it as a *prosodic* device: "If [a contemporary poet] wishes a pause so light it hardly separates the words, yet does not want a comma—which is an interruption of the meaning rather than the sounding of the line—follow him when he uses a symbol the typewriter has ready to hand: What does not change / is the will to change."[14] "Turn it backwards / see, see what I mean?" Baraka writes in "In Memory Of Radio," an early poem that also utilizes the open parenthesis; I count some half dozen poems in *Preface to a Twenty Volume Suicide Note* that do so.[15] Apparently, "how you sound" in the early 1960s is a lot like Olson—although with profound differences.

How does a parenthesis *sound*? As a prosodic device, it is a sonic modulator: in affording a sense of intimacy with the writer, an "aside," it produces a *sotto voce* drop in the reading voice. The writer lowers their voice, inviting the reader into their confidence: the drop in sound that a parenthesis initiates corresponds to the figurative descent of the reader into an enhanced intimacy with the writer. We listen more *closely*. After a closed parenthesis, the reading voice typically rises again, as if ascending from the depths of the writer's interior back to the more public surface of the page. Parentheses orchestrate the *sounding* of a poem.

But what happens when the parenthesis does not close? In this case, the writer's voice remains *sotto*; it does not rise to its former pitch, and the reader correspondingly remains figuratively within the writer's confidence, intimate with their mental machinations. In Baraka's poetry, we can become trapped by an open parenthesis, and the closeness can be suffocating: we never get out of the dialogical splitting of the self-contradicting consciousness depicted there. A good example of this dynamic appears in "The Insidious Dr. Fu Man Chu" (1961), a kind of precursor poem to "An Agony. As Now":

> If I think myself
> strong, then I am
> not true to the misery
> in my life. The uncertainty.
> (of what I am saying, who
> I have chose to become, the
> very air pressing my skin
> held gently away.[16]

Appearing abruptly after a period closing off a decapitated noun phrase, the open parenthesis here cups a suspended dependent prepositional phrase qualifying and complicating the speaker's *uncertainty*: if I am uncertain of what I am saying, then by default I am uncertain of my very uncertainty, even as I consider that uncertainty in terms of who "I have chose to become." Identity is apparently a matter of choice and therefore already indicates a split in consciousness: I am the I whom the I who I am chooses to become. Who in the hell I *really* am is a problem, even to the point of alienating me from the very air around me. All of this uncertainty is choreographed by the lurching syntax and weird punctuation of the lines in a kind of dark jazz of multiplied consciousnesses. The parenthesis never closes in this poem, leaving us in these unresolved uncertainties of a mind spinning in contradictions and second thoughts. It is not far from here to the burning man shrieking through the slits in his iron.

In "An Agony. As Now," Baraka uses open parentheses to wind us deeper down into the ever-qualifying thinking of his agonized robot, nesting parenthetical comments, both open and closed, within one another, in a vertiginous spiral into the doubled and redoubling consciousness of the speaker. The dynamics of this ongoing modulation are fascinating and well worth perusing. The first three parentheses in the poem are all unclosed, and each initiates a dramatic twist in the thinking of the man in the iron mask. Within the first parenthesis, the speaker qualifies this enclosure as *flesh*; we are brought into his more intimate point of view—we are in a human body apparently inside a metal body, which might actually be the same body. He then immediately qualifies this body's sense of "Touch. (Not mine.": so he is in a metal body, no wait, a flesh body that has a sense of touch (that by the way is not his. "Or yours, if you are the soul I had / and abandoned," then, "(if he is beautiful, or pitied." We have now coiled three levels deeper into the mind of the speaker, whose voice at this point barely rises to a whisper, and who in a series of open parenthetical asides assures us that the metal he is in is flesh, that the touch it has is not his, and that it does not belong to the second-person addressee he apostrophizes, who might or might not be his abandoned soul—well, that is if he is beautiful or pitied. *If*? Who is "he"? Twisted deeply into a consciousness that continually feels the need to discriminate and turn the objects of its thinking, we are far removed from the metallic eye slits at the surface of the page. And we remain at this third level of the speaker's agonized reflections for the entirety of the subsequent fourth verse paragraph, the long passage punctuated by "Or pain." Three separate fully closed parenthetical comments appear here, qualifying respectively the pain "(As now, as all his / flesh hurts me)"; "the other" (presumably the soul); and the cold men in their gale. A full eighteen lines later, the stanza ends with a single right parenthesis, which traced back closes "(if he is beautiful, or pitied." Narratively, we are at the level of "Touch. (Not mine."—which is precisely where we feel the burn and scream. How you sound has everything to do with *where* you sound. The shimmering acoustics of "An Agony. As Now" play out in the sonics of multiplied consciousness.

It is hard not to read Olson all over this poem. "La Préface" is a paean to the dead of the Holocaust's concentration camps that is simultaneously a call for a new dispensation of consciousness ("Buchenwald new Altamira cave"), and the open parenthesis is the punctuation pointing Der Weg forward: "The closed parenthesis reads: the dead bury the dead / and it is not very interesting. / Open, the figure stands at the door, horror his / and gone, possessed, o new Osiris, Odysseus ship."[17] Baraka's metal man also stands at the door in horror, although he speaks from *inside* the oven, a Black Osiris trying to rise from the dead and howling like Olson's Blakean Babe at visions of unimaginable violence and hatred; Odyssean renewal in this case is not an option. "As the metal is hot, it is not, / given to love" echoes another Olson poem that speaks of initiation and redemption:

> Off-shore, by islands hidden in the blood
> jewels & miracles, I, Maximus
> a metal hot from boiling water, tell you
> what is a lance, who obeys the figures of
> the present dance[18]

Olson's hot metal man marshals us with his lance to love—love of the redeemed human body, projective agent of proprioception, qualified by its own open parenthesis: "love is form, and cannot be without / important substance (the weight / say, 58 carats each one of us, perforce / our goldsmith's scale."[19]

How different is this metal hot from boiling water from Baraka's burning metal not given to love! Baraka's open parentheses lead not outward and forward but down and in, to an agony as now. The Black Holocaust is a slow burn, still blazing half a century after the poem was written. And an African American person is still perhaps a human cylinder that screams—sometimes barely at the level of a whisper:

> Sometimes they will imprison you in paper or sounds, or
> sometimes
> They will imprison you inside yourself. There you be
> screaming but
> Cannot hear yourself. Such as it be. Such as you cannot see.
> Call me
> A black whole, call the world a mystery.[20]

RA-MAÑANA: SUN RA'S AFROFUTURIST PSALMS AND PARABLES FROM THE COSMO SPHERE:

> "The black pirates of Barsoom, O Prince," said Thuvia.
>
> —Edgar Rice Burroughs, *The Gods of Mars*

> What is one to do in an alien planet
> where the people breath New Ports?
> Where is my space helmet, I sent for it
> 3 lives ago . . . when there were box tops.
>
> What has happened to box tops??
>
> —Amiri Baraka, "Look For You Yesterday, Here You Come Today"

Baraka's tongue-in-cheek evocation of the kid friendly, breakfast cereal side of science fiction—*send in ten box tops and get a cool free space helmet!*—brings us to that other critical aspect of sci-fi, its pitch toward humor, kitsch, and corn (pops). Sun Ra might be the original Black Captain Crunch of this corner of the sci-fi galaxy—although the wry comedy of the Arkestra is always pointed with deadly seriousness and polished by a professional musicianship that simultaneously animates and pierces all the spangle and fun.[21] It is hard to describe what Ra calls "the moving panorama of the outer spacite program"—the Arkestra playing gas music from Jupiter in bejeweled and glittery neo-Egyptian outer space alien outfits, swaying and chanting while June Tyson in aviator glasses sings and twirls, Ra meanwhile in robes and chainmail headgear blasting cosmo sounds on his synthesizer, surrounded by dancers in kitschy pharaonic masks—and this difficulty is part of Sun Ra's genius, his uncanny ability to be in or at two or more places at once. He is both a Black man in racist America and an intergalactic space traveler, born in Alabama and a citizen of Saturn, a brilliant interpreter of jazz standards and an artist playing at the farthest reaches of the avant-garde, shaman and carny barker: alien visionary of cosmic good vibes who always carried a concealed weapon. An Astro Black American.

> *The First Born of Barsoom are the race of black men of which I am Dator or prince. My race is the oldest on the planet. We trace our lineage, unbroken, direct to the Tree of Life which flourished in the centre of the valley Dor twenty-three million years ago. Countless billions died before the first black man broke through his prison walls into the light of day. Prompted by curiosity, he broke open other shells and the peopling of Barsoom commenced.*[22]

In many ways, Sun Ra fulfills the second half of Yaszek's formula for Afrofuturist sci-fi: he points the way to a new and promising alien future, his music and his poetry both predicated on Black liberation and an impossible utopia figured in the stars. The spectacular complexity of his art makes it the potent constellation of affect, information, and sheer pleasure that it is. How to measure this altogether immeasurable equation? Sun Ra's self-penned job description lays out the difficulties of his mission:

I'm working under a compelled determination
On a sundry plane
        Of
Duplicity-parable-paradox
        Where the sun strives
            With the ignorance of masses
                And the difficulties of tongues
        Yet, indeed will achieve
                Invincible stance
    Bringing all into the dark-cosmo-light
        Of a sudden burning celestial-fire[23]

In his poetry, Ra strives with the ignorance of masses and the difficulties of tongues in order to articulate the *plane of duplicity* that is at the base of his sci-fi version of a visionary diploetics, predicated at once on the double meanings inherent in the *parable,* with its interlocking tenor and vehicle, and the internal mirroring of *paradox,* with its inherent self-contradiction. Doubles and twins, masks and dualities, opposites and parallels, puns and homonyms litter Sun Ra's poems, propelled by the "duality meaning presence (or meaning of words)" of "the wisdom of the double-knowledge" that is "the presence of duality / In all it's infinite and splendid reach / It's reach potential is everywhere."[24] In a poem that itself doubles its doubles, he speaks of "Dark meanings brought to light / See the mystery / Hear the sound duplicity / The double opposite parallel / Hear the sound duplicity / The double opposite parallel."[25]

THE MAN IN THE IRONY MASK

> *I had an excellent opportunity to examine the black pirates of Barsoom. They were large men, possibly six feet and over in height. Their features were clear cut and handsome in the extreme; their eyes were well set and large, though a slight narrowness lent them a crafty appearance; the iris, as well as I could determine by moonlight, was of extreme blackness, while the eyeball itself was quite white and clear. The physical structure of their bodies seemed identical with those of the therns, the red men, and my own. Only in the colour of their skin did they differ materially from us; that is of the appearance of polished ebony, and odd as it may seem for a Southerner to say it, adds to rather than detracts from their marvelous beauty.*[26]

Like Baraka's burning man peering through his metal slits, Sun Ra wears a mask—although he immediately puns on the word, splitting its meaning in two and then into three and pitching it into wholly different registers: "I'm working under a mask / There are some of another masque / Where the sun strikes the towers / Beyond the mosque."[27] In a masterfully concise passage torqued by visual and aural puns and near homonyms (mask-masque-mosque), Ra takes us from the personal (Gk. *personae*: mask) to the performative (theater) to the religious/political (Muslim!) worlds, first via the consonant shift from final -k to -que, which only registers visually, not aurally; and then in the internal vowel shift from -a to -o (masque-mosque), which we *hear*. Hence the sound duplicity of double opposite parallels. As Ra puts it, "When the word was spoken, / It was balanced on the pivoting planes of sound. . . . . . . / When it was written, / It reflected one plane of sight. / Thus the triple meaning with it's multi-divisions / was no longer apparent."[28] That is, when a homonymic word is spoken, we cannot tell which meaning it intends (*mask* or *masque*?). Once it is written down, however, the ambiguity disappears; the printed word reflects only the one plane of sight; the other two meaning planes vanish. All of this is couched in a distant echo of the opening lines of a poem from another visionary poet, Omar Khayyam of Naishápúr: "Wake! For the Sun, who scatter'd into flight / The Stars before him from the Field of Night, / Drives night along with them from Heav'n, and strikes / The Sultán's Turret with a

Shaft of Light."[29] Pivoting planes of sound indeed, and what exactly lies "beyond the mosque"? Somebody is staging a ritual drama, a costumed parable of some sort, over there. But Sun scatters and drives, working under a mask in a masque on *this* side of the Sultán's turret, which he strikes along with the towers beyond, lighting them up in his burning celestial fire.

Masks and masques are of course already doubles—a mask is a second face; a masque is a narrative spectacle that points to a supplemental, parabolic meaning—but Ra's mask is different from Baraka's: it hides a wily masquerader, not an agony as now. Sun Ra's iron is irony, doublespeaking with a deadly twist. His sense of a fundamental doubleness, of a splitting and twinning in the core of reality itself, pervades the entirety of his art. Ra even describes himself as doubled: "I am the fantasy-image of the differential projection, / Yet I do exist / Twin in spirit-being . . . / Yes, I am here but I am also there / Some far off celestial dimension there. . . . / Some omni-splendid myth—world's there."[30] The very age we live in is a twin of the future: "This is the space age. / This is the disguised twin of tomorrow," he writes, in what reads like a definition of science fiction—the disguised twin of tomorrow!—in a nutshell.[31] Out-of-phase temporal and spatial displacements—time warp and space travel—find their analogues in Ra's music, which is itself a twin of language: "Music like other languages in relationship to each other is of a different system of sound and phonetic differential. The permutation of the series of scales and notes of chords is just as real as that which happens in words/alphabetical arrangement-formation version and condensation": "The music is a journey, the journey is endless / It is sound endlessness communication language point."[32] Sun Ra's music is a time ship and a space machine that speaks to us: when we listen to the Arkestra, we mentally travel the spaceways of astro-thought in mystic sound. Music is *cognition* for Ra, who declares that "poems are music, and that music is only another form of poetry"—whether it be the songs "Of the Ultra-Cosmo-Standards"—after all, "bop is a spaceship lullaby"—or the music of the heliocentric spheres.[33] Grounded in the jazz standards of the past, to which it constantly returns, the Arkestra is also known for playing the sounds of outer space, music made of clash and dissonance, improvisation and long loopy synthesizer solos:

> *interplanetary music, where the next stop is Mars, the second stop is Jupiter, and then on to Saturn's moon and Plutonian nights—have you heard the latest news from Neptune?—traveling strange celestial roads of endless heaven, on to the Pleiades, the other planets of there, the twin stars of thence, and a cluster of galaxies somewhere in space, to the outer nothingness of the interstellar low ways. When the space ships appear, the Nubians of Plutonia travel the spaceways on rocket number nine, tracing*

> *the tapestry from an asteroid, interplanetary travelers taking a journey to the stars on a planetary search for provocative celestials who dwell on other planes. There they learn the dance of the cosmo-aliens, the dance of the extra terrestrians, the dance of the language barrier.*[34]

An ongoing dance at the extraterrestrian language barrier, Sun Ra's poetry is a choreography forged in the vocabulary of science fiction, the only writing with enough torque, with enough twisting force, to convert such an elusive referent into an object available for representation. For only such writing, in which science fiction tropes are systematically turned into poetic forms, can accommodate referents so averse to representation. By formalizing science fiction literalities, Sun Ra's sci-fi poetics provides a representational home for referents that are themselves neither purely literal nor purely figurative. They hover in the infrathin space of doubleness between figure and letter, here but also there, pivoting on planes of sound and sight, twins in spirit-being.

THE DIPLOETICS OF IRREALIS

> Would you to know? Would you to know,
> The things you would to think you should?
> You Would?
> I thought you would.
> I thought you would . . . I thought you would.[35]

Ra often pitches his poetry along the subjunctive, the grammatical mood used for expressing wish, desire, and longing and for discussing imaginary or hypothetical events and situations—the would thats, should yous, were you tos, and had it been sos of language: *the things you would to think you should.* Were it possible to translate grammatical modality into larger literary modes of genre and narratology, all science fiction might be construed as working in the subjunctive mood—certainly Yaszek's sense of Afrofuturism's vatic fantasies of impossible tomorrows fits the mold. Longing and desire for a better future discussed in imaginary or hypothetical terms is what Afrofuturism fundamentally *is*. The subjunctive is the grammatical ghost locked inside the skeleton of the sci-fi device: in Black sci-fi poetry and music, this ghost is on fire. Baraka's burning man and Ra's cosmos-light are both spirits of intense desire, longing that stretches reality to the breaking point: these poets and the sounds they make warp into shrieks of sheer reaching.[36] Theirs is an ecstatic art, a shuddering of the stasis that keeps the racial status quo set. Ra's music is frightening, terrific, mind blowing. It angers people, like Miles Davis shredding Broadway tunes at breakneck speeds or Jimi Hendrix making the national anthem Bold as Love—or Albert Ayler's haunted military march of ghosts.

> *Without exception the blacks were handsome men, and well built. The officers were conspicuous through the wondrous magnificence of their resplendent trappings. Many harnesses were so encrusted with gold, platinum, silver and precious stones as to entirely hide the leather beneath. The harness of the commanding officer was a solid mass of diamonds. Against the ebony background of his skin they blazed out with a peculiarly accentuated effulgence. The whole scene was enchanting. The handsome men; the barbaric splendour of the accoutrements; the polished skeel wood of the deck; the gloriously grained sorapus of the cabins, inlaid with priceless jewels and precious metals in intricate and beautiful design; the burnished gold of hand rails; the shining metal of the guns.*[37]

The subjunctive is one of several grammatical moods that linguists term *irrealis*: irrealis moods are used to indicate that something is not actually the case or that a certain situation or action is not known to have happened at the time the speaker makes his statement. Irrealis verb forms are thus used when describing an event that is not likely to happen, has not happened, or is far removed from the real course of events or is otherwise impossible, in other words: science fiction! Sun Ra's poetic visions of travel to the outer limits of the cosmos are deeply irreal, and like a technician who knows his tools, he attunes his spacecraft to the finest modulations of grammatical mood:

> Would I for all that were
> If all that were is like a wish.
> Would I for all that were
> If all that were is that which never came to be;
> For the image of the world that was
> Is the light of the darkness today . . .
> And all that were is not what I wish it were. . . .
> Would I for this wondrous thing
> A new decree of happiness
> Better than, any liberty this world has ever known.
> A Cosmic weigh
> That opens the way to the worlds that are:—
> The Kosmos worlds of endless galaxies.[38]

Ra weighs his cosmic words carefully—"My watchword is precision," he writes, and *precision*, often in the company of *discipline*, even hyphenated as *precision-discipline*, appears frequently in his writings and song titles.[39] He weighs his words with care because they open the way to the "Kosmos worlds." Words are the literal gears and pistons of the engines of his craft as it races through space propelled by the rocket fuel of the subjunctive: would he for all that were if all that were is like a *wish*, a wondrous thing that opens the way to the worlds that are.

The subjunctive mood is also a doubling: a wishing for something other than what is here or otherwise present; a fantasy of some other place, time, or circumstance; a something that is not actually the case. If, in Wittgenstein's formula, the world is everything that is the case, then what in the world would a world that is explicitly *not* the case *be*? This is what Ra calls the "Lightning Realities" that his art is designed to address and discriminate:

> All lights are rays of being
> Lightning realities touch
> Intense vibrations. . . . voice of the silences-sound
> All lights are of rays . . . beams
> Projection from subtle hidden sound field
> To feel-synchronization
> That moves from rays to race to rays to race to rays
> To beams of beings. . . . .
> Thus, through the medium of light
> From sundry cosmo-planes,
> We can move to spheres in the vast endless abyss. . . . . . .
> The vast endless abyss of Outer Space. . . . .
> The approach of the Eon of adjustment is at hand
> Transition-adjustment . . alter interpretation. . . . . .
> Equational-precision
> Cosmo-Visions Magic . . . abstract translation
> To other waves of thought-feeling-atunement . . .
> "The lifting up shall be the casting down",
> 'Tis thus it is written. . . . .
> Look outward at the eternal pit of Out-Space. . . . .
> Out-Space is at first for bold outcast pioneers . . .
> Cast Out from the earth into the bottomless pit.[40]

Turning the book of Job on its head ("When men are cast down, then thou shalt say, There is lifting up," Job 22:29), Ra begins his fireside chat with Lucifer: the bottomless pit it turns out is not a fiery furnace in the center of the Earth but the black and infinite abyss of outer space. Ra pens a wickedly ironic satanic psalm here, firmly in the visionary company of Shelley and Blake: being a bold outcast pioneer cast into the eternal pit that is the cosmos requires a transition-adjustment based on an alter interpretation, an abstract translation of the poetic texts of the Bible. Lucifer in this view is the solar light bringer, the Sun Ray, cast out of heaven for rebelling against the Power that be:

The delusion is the God—idea . . . . . .
The deception is the conception-certified
Or the certified conception of the God-idea
Cast the outworn God-idea out of your mind
The outworn God-idea
Is the control center
Which has been used to mold the minds
Of the complacent, the unwary
And the unsuspecting . .
It has destroyed the innocent
As well as
Trapped the guilty . . . .
The outworn God-idea
Has really been the creator
Of the world as it is today . . . .[41]

Like Lucifer, Ra is a Promethean intruder with an "idea, the calculated knowledge of it / Eternally balanced by the uncalculated presence of / The intuition potential intruder/the beam / Harmonic precision celestial being / Chromatic rays race. / There are angels. / There are angels!"[42] For such an Angel or Demon at play, light and sound, seeing and hearing, are rays of real being—actual things that beam from their hidden fields to materialize and synchronize in feelings attuned to thoughts, most forcefully through the measures of poetry and music, which are wholly *creative.* Such rays alter interpretation and make new worlds: "New sounds cause new vibrations / Like ripples on a lake / They branch out from the propulsion / Point of activation. / New sounds! / New sound crash the shield of illusion-hypnosis / And one can plainly see / That the 'life' of the world / Is only the manifestation / Of a particular interpretation."[43]

For Ra, to create is to *beam,* a key word in his visionary lexicon. A beam is a projected and directed vibration of light and sound: "Every light is a vibrational sight and sound: / It is rhythm in harmony with beam/rays/intensification and projection visibility."[44] The sun beams, its rays lighting up reality and thereby rendering it visible: Sun Ra beams, his rays lighting up irrealities and thereby rendering them visible (and audible): "For since I hear the music / Upon the beam I trace the sound / And always the beam vibrates / The meaning of the sound."[45] In classic Ra fashion, he breaks the word *beam* into two: "For we who are know we are to is . . . / To be and am / We be am / To beam-synchronize / Within its energy-rays."[46] To beam is to *be am*: again a doubling, this time of the very plane of existence itself, which here is twinned into an enhanced life, a living in the visionary projective Sun beam as opposed to mundane solar earth light. To beam is to be at once *is* and *are* (*be am*):

If I to be am
Then to be is and are.

Why did other voices speak to you
And enchant your mind. . . . . . ?
It is what your mind is must seek to understand
Beyond the planes of earth-light love. . . .
I have known a heaven all my own. . . .
How bitterly long have I searched
For all that is mine: Now I must be, I must be:
        And mine is mine. . . . .
My immortal pure idea
My sound idea.[47]

Ra's revolutionary project, his cosmic weigh then, is to crash the shield of illusion hypnosis and break the spells that enchant the mind: his visionary beams of music and poetry issue a "new decree of happiness / Better than, any liberty this world has ever known."[48] As an Astro-Black American, he is out to free slaves, his beams projecting from subtle hidden sound fields to feel synchronization that moves from rays to race to rays to race to rays: "My measurement of race is rate of vibration-beams . . . rays. . . . Hence the black rays is a simple definition of itself/phonetic revelation."[49] Indeed, if "The third heaven of the heavens is called earth / It is heaven # three," then Ra has questions: "The third heaven slaves? / Who, and what and why are they? / I see places of disguise / Hidden monarchs of the past hid them."[50] If the idea is that "We Free Kings," in the words of yet another visionary musician and poet, Rahsaan Roland Kirk, then Ra's Black phonetic revelations "can teach a king / To smash tradition's fort / Cross the moat / Of feudal futile passe defense / And bring to naught / The bounds of planned confusion's / Languages. . . . . / That separate and demean / The brothers of the Sun."[51]

POLISHING THE GEMS OF A LOVESICK EYE: SUN RA'S OPEN FIELD REVISIONS

On four sides of the throne and several feet below it stood three solid ranks of heavily armed soldiery, elbow to elbow. In front of these were the high dignitaries of this mock heaven—gleaming blacks bedecked with precious stones, upon their foreheads the insignia of their rank set in circles of gold. On both sides of the throne stretched a solid mass of humanity from top to bottom of the amphitheatre. There were as many women as men, and each was clothed in the wondrously wrought harness of his station and his house.[52]

One way of understanding Afrofuturist diploetics is as ongoing revision, constant reseeing: Baraka's burning man in "An Agony. As Now" continually changes his mind, turns his thoughts, qualifies his statements: revising what it is he knows and feels. The poem twists around "or," the conjunction of alternatives—it's either this *or* that *or* neither *or* both: there is never just one way or view. It's the ongoing thinking of the mind caught in its deliberations, the human condition of mentally moving through time and space and adjusting to the circumstances that appear before one, momently. This is a poetry that *sets out*, aiming to encounter the world and its contingencies as they unfold in one's literal line of sight, or insight: what one knows in the process of coming to know. It doesn't stop: consciousness *as* it doubles; alter-interpretations on the fly.

Sun Ra's poetry works in the same way, but it is torqued more often around *and*—also a conjunction of doubling, albeit more inclusive and forgiving than Baraka's harder *or*—and *if*, the conjunction of condition and the conditional:

According to nature's laws and law
I be as I am and what I am not even
Because and yet not even because
Because and yet not even because
Because, for, and, that is .. why ..
Then and so
Perhaps
May
If I do I will
And if I don't I won't
Either way I do and I don't perspectively
Why, when how, what, which
Yes, no. . . . . neither.[53]

How many Ra's are there? He is what he is and what he is not because, and yet not even because, for—and, that is, why—then and so, and maybe: if he does and if he does not, *perspectively*, when how, which; yes, no . . . neither. This vertiginous mental spiraling pivots around the poem's two center words: *perhaps*—maybe, could be—and *may*, the modal verb used to declare both intention and permission ("I may go, I'll see" versus "He says I may go"). It's a matter of perspective: He can, and if he does, he will: Depends, I guess.

This is not so much a depiction of a profoundly indecisive mind as it is an acknowledgment of a radical freedom of choice and self-determination: nature's laws and law (what exactly is the difference?) is *lawlessness*, says bold outlaw Ra: what's all this about *because*? To be or not to be, what's the problem? Perhaps I may, perhaps I may not. It's actually none of your business. Smash the forts and cross the moats and bring to naught the bounds of planned confusion's languages. Teach the king: *that's* the plan. In the meantime, get off my case.

This acknowledgment of the fundamental and universal freedom to *vacillate* —to change and choose one's mind, at will and even capriciously; to shift perspective and remain flexible and responsive to the world and one's sense of it—is at the center of Ra's immortal pure idea. Couched in the rhetoric of science fiction, it is also key to his poetics, his diploetics of the sound duplicity of double opposite parallels. Poetry is where we dance at the extraterrestrial language border, the place in space where words are revised, reseen, reheard, made fresh, and recast into the verbal means to reach the outer limits:

> The Word . . . words. . . . words made fresh . . .
> Made again. . . . . The recreate . . . the recreation
> The Word was made fresh. . . . . .
> is the Cosmic reach. . . . .
> Dark meanings brought to light. . . . . [54]

Again, a densely packed stanza, replete with biblical allusions: making words fresh in poetry is both play (recreation) and at the same time the deadly serious work of ongoing Creation, of making Word flesh, of freshening St. John's living Word that in the beginning made the heavens and the Earth. Words are our means for reaching the cosmos, the verbal sound/sight/mind rays with which we long and stretch for and illuminate other worlds. If presently we see through a glass darkly, the word is the way to bring darkness into light: black unto white, cleansing the sight, making things right, changing the rite:

> Projecting the words: right, write and rite.
> Those who in ignorance seek rights
> From the hand of man receive rites
> So that equal rites are equal rights and equal writes. . . .
> Equal writes can be equal written words. . . . .
> The right word can be considered as the write word:
> The written word.[55]

Ask for rights from the Man, and all you get is rites, the masque beyond the mosque. Instead, equal writes is the way to equal rights. The immeasurable equation is an equal sign, and it renders whatever appears on either side of it an equivalence. Some words are dead ends, according to how they are arranged; they do not line up in the equation:

> Some words are dead ends according to the arrangement like book ends are to books, such words are so to other words; this is not to say they do not mean anything at all, but rather they are not of the equational bal-

> ance continuum. Other words move in an eternity cycle/circle. Like the words are the music, like the music are the words. They are translations, each of the other. They move in designs/different shapes.[56]

The point is to make words point, to each other, to music, to eternity. One of Ra's most gnomic poems makes exactly this point:

> *[Point Equal Aim]*
> · = aim
> · = end
> · = period
> · = time
> · = era
> · = age
> · = cycle[57]

To point equals to aim; an aim points to an end; the point at the end is a period; a period is a length of time; a length of time can be an era; an era is an age; an age is a periodic cycle. These are words in an equational balance continuum moving in an eternity cycle/circle. Translations of each other, each of them revises the next. This is the way we write when we write with design, laddering on equivalences that spiral upward and out:

> The code
> Projection sensitivity
> Force reach decision
> Perpendicular spirals
> Galaxies, planets, earth
> Man and his world
> And the other world of man
> Comprehension response
> To the world of angels[58]

LINES, DESIGNS, PATTERNS, SHAPES

I want to address Sun Ra's statement that his living cosmoworld words "move in designs/different shapes" because not only does he revise the language of his poetry time and again over the course of his writing life, but beginning in 1980, many of his poems appear in radically altered shapes and patterns. Departing from the generally standard lineation of earlier versions—hard blocked rectangles of lines, left-justified, after the manner of most traditional poetry written since forever—he construes the poems anew, variously across and down the page, breaking up and indenting and spacing stanzas, punctuating lines with ellipses or long rows of periods, or tabbing them into sharply shaped chevrons or other systemic designs. Sun enters the open field, reforming his poems into dynamic and mobile objects that excite the eye and ear as the reader travels the space ways of the page, where the doubled visions/versions of diploetics forge a close and exacting unity between poetic form and science fiction content.

A good example of Ra's process of revision can be seen by comparing the first stanza of the 1972 version of "Would I for All That Were," his paean to the subjunctive, with the version of the same stanza from 1980. The first is published as a standard left-justified lyric, typical of the poems one might find in most anthologies and magazines of the day:

> Would I for all that were
> If all that were is like a wish
> Would I for all that were
> If all that were is that which never came to be
> For the image of the world that was
> Is the light of the darkness today
> And all that were is not what I wish it were
> All that swirls anon in the world of dreams
> Boundless in thought and fruitful reminisce.
> Would I for all that were
> All that words cannot express
> All that pleasant dreams cannot remember
> The enchantment and warmth of rare content
> Would I for these and these alone
> That I might live as cosmic thought insists I should
> As it were right to be as I wish to were.[59]

Almost entirely unpunctuated, the poem looks and reads like a list, the eye tracking quickly and unhampered in a largely uninterrupted flow from the end of one line to the beginning of the next. Line length is determined by the borders of syntactic units: prepositional and adjectival phrases make up the bulk of these, while aside from the four subjunctive "would" clauses, only a single declarative verb, "is," leads off the one hard enjambed line in the stanza. No line has caesura, and the metrical units are each of a piece; the rhythm is consistently iambic, and the feet range from trimeter to tetrameter to pentameter, with two lines—the fourth and the penultimate—making hexameters. The stanza is a model of poetic modesty and restraint; any semantic dynamics are contained and framed by its metrical schema and the iron mandate of the left margin.

In the second version, Ra liberally uses the typewriter tab key along with punctuation, some of it unconventional, to produce a much different looking—and sounding—poem:

Would I for all that were
If all that were is like a wish. . . . .
Would I for all that were
If all that were is that which never came to be.
For the image of the world that was
Is the light of the darkness today;
And all that was is not what I
wish it were.

Would I for all that were: All that words cannot express;
All that swirls anon in the world of dreams. . . . .
Boundless in thought and
fruitful reminisce,
All that pleasant dreams cannot remember:
The enchantment and warmth of rare content.
Would I for these and these alone
That I might be as cosmic thought insists I should,
As it were ideal-meant to be as I wish to were.[60]

The regularizing of the punctuation here—particularly in the introducing of periods, colons, and semicolons into the verse—produces hard stops and distinct pauses, making of the stanza a much more hesitant, jerky, and finally discursive object than the first version, which has no such markers: the *sounding* of the *meaning* of the poem is different. The stretched ellipses—twelve and ten spaced points, respectively (· = pause?)—simultaneously lengthen the elliptical hitch and suggest an extended, unfinished thought, the longing of the subjunctive: *if all that were is like a wish* dot dot dot dot dot dot dot dot dot dot dot dot. The poem points out of itself and toward the silence of an inexpressible desire, all that swirls anon in the world of dreams. The variable-foot iambic pattern stays the same as in the older version, with the exception of the eighth line, which is in heptameter, with a strong caesura. Ra takes the clunky suspended ballad measure 3 x 4 of "Would I for all that were / All that words cannot express" and turns it into a muscular independent clause driven by the logic of its colon; the line's seven beats, broken in uneven halves by the caesura, effectively snap the singsong monotony of the iambic that up to this point dominates the verse.

But all of this appears against the vivid patterning of the writing across and down the page. The poem's meticulously slanted and alternating stanzas veer and snake in a crazy vorticist dance, a visual analogue to the twisting temporals and conditionals of "Would I for all that were / If all that were is that which never came to be." And there is a deeper logic, rooted in the way syntax initiates and carries semantics, to the breaking and spacing of the lines here.

Olson's comments about composing on a typewriter in "Projective Verse" can help parse this:

> Observe [the poet], when he takes advantage of the machine's multiple margins, to juxtapose:
>
> "Sd he:
> to dream takes no effort
> to think is easy
> to act is more difficult
>
> but for a man to act after he has taken thought, this!
> is the most difficult thing of all"
>
> Each of these lines is a progressing of both the meaning and the breathing forward, and then a backing up, without a progress or any kind of movement outside the unit of time local to the idea.[61]

In other words, to move from dreaming to thinking is a moving forward in *meaning*—thinking is more active and volitional than dreaming, which is largely passive and involuntary, but the move from one to the other is relatively easy. To move from thinking to acting, however, is much more difficult because it involves no longer merely speculating but putting speculation into action, projecting it forward and *realizing* it, in the world. The stepped lines of the poem embody this moving forward by the fact of their ongoing indentation: you move forward in meaning from dreaming to thinking to acting, *literally*, as you move further rightward across the tabbed stops of the page. There is also a "breathing forward" in sequence: speak the lines, and you can feel the momentary hitch and lift of the last word of each as you breathe forward to the next. The line beginning with the qualifier "but," however, takes us *back* a step: this doubling conjunction initiates either a contrast with or a response to something already said. Hence on the page we literally face around and move back: we hesitate as we back up to summarize and consolidate the poem's meaning up to this point, and we breathe the longer pause, mobilized by both the stanza break and the shortened left tab return, between "difficult" and "but." Projective verse sets out to produce a literalized physiognomy of thinking in writing: Olson's poems are formal icons that imitate in their shapes the dynamics of their semantics.

Sun Ra's shaped poems operate in much the same way. Consider again the stepped breaks in the first stanza of "Would I For All That Were":

> Would I for all that were
> If all that were is like a wish. . . . .
> Would I for all that were
> If all that were is that which never came to be.

For the image of the world that was
Is the light of the darkness today;
And all that was is not what I
wish it were.

The second line is a moving forward of the thinking in the first, a qualification of the double subjunctive "*Would* I for all that *were*" that is initiated by "If." From there we move back to the original question and, appropriately, step back to the left margin. This is followed again by an indented prepositional qualification in the fourth line, which in turn is followed by another prepositional phrase, a second qualification in the line of thinking, initiated by the preposition "For." The enjambed verbal "Is the light . . ." then finishes and brings forward "the image of the world that was," and this is followed and qualified finally by a conjunctive ("And") clause (preceded by a semicolon). The logic of the poem's rightward drift is locked in and determined by its syntax and punctuation.

Or observe the patterning of the "be am / beam" passage in "The Other Otherness":

For we who are know we are to is . . .
To be and am
We be am
To beam-synchronize
Within its energy-rays. . . .
To rise above
The
Revoluted-eternity. . . . . .

Here we see a series of lines and groups of lines systematically offset one from the other. The second line is centered in regard to the first and is a qualification of it: *be* and *am* are versions ("translations") of *is*: the spacing produces both an equivalence and a stepped movement forward from a specified "we" to the abstract universal of the infinitive "To be." The third line then extends the meaning of the second by translating the infinitive into the equivalent but more concretely specific and active pronoun construction "We be," and is accordingly stepped forward. Line three collapses "be and am" into "be am," which then subsequently synchronizes into "beam" in "beam-synchronize" in line four. This compacted description of itself translates and aligns with line three. The opening preposition "Within" of line five then marks a movement forward and inward from line four's infinitive "To" (*to beam / within*), which is echoed in line six's "To rise above" in a stepped qualification of "To beam-synthesize." The two subsequent lines are then centered in regard to this line in order physically

"To rise above / The / Revoluted-eternity." The entire stanza is constructed as a turning of the screw, a winding in and down *without a progress or any kind of movement outside the unit of time local to the idea.*

After all, if I were going to write a science fiction poem about *beaming* as a projective condition of *being,* how else would I place the words on the page in order to have them participate in the circumstance of that occasion? Ra's poetry, like his music, integrates time, space, sound, and thought in an equational continuum balanced on pivoting planes of sound and sight. Sci-fi diploetics is a precision discipline of the highest order, its double vision our ticket out of the book and off to the stars:

> This is the Space age——
> Prepare for the journey!
> You have a rendezvous
> With the Living Wisdom
> Of the unadulterated fate.
> Prepare for the journey!
> Like a happy child
> You will step out of the pages
> Of the blinding blend of the Book,
> And gaze astounded
> At the endless space of the
> Cosmo-Void.[62]

> *The black led us rapidly through the inner chambers of the temple, until we stood within the central court—a great circular space paved with a transparent marble of exquisite whiteness. Before us rose a golden temple wrought in the most wondrous and fanciful designs, inlaid with diamond, ruby, sapphire, turquoise, emerald, and the thousand nameless gems of Mars, which far transcend in loveliness and purity of ray the most priceless stones of Earth.*[63]

FEEDBACK, KALOOKA, HARMOLODICS: JIMI HENDRIX, YUSEF LATEEF, ORNETTE COLEMAN

> Before ancient Egypt, there were moon trips
> —Jimi Hendrix, "Valleys of Neptune"

A primary thesis of this book is that science fiction creates a tendency in poetry and poetics toward a kind of enhanced distortion that plays out in formal as well as in thematic registers: cognitive estrangement torques sci-fi poetry at levels of syntax, line, stanza, shape, and pattern that are intensified and even specific to the genre. This present chapter argues that these affects are in effect doubled in Afrofuturist writing: given the formal principle of cognitive *ostranenie* basic to science fiction, the always already alienated figure of the Black person is alienated yet once again, intensifying and further distorting the texture of the image and the language and the voice (Baraka's "how you sound") of the Black writer. Or musician, in the case of Sun Ra, in whose moving spacite panoramas the distortion deepens to blend into the very fabric of the spectacle itself, warping space and time travel into the audio-visual dynamics of the present of the performance.

This can be heard palpably in Ra's music: every time the Arkestra heads to the outer reaches of the galaxy, the sounds it makes become increasingly dissonant, angular, raucous, and abstract, with Ra gleeking and blaring on his synthesizer, as if cacophony were the music of the spheres and intense racket the noise of the cosmos beyond—or at any rate, as if the sound of the craft *traveling* to them were—in a non-Euclidean scrambling of the proprieties and pieties of terrestrial orders, a bold advance into the irreal. Here one thinks of numbers like *Cosmic Chaos, Voice of Space, Cluster of Galaxies, The Outer Heavens, Infinity of the Universe, The Cosmic Explorer, Heliocentric Worlds, Continuation to Jupiter Festival, Space Probe, Pathways to Unknown Worlds, Next Stop Mars, The Second Stop is Jupiter, Astro Black*, and many others, where space and space travel are signified by a furious and glorious free jazz driven to extraordinary limits of sheer expressiveness. The cosmo-sound is Promethean music unbound.

What follows are brief discussions of three other occasions in Black music where science fiction impels extremes of formal distortion, both in sound and in song, instrumentation, and lyric. Science fiction in these cases drives musicianship and song craft to audio limits that stretch to where language itself smears, breaks, cracks, and clacks into the alien indecipherable.[64] In these excruciations of sound and meaning, Afrofuturism leaves its profoundest formal marks on both music and poetry.

ASTRO MAN

> Imagination is the key to my lyrics. The rest is painted with a little science fiction.
>
> —Jimi Hendrix, *Starting at Zero*

Sometime in the late 1960s, a Mr. Paul Corusoe, an odd-looking fellow and putative expert on extraterrestrials, was interviewed on British radio station EXP:

> ANNOUNCER: Good evening, ladies and gentlemen. Welcome to radio station EXP. Tonight, we are featuring an interview with a very peculiar looking gentleman who goes by the name of Mr Paul Corusoe, on the

dodgy subject of are there or are there not flying saucers or . . . ahem. UFO's. Please Mr. Corusoe, could you give us your regarded opinion on this nonsense about spaceships and even space people.

Mr. Corusoe: Thank you. As you all know, you just can't believe everything you see and hear, can you.

At this point Corusoe's voice begins to distort and slur electronically; then:

Now, if you'll excuse me, I must be on my way.

Announcer: Bu . . . but, but . . . glub . . . I, I don't believe it.

A barrage of sustained guitar feedback follows, fading in and out and panning between left and right channels, as Corusoe blasts off for the outer limits:

Mr. Corusoe: Pfffttt!! . . . Pop!! . . . Bang!! . . . Etc!!!?[65]

Thus opens *Axis, Bold as Love,* the second studio album by the Jimi Hendrix Experience, released in 1967 and featuring a number of technical innovations at the time, including experiments in microphonic and harmonic feedback and the stereopic panning effect mentioned above. All of the contemporary resources of the art and its evil twin, mechanical reproduction, were exploited at the time to produce a recording the likes of which nobody had ever heard before. Science fiction boldly strode into psychedelic rock and roll in 1967, converting the electric guitar into a spaceship and the studio into a time machine while introducing hard core electronic distortion as the sonic analogue to outer space travel.

Like Baraka and Sun Ra, Hendrix dons various sci-fi masks and personae, and science fiction operates for the Experience as a framing device for exploring double consciousness via music and lyric. Like his fellow spacemen in the arts, Hendrix was aware of the kitsch elements of sci-fi: in "Astro Man" he becomes the avatar of Mighty Mouse (he kicks off the song by yodeling "Here I come to save the day" in a wavering falsetto), the rodent superhero who rescues threatened humanoid mice while making his home on the moon. The song is a compactly sardonic portrait of a fractured consciousness that in its turn becomes a spirit of violence and revenge: "A little boy in a dream just the other day / His mind fell out of his face and the wind blew it away / A hand came down from heaven and pinned a badge on his chest / It said 'Get out there, man, and do your best.'"[66] Having your mind fall out of your face is no doubt harrowing enough: Hendrix depicts a profound split in the boy between depth and surface, skin and brain. We are close to the troubled doubling in Baraka's traumatized robot. But the clincher is in the next two lines, in the mocking cynicism of the hand reaching down from heaven to pin a badge on the boy's chest: the blazon of race become the tin star of the antihero, who decides to do his best—his best, that is, to screw things up:

> Oh, they call him cosmic nut
> And he's twice as dense as Donald duck
> And he will try his best to screw you up
> The rest of your mind
>
> look out, my guitars . . .
>
> He's going to blow out the rest of your mind
> Talking about looking for peace of mind
> Astro man will leave it in pieces . . .
> May you fly around in pieces
> Blow out the rest of your mind

Astro Man is a dark animus who, having internalized the wound of race, turns it back on his attackers, pledging to screw them up in turn. Hendrix uses outer space to articulate inner space: the man from the stars it turns out is in your very midst, attacking your peace of mind with his music and blowing the rest of it away, an incendiary alien with a bomb set to go off and wreck the world.

In his most fully realized sci-fi musical extravaganza, "Third Stone from the Sun," Hendrix does just that—destroy the world, that is. In this epic song, he poses as an astronaut from an alien planet exploring Earth in a scout ship. The cut begins with a dialogue between the pilot and the "star fleet" mother ship, recorded at half speed and so for all intents and purposes unintelligible to the listener:

> "Star fleet to scout ship, please give your position. over"
> "I am in orbit around the third planet from the star called the sun. over"
> "You mean it's the earth? over"
> "Positive. It is known to have some form of intelligent species. over"
> "I think we should take a look."[67]

The distortion here marks the voices as alien, sound and sense blending into a sci-fi audio slur. As the scout ship descends to the surface of the planet, the pilot speaks again, this time with absolute clarity, as if we were hearing him through a Star Trek universal translator. He then repeats himself in distorted alien mode, reporting back to star fleet that he wishes to examine the Earth's mysterious mountains up close and land his "kinky machine." As the ship lowers to the ground, Hendrix rips the sounds of its engines in grand sweeps of feedback and vibrato, his guitar shrieking and grinding; one pictures the spacecraft hovering and gliding over the planet's surface. Then comes the pilot's doomsday verdict: "Although your world wonders me / With your majestic superior cackling hen / your people I do not understand / So to you I wish to put an end / And you'll never hear surf music again."

Bummer. The Earth is annihilated in a vortex of sonic destruction, as if Baraka's metal scream were blasting from the slits in his mask to wipe out the (White?) world and its insipid surf music. At any rate, that's one way to read it. For Hendrix, science fiction is a means for imagining not an extraterrestrial utopian future on distant planets but a domestic sci-fi apocalypse. Mighty Mouse descends from the stars with a death ray to save the day. Or waste it!

KALOOKA KALEEKA

> The number that we're about to play has a message in it for all mankind. It says let's not be taken in with our advances and technology to the degree that we forget to be human beings. Let's not become robots and forget our fellow man. Let's not forget to help those that need help—simply to be brothers and sisters to everyone and to each other.
>
> —Yusef Lateef, "Robot Man," live performance

Thus Yusef Lateef introducing his song "Robot Man" on a Norwegian television program in 1972.[68] Decked out in a traditional Fulani hat and West African robes, he begins the number with a soulful wooden flute solo before delivering his introduction, accompanied by the space boink sounds of Patrick Gleeson's synthesizer. Then, as the band begins the song's fat bass funk riff, Lateef mimes a robot moving in jerky mechanical syncopation to the beat. He intones the song's lines with marked pauses between phrases and words:

> Robot man
> will you sing
> Robot man
> will you sing
> I
> am not swayed
> by emotion
> I
> am a seeker
> of perfection
> I
> am only
> a machine

I
have been programmed
by my
commander

Lateef's robot man is closer to Baum's Tik-Tok or the Nome king's iron giant than he is to Baraka's overheated metal soul: the mechanical mind depicted in the lyrics here is emotionless and cold, a figure for organization man, preprogrammed for the institutionalized mimetic rationality of the administered world, an Adornian drone. Robot man has traded the complexities of human life for unreflecting obedience to the commander: as he says, "In robot life / attitudes / toward the world / do not matter." The robotic human represents one of the most familiar and hoary themes in the sci-fi canon: the question of the limits and boundaries surrounding the agency—or the lack thereof—of artificial intelligence, in this case used as an allegory for faceless modern functionalism. Robot man is the direct descendent of the futurist automaton, the legacy of Marinetti's multiplied man and Mina Loy's passionless human cylinder. All business, he is no fun, or any help to any brother or sister.

The linguistics of this sociopathic robot's speech are interesting; it is clear that he can talk a kind of simple preprogrammed English, which he painstakingly delivers in clunky word-by-word sentences, but his language has a deeper structure that is based on the sounds of his inner working parts. After Lateef once again asks robot man to sing, we hear him do so:

Bam boom zoom pop
bim bam boom
Bam boom zoom pop
bim bam zop
Robot man
will you sing
Robot man
will you sing
kalooka kalooka kalooka kaleeka
kalooka kalooka kaleeka kalooka
kalooka kalooka kalooka kalooka

This automated speech-song, imitating both machinic gear clack and electronic zip, is followed by a lush saxophone solo, as if Lateef were answering robot man with sheer sonic expressivity, reminding him and us of what it sounds like to be human: humans inflect language emotionally through vocal modulation, which, intensified and exaggerated, begets singing. What robot man cannot do is *sound*, in Baraka's sense of the word. A fraught doubleness appears in the song: the lines traded back and forth between Lateef and robot man are both spoken in the first person, as if Lateef *were* robot man, or were speaking to an aspect of himself, a dangerous internal doppelgänger—a possibility corroborated by his mechanical dancing: Are those Yusef's moves or his inner robot's? This infrathin proximity to the automaton within is precisely what Lateef warns us about in the introduction to his song. We might not be inside robots, but robots are inside us.

Can a robot sing? Or is it just imitating sounds? What is the difference, exactly? Lateef's question is a different one again, however: he asks *will* robot man sing. Here the issue is not ability but intentionality: When and how does a purposive or deliberate mental state appear out of the clacks and zips of the gears and circuits in a machine's "head"? What would it take to make a robot actually "sing," to be "swayed" by emotion and express it in musicalized speech? Can a robot *swing*? Will it ever? And if it can't or won't, don't it mean a thing? It all depends on what a "song" is, and what it means to mean or to "feel," altogether. And then there is the issue of transcoding, of moving from the unimaginably complicated nexus of human syntax and semantics to machine language:

> Robot man
> will you sing
> I
> will have to decipher
> your language
> in order to
> understand
> your lin
> guis
> tic
> pro
> ces
> ses of
> communication

The robot is a kind of translating Turing machine, a mechanical device that decodes and then recodes what is in this case sonic input. But what exactly are the "linguistic processes" of *song*? Robot man's diction disintegrates into syllables, as if he were trying to reduce words to their smallest phonemic particles, which of course can never get to the gist of "meaning": What does "guis" or "ces" *mean*? Surely words are more than the sum of their phonemes, and a song is more than the sum of its words. A seeker of perfection, robot man gets it all wrong. Songs *sway*, imperfectly. The soul appears in the flexing timbres of the voice, but robot man can only mechanically stretch and multiply syllables, as in extending *click* into *kaleeka.* Similarly, dissolve writing into its alphabetic grains and you have exactly nothing, atoms that carry no meaning: Blake's sand on the Red Sea Shore.

Asked one last time if he will sing, robot man starts in again with his zoom pops and kalookas—but then suddenly Lateef breaks into astonishing scat, zeedle doo dipping and whooping and grunting, only to end in a swirling catastrophe of growls and uh-uh-uh-oh's as the music disintegrates into a whirlpool of dissonance while he lurches his dancing down, slumps, and finally freezes in place, robotic arms half lifted. The stress of trying to sing has apparently caused robot man to overload; he blows a fuse and switches off: Tik-tok winds down. Robots, it turns out, will not sing—they *can't.* They can keep time, but they can't groove. For one thing, they don't breathe; they have no *anima.* Lateef then slowly picks up his sax and blows a robust, lush, heartfelt ballad. Human language as distinguished by its emotionally expressive sonic textures—and in fact music as the pure rush of those textures—wins out over the empty clicks of the machine. The dangerous robot double disappears in the expire of human breath.

There is another level of doubling to the story: five years later, in 1977, Lateef recorded "Robot Man" again, this time in a revised, hyped-up, super slick disco version of the number, suggesting that the song's target has shifted from hollow corporate clone to glittery hipster tripping the light fantastic under the mirror ball, part of the slide from early 1970's activism to the self-indulgence and narcissism of the later half of the decade's apolitical malaise, for which the figure of the soulless robot is still entirely on point. The droning monotonous thump of techno is not far off—sheer sonic perfection: no human players invited. You'd only make mistakes. For Lateef, science fiction once again becomes the occasion for Afrofuturist diploetic critique of the double, the robot embedded in the human and forever threatening humanity's music, the bend in the quaver of our indelibly imperfect voices.

SPACE SHIP AIR CHURCH

Ornette Coleman's record *Science Fiction* caused quite a stir when it was released in 1971, and it still does: critics describe it as an unprecedented work of brilliance and creative advance and a prescient herald of the music to come, not only in Coleman's repertoire but also for the future of jazz, funk, disco, punk, and many of the myriad posts- that lay ahead. Coleman and his intrepid band step forcefully into a brave new world of electrification, overdubs, spacey vocals, and rock-derived modalities: Bill Milkowski even notices Charlie Haden playing a Jimi Hendrix "'Purple Haze'–styled bassline through a wah-wah pedal."[69] Steve Huey calls the album "a stunningly inventive and appropriately alien-sounding blast of manic energy."[70] But other than its all too human "alien-sounding . . . energy," what makes this album a work of science fiction? The fact that music might be experimental or that it expands into new sonic territory does not necessarily make it sci-fi, although employing evocative metaphorical phrases to describe it like *taking off, heading for the outer limits*, or *knocking it out of orbit* massage the message that way. It is not clear to me, at any rate, how *Science Fiction* is science fiction, other than in its adventurous novelty.

Except, that is, for the eponymous title track, which fits the sci-fi rubric beautifully and especially its Afrofuturist component. Against a background tornado of intense free jazz delivered by two trumpets, bass, drums, and tenor and alto saxophones, the poet David Henderson reads his cosmic poem of conception, birth, race, and civilization, paced slowly word by emphatic word in a voice electronically reverberating in a fuzzed-out echo chamber and punctuated periodically by the sound of a crying baby:

> No
> mother
> to
> be
> and
> no
> father
> to
> feel
> there
> I
> stood
>
> [baby cries]
>
> humans
> they
> said
> are
> made
> from
> two
>
> one
> being
> me
> the

other
one
you

How
many
enemies
make
a
foe

[baby cries][71]

Humans, Henderson intones, are made of two. The baby cries twice: once upon being born from its two parents ("there I stood") and then upon itself dividing into two, a me and a you. Here the doubles we watch burning in Baraka, playing in Sun Ra, raging in Hendrix, and dancing in Lateef appear immediately in the figure of a single split I, a subject (me) aware of itself as an object (you). A male ("no mother to be") without a father ("to / feel"), Henderson's manchild is an involuted enemy of itself materializing in the play of the mirroring of double consciousness. But this mirror then flashes outward, as the poet addresses a third party:

Don't
race
my
face

to
flash
my
way

How do you race a face? to flash his way? Henderson torques the verb into a new direction: you race a face by declaring it as such—as *a race face*. The verb activated becomes an adjective. This is close to Hendrix's boy who dreams that his mind falls out of his face, except that Henderson's mind is flashed back into his face. Here again Yeats's lines cribbed earlier fit the scenario: How do you escape that defiling and disfigured shape the mirror of malicious eyes casts upon your eyes, until at last you think that shape must be your shape? The flashing mirror of bigotry casts race back into the face of the speaker: already doubled by his split consciousness into a me and a you, he now has to face race, that other more vicious, debilitating, and fatally cracked mirror.

The song ends with a literal and formal declaration of doubled life:

my
life
my
life

and an abdication of self so profound that it can only be proclaimed against the horns shrieking behind it:

my
mind
belongs
to
civili
zation.

Black Americans have always lived science fiction, in the form of the internalized alien, forever a stranger in White civilization and out of phase with *themself,* in this case the awkward plural pronoun is entirely apt.

And here I am going to take a speculative stab at answering Henderson's curious and beguiling question: How many enemies does it take to make a foe? What exactly is the difference between the two? *Enemy* is a Latin word, derived from *inimicus,* "non-friend": -in + amicus. An enemy it appears can turn into a friend; it is literally a matter of reversal. "Foe," I would posit, is a heavier and more emphatic word, deriving from the Anglo-Saxon *fah,* to feud. Feuds can be deadly: in ancient Germanic cultures, they most often signified *blood* feuds, vendettas, wergild, and revenge. The first definition in the OED is "one who hates and seeks to injure another: a personal enemy." A *personal* enemy, not just any enemy: an enemy who is in your face because it is *your* face. You can negotiate with an enemy, but foes are implacable. My enemies within I can deal with; my foe outside is my *mortal* enemy, with whom I am locked in a struggle to the death, a death wish. Feuds are notoriously difficult to bring to finish; they last for generations and for centuries: for life times.

If my mind belongs to civilization, then it does not belong to me: I am outside looking in. What I see is my mind reflected back at me as the face of race. It takes at least three enemies to make a foe: me, you, and that other you, looking back at me from out there.

ATHABASCAN SCI-FI: SHERWIN BITSUI

A new wing emerging from the lips of these Indians,
who are no longer passing thoughts in the paragraphs of an oil-soaked dictionary
—Sherwin Bitsui, *Shapeshift*

Along with African Americans, Native Americans and the myriad other Indigenous peoples of the New World have lived the terrors of science fiction in their flesh, blood, and bones. The list of real-time historical events that evolve into sci-fi literary tropes is nigh endless: first contact with aliens bearing unknown and lethal technologies; the frontier as liminal cultural space and ever-expanding border; aggressive colonization and settlerism leading to enslavement and genocide; biological and viral warfare and enforced assimilation; Indigenous peoples classified and treated as subhuman aliens in Native homelands that are pillaged, exploited, poisoned, stolen, and destroyed—the history of the Americas over the past five hundred years plays out as one horrific, relentless, ongoing sci-fi scenario, the bulk of it *avant la lettre.* It is important to remember that science fiction in no small measure develops out of the Western and that many of the themes and issues that characterize the latter migrate easily into the former, where they are broadcast into outer space or plunged into inner Earth and projected into ever stranger forms and trappings, as in *Princess of Mars* and *Phantom Empire.* Science fiction and Native Americans have been intimates since before sci-fi was conceived. If anyone's mind belongs to civilization, it is theirs.

But contemporary Native writers reverse the terms of this all too symbiotic relationship: rather than depicting Native peoples as forever fated to playing the roles of hapless victim or enemy alien, Indigenous authors use science fiction to explore their own tribal identities, histories, and cultural metaphysics, forging a potent mix of traditional modes of storytelling, myth and legend blended with sci-fi into a hybrid literature of Indigenous futurism.[72] Native American story often already shades into the fantastic and otherworldly: the alien, the weird, the strange; shape-shifting and astral travel; time warps and alternate existential dimensions. The casting of these narrative epiphenomena into the forms and contours of science fiction makes this literature increasingly resonant and relevant.

But what about poetry? While a great deal of critical ink has been spilled concerning Indigenous futurist stories and novels, one rarely if ever hears about Native science fiction poetry—is there such a thing? And how to determine what is mythopoetic in it from what is sci-fi poetic? The very intimacy of the blend, the tight braiding of the two genres, makes this question complicated: both science fiction and mythopoesis rely on cognitive estrangement to build their worlds; add surrealist *ostranenie* to the mix, and it gets difficult to tell the literary forest from the trees.

I nevertheless want to make an argument for an Indigenous science fiction poetry, by examining poems by Sherwin Bitsui, Navajo writer of an arresting body of work that ranges over reservation life, historical trauma, ecological damage and resource extraction, and Native American consciousness—and perhaps even the American *unconscious*—more generally. Dreamlike and congealed into knots of vivid oneiric impressions, his tightly packed images have been called surrealistic, although Bitsui insists that they derive more directly from the contingencies of his Native heritage.[73] So what contribution, if any, might sci-fi make to his poetry? Or, phrased differently, what would it mean to read Bitsui's poetry as science fiction? Or should we read his work as a limit case for an Indigenous sci-fi poetics? These questions formulate across the fractured landscapes of Bitsui's poems, landscapes at once geophysical and sociohistorical, comprised largely of the red rock canyons, brushy arroyos, and mesa strewn badlands of the high southwestern desert but at the same time marked by tribal sensibilities and memories and scarred by colonial histories implicit in the ongoing traumas of reservation life. Scenes play out in remote hogans and along the sandy dirt roads of Canyon de Chelley but also "against the drooping bones of / arthritic HUD houses," in Indian Health Services (IHS) clinics, and around hard-bitten border towns like Gallup and Farmington. The scourges of reservation life—endemic poverty; alcoholism; joblessness; White prejudice and bigotry; and lingering health problems from a century of uranium mining, gas and oil extraction, and coal firing—figure side by side with blooming cacti, smells of rain in the canyon floor, the blue mountains west of the Rio Grande, the nebula of the roadrunner's beak, ravens, red ants, and "Coyote biting his tail in the forklift." Bitsui's poems are spooky, haunted, acutely nostalgic, and shot through with pain, wreckage, and menace. They beam to us, as he puts it, "from the galaxy closest to the argument."[74]

But what about science fiction? Sci-fi *inheres* in these composite landscapes, providing a ghastly backdrop that is at once antithetical to Indigenous sensibilities while crimping them into the grotesqueries of a world profoundly at odds with itself. Sci-fi appears here most forcefully in passages involving images of the White world with its corporate interests and the tissue of machinery—oil derricks, forklifts, train tracks, water towers, pipelines, mine trailings, Coke cans, and the West's ever-ubiquitous barbed wire—that civilization drags along in its wake in order to establish proprietary boundaries and maintain property relations. This is a world where "We are speaking inside the nervous system / without nerve endings to call our own. / Children born with teeth chewing into incubators, / not knowing walls, / or the beating heart of an owl / hovering over the gates of her belly."[75] In the seismic clash between the incubator and the mother's belly, refiguring the earlier dialectic between the robot and the egg, science fiction teeth and nerves are put on edge. The extended metaphor in this passage is just barely visualizable: we can imagine babies gnawing at machines as easily perhaps as we can an owl hovering over the body of a parturient woman; the Native and the sci-fi are in hard tension here, disparate energies indeed. Samuel R. Delany argues that reading science fiction "code" often comes down to a matter of interpreting metaphorical phrases—for instance, "Her world exploded"—literally.[76] Children born with teeth chewing into incubators derive from the codes of science fiction: the phrase brings technology and a deeply estranged humanity into dead heat proximity. The incubator evokes images of the mad scientist laboratory, replete with umbilical cables and machine hum, dials and flashing lights; we are in the world of Frankenstein or artificially grown pod people. The Native estrangement of Bitsui's Indigenous perspective is estranged yet again as it gets entangled in the nets and networks of alien machinery and technology; the hybrid figure that emerges, an alien/Native cyborg wandering the deserts of Arizona, is pure science fiction.

"Asterisk," the first poem in *Shapeshift*, Bitsui's first book, illustrates the ways in which his complicated landscapes and images crisscross and collide in order to produce an hallucinogenic sci-fi inflected nexus of innuendo and danger. There is something mean afoot in the world: in fact, the poem torques around the word *something*, ringing the changes on its pronominal ambiguities: what thing is this *something*? The first lines refer to a vaguely remembered date and an unnamed event, as if the poem were avoiding saying something by saying "*something*":

> Fourteen ninety-something,
> *something* happened
> and no one can pick it out of the lineup[77]

"Lineup" suggests a criminal lineup—what crime was perpetrated? When? *Something* happened in fourteen ninety-something, but no one can pinpoint or quite remember what it was.

> But look—
> something lurking in the mineshaft—
> a message, ice in his cup,
> third leg uprooted but still walking.
> It peers over his shoulder at the dirt road dug into the mesas's skirt,
> where suguaro blossoms bloom nightfall at the tip of its dark snout,
> and motor oil seeps through the broken white line of the teacher's loom.

In a series of twisting whiplash turns, *something* goes from indicating a date, to naming an event, to describing a monster lurking in a mineshaft. Here we see Indigenous history torqued into a concise spiral—the date: 1492; the event: first contact; the monstrous offspring: uranium poisoning. *Something* in the mine has an icy message, and while it has been uprooted, it still walks the countryside on its three legs, peering over your shoulder, the way sickness stalks a community exposed to the dark snout of an abandoned and poisonous mine. The stanza's last line is a marvel of poetic condensation: motor oil seeps through the Navajo weaver's loom, spoiling the web and breaking the line of tradition's thread. Dreadful creatures born in underworlds of dark machinations are abroad in the world, bringing suffering and death and wrecking cultures.

Something then morphs from monster to occurrence:

> *Something,*
> can't loop this needle into it,
> occurs and writes over their lips with thread;
>   barnacles on their swings;
>   fleas hyphened between their noses;
>   eels asphyxiating in the fruit salad.

OK, this gets weird: this *Something* is something like a temporal writing machine, a looping shape-shifting body without organs that *occurs,* in the process usurping the needles of the teacher's loom, sewing lips shut, and silencing the Diné. The conflation of codes and registers in this passage is breathtaking—literally, since nothing can be said. And the bizarre objects that follow—barnacles (in the desert?) on swings; eels (in the desert?) suffocating in fruit salad (or is that *dessert*?); and then how exactly does a flea hyphen between a nose or noses?—are taken straight from the surrealist playbook, or from the Indigenous perspective. Take your pick. But the third "leg" on which this ungainly creature stumps around belongs to science fiction: a monstrous alien *something* with a dark snout that lives in a mineshaft, or *is* a mineshaft. The sci-fi stuff of nightmares.

At the end of the poem, "fragrant rocks in the snout remain / unnoticed in the bedroom, / because the bridegroom wanted in, / Pioneers wanted in, / and the ends of our feet yellowed to uranium at the edge of fear." The rocks in the mine monster's snout even stalk the procreative bedroom, poisoning generation and generations, all because pioneers wanted in. But "a new wing [is] emerging from the lips of these Indians, / who are no longer passing thoughts in the paragraphs of an oil-soaked dictionary": and a raven's quill makes a very sharp pen indeed. In Bitsui's poetry, science fiction filters and inflects the language of Indigenous perspective. What is an *asterisk,* after all, but a star, a * indicating *something* that has been omitted?

6

Dancing at the Language Barrier

Clark Coolidge's Alien Tatters

> The more languages you know, the more building blocks the Martians have to play with.
>
> —Jack Spicer, Vancouver Lecture 1

Well, that's gotta be true. If language, as William Burroughs puts it, is a virus from outer space, then the Martians currently have somewhere in the neighborhood of 6,500 different sets of viral building blocks to play with—quite the arsenal for infecting a planet! And while every terrestrian language is its own diabolically complicated array of sounds, words, grammar, syntax, and semantics, all of them are created equal, each one perfectly suited for expressing the human mind in all of its convolutions. The individual building blocks of each particular language lock together beautifully with one another, but each set of blocks is as differently designed from every other as you can imagine. Languages are not codes—they cannot be "broken," as the Japanese military discovered when it tried to decipher Navajo code talkers or as any puzzler over Linear A will tell you—they are hermetically sealed, self-contained word worlds. Mutually unintelligible, they all build to say the same thing. But to understand any one of them, you need a gateway: a Rosetta stone, a native informant. Otherwise the runes stay mute, the talker unintelligible. The Martians have their work cut out for them.

The question for science fiction is what would an alien *say*? What would such a being talk "about"? Human languages are all translatable into one another—but that is because they are *human.* We are all wired the same way: we each have the same brain, the same five senses, the same upright bipedal bodies, opposable thumbs; we share the genome and a planet: it has one moon; everyone dreams; and we all have the same innate faculty for language. One big happy family in Babel, a city with 6,500 towers. But what would an alien who shared none of our terrestrial or biological features have to say, as they say? This is one literary venue where science fiction ostensibly has something to contribute:

imagining nonhuman languages takes us to the outermost limits of intelligence and intelligibility. And if the poetic function, as Roman Jakobson tells us, is "the set (*Einstellung*) toward the message as such, focus on the message for its own sake," then by definition poetry would be the best genre for exploring the parts and particles—the syllables, words, phrases, clauses, rhythms, tempos, sounds, moods, modes—what Jakobson calls "the palpability of signs"—of fantastical languages.[1] Like Baraka's metal man with his twisting thoughts, poets *turn* language, but they also *re*turn it: the coil of the poem can take language out, but typically it brings it back in, back to what we think it means to be human. Sci-fi poetry by contrast would conceivably keep spiraling further outward, to unknown spaces and wholly unfamiliar existential states—to the utterly defamiliarized strangeness of the alien. The tendency in much science fiction is to *domesticate* aliens, to render their lives and worlds into warped mirrors of our own—something of a diminished ambition, and one implicated in what we have already seen as the settlerist and imperialist fantasies of outer space "exploration," which as often as not comes down to a search for slaves, precious resources, or "empty" New Worlds to colonize, under the guise of scientific investigation and adventure.

If science fiction in Deleuze's formulation is writing at the frontiers of knowledge, then crossing those borders should have a linguistic component as well: languages have frontiers too, edges that we edge up to when we write at the lines that separate our knowledge from our ignorance and transform the one into the other. New worlds require new words—even new *shapes*, in the case of a writer of sunbeams like Sun Ra. Under the pressures of sci-fi's mandates of estrangement and first encounter, language stretches to accommodate what it meets, or conjures, and this is especially true in science fiction poetry, where how you sound and how it looks become weird as a matter of the generic occasion. The foregrounding and managing of science fiction poetic language has been one of the principle themes of this book: from what Benjamin calls the "completely new language" of *Lesabéndio*, to futurist *ostranenie*, to the surrealist's magnetic fields, Burroughs's cut and spliced *Nova* texts, Smithson's fourth-dimensional entropic hilarity crystals, Coolidge's poems that work like outer space toys, Reilly's blob Styrofoam writing, Andrews's oozy rhizometrics, and Lateef's robotic kaleeka lyrics. Science fiction poetics work to project cognitive estrangement and dissonance into the textures of language itself.

Conceptualist poet Christian Bök actually invented an alien language—Taelon—after he was commissioned to do so in 1997 by the producers of the television series *Earth: The Final Conflict*. In his essay "The Alien Argot of the Avant-Garde," Bök describes his artificial language as an unabashedly Whorfian fantasy: it turns out that, unlike any actual human language, Taelon expresses a "model of the universe,"[2] this time that of a race of "celestial Buddhists."[3] After dismissing that other most successfully created sci-fi language—Klingon—as "nothing more than a simple cipher for English with a reverse grammar and a Germanic emphasis," Bök turns from Worf to Whorf and his versions of Amerindian languages for his model, describing Taelon as something like a mash-up of Uto-Aztecan and Algonquian, framed by Austro-Aboriginal dream time and chased by stiff shots of Heidegger and Deleuze. As in Whorf's long-discredited account of Hopi, Taelon has "no tense, except the present tense. There is thus no way to express an action that takes place in a yesterday or a tomorrow. Time, for the aliens, is defined not through a 'sequence' of causalities, but through 'rhizomes' of coincidence."[4] "The Taelons have no cognate for the word 'reality,' except a gerund that roughly translates as 'thinking' or 'dreaming.' The language does not describe a universe that exists beyond the character of language itself: there are no things that endure (no 'states'); there are only traits in action (only 'events')—no existing, only becoming. The aliens have no concept of representation. For them, things do not 'imitate' each other; instead, they 'connect' with each other."[5] After the manner of classic science fiction, this is the American Indian—or at any rate a deeply confused version of New World language—projected as an alien in outer space with a vengeance. No doubt John Carter's red Barsoomians express themselves in just such an argot. As in standard Arapaho, "predicates are not composed of nouns and verbs; instead, every sentence is reducible to a word that synthesizes noun and verb into a kind of 'adjectival infinitive.'" "Such a 'nounverb' is a trait in action, referring simultaneously to a quality and its conduct." Described as "aliens who embody an inhuman science of enlightened tranquility," the Taelons are whispering Heideggerians, who "do not even believe that they use their language; instead, they say that the language uses them. It is, for them, an entity with a life of its own. It is not a tool used to express ideas; instead, they see it as an ideal virus that uses their own minds as a means for replicating itself through the act [of] communication."[6] Even William Burroughs's idea that language is a virus from outer space gets a shout-out here. Warped by their corny grammar into inflated caricatures of exotic others, like Buddhist monks and Yaqui shamans, the Taelons sport the enormous bald heads and exaggerated cranial features long associated with extraterrestrial intelligence and Asian sages. They are often shown flashing mudras, sure sign that we are among the enlightened. One wonders how many words for snow they have.

In other words, Bök's sci-fi language is hardly what he describes as "a truly alien argot with no earthly cognate": Taelon is cognate with an all too Earthly idea of language grounded in theories of linguistic determinism current during the first half of the twentieth century. All of the force of Benjamin's dialectical image comes rushing toward us in the picture of a prison house of language projected from the past to explode into the present from a fantastical sci-fi future. Its sartorial equivalent is the kitschy glitter on the purple nehru jackets sported by the bobble-headed aliens.

Given the unmotivated and arbitrarily symbolic nature of human languages, perhaps nonhuman alien languages should necessarily be conceived as motivated and iconic: after all, nothing could be further from terrestrial language, and the Taelons' grammar and their worldview would then indeed be ineluctably locked in some sort of fatal symbiosis. But to construe what the producers of *Earth: The Final Conflict* characterize as a race of "electroplasmic superorganisms" as Buddhist Pueblo Indians—and to do so based on a romanticized notion of human language that decades ago fell into disrepute—is surely to return these extraterrestrials to the very planet that it was so important to distinguish them from in the first place. For a linguist, Taelon is a kind of excellent joke. And that is part of what makes it okay for science fiction, which, to reiterate the words of Csicsery-Ronay, "continues to construct 'sentimental' myths that simultaneously satisfy readers' needs for complete world-pictures, and call ironic attention to their ludic and constructed character."

For earthlings, the issue for sci-fi language ultimately has to come down to the question of *translation*: How can I say what I understand that alien to be saying? Perception, attention, intention, purpose, attraction, fear, pleasure, disgust, motivation, intuition, knowledge, humor, and every other shade and mode of intellection and feeling are ostensibly involved, even though any or all of these might turn out to be inapplicable to nonhuman life. What in the world would an alien make of our world? And how to *repeat* that? The estrangement once again redoubles: here Benjamin's sci-fi dialectical image is not so much a temporal index, flashing between the poles of the past (the writing), the future (the fiction), and the present (the reading), but a linguistic one: If translation is a kind of mirroring, then what happens when my words strain to reflect what is irredeemably estranged? The pressures on language in such a case are considerable. In *Alien Tatters*, Clark Coolidge's awesomely bizarre collection of poetry based on the language of alien abduction narratives, he puts the dilemma like this:

> Speaking in terms not understood but grasped. They do not have this as a language. But we grasp the stuff that they do. There is nothing else this close to the perimeter.[7]

It is the issue of the proximity to the perimeter that we are interested in grasping here: How close to alien speech can we get? Since *Alien Tatters* is, so far as I know, the longest, most ambitious, and most fully realized attempt to get extraterrestrial language—where terms are not understood but grasped—into poetic writing, I will end this book with it. What do aliens say, and what can be said about them?

THE RUNIC SHELVES OF PARTICLE PLENTY: CLARK COOLIDGE REDUX

> The Singularity presents itself, in deadpan apocalyptic tones, as science-fictionality purified of fiction.
>
> —Istvan Csicsery-Ronay Jr., *Seven Beauties of Science Fiction*

Coolidge uses science fiction lingo explicitly in order to further his ongoing project of writing innovative poetry: sci-fi is the scaffolding, and first contact and abduction narratives are the means for an avant-garde compositional practice firmly grounded on *ostranenie.* Coolidge frames *Alien Tatters* as generic science fiction while using all the registers of estrangement that such extraterrestrial encounters imply as the main tropes of his poems. Describing his "huge desire to participate" in the "vast chatter" of alien abduction accounts, Coolidge outlines his purposes in his afterword to the book: "If I couldn't go, then perhaps at least I might learn to speak the language, and use it to take myself further in, or out, to what? The brain bred up a notch to apprehend things it can't yet identify? Or is this just the human again but seen through an alternate rift, given a different spin? At any rate that relentless need for the Other."[8] Coolidge poses the grounding question of sci-fi as a dichotomy: Is it fundamentally about us, or is it about them? Is science fiction a cosmic stage for "just" representing ourselves, where we yet again witness the human condition mirrored in "an alternate rift"? Or is it a means for apprehending what we cannot yet identify, for writing those things that one does not know, or knows badly, for imagining radically nonhuman "things"? Coolidge puts it succinctly in the afterword: "Anything that helps shed limitations suits me. You guys listening?"[9] Science fiction as cognitively estranging activity makes it a potent genre for poetry: *Alien Tatters* is science fiction *on.*

Coolidge's book is divided into five sections, each marked by subtly different moods, modes of address, formal features, and ostensible speakers; and an afterword, which is where we learn of the poems' genesis in accounts of alien abduction, particularly in books and audio tapes written and recorded by the UFO-ologist Budd Hopkins, as Coolidge explained in an interview with Tom Orange.[10] When asked about the book's sources, Coolidge replied that he "debated for a while putting a list of sources at the end but I finally decided that was tying it down too much," at the same time pointing out that his "work often comes from a lot of different sources, not always just alien scenarios or whatever." Indeed, much of the writing in *Alien Tatters* is not recognizably derived from abduction narratives; plenty of other kinds of language appear, but then the point is to avoid tying it down too much: *Alien Tatters* is not "about" alien abduction; it is a text written *through* it.[11] Coolidge claims that he wants to learn to speak the language, and presumably one would use such a language to say many—any!—sorts of things. After all, as he tells us, he himself has never suffered abduction by aliens: instead, *his language has been abducted by the language of alien abduction*, which literally invests his poetry, forcing it into registers ever more weird, infecting it to the core: a virus from outer space. Abduction and first contact entail disorientation, uncertainty, surprise, fear, confusion, helplessness, paranoia, and feeling unsure or threatened. The question is, what might such a viral language lead one to say? Surely not "take me to your leader," which is no doubt what the Venusian woman in the skisuit in the backyard would utter.

In the book's fourth section, "Puzzle Faces," we find a hilarious list of classic sci-fi alien clichés, enumerated by an exasperated and apparently female voice:

> But why do they have big heads and little necks? Why do they have big dark eyes at an angle? Why do they have shrunken grey bodies that remind us of camp victims? Why ski suits? Why cosmic genetics? Why do we have to deal with outlines? What's washing in the bottoms of their sinks? I doubt I could blow a nose beyond this and stay tawdry. The grey ones take a pick from my eyeliner but theirs is not in this salad. Let's go hopping, they say. Let's part and then snap back together, they command. I know of no one with so large a ledger. I hear of no slam hand. With gimbals they go traveling slinging us past. Worlds, what worlds? Can you say, Rasher Meats?[12]

I am not sure what Mr. Meats might answer, but the speaker's questions are not idle: Why do aliens so often resemble the iconic green humanoids from Roswell, New Mexico? Coolidge pokes fun at a century of the kitschy, low-budget mysticism with which films like *Earth: The Final Conflict* endow their aliens: the go-to extraterrestrial for Hollywood has always been the green man in a ski suit: ray gun, angled eyes, pointy ears, big head, nehru collar, exotic wisdom. But if aliens use salad eyeliner, like to "go hopping[,] . . . part and then snap back together," and carry around outsized ledgers in their slam hands, then we need to rethink what it is that we are looking at. What are they pivoting inside their "gimbals" as they go "slinging us past"? Shedding limitations in order to take oneself further out and breed the brain up a notch calls for a different order of proceeding.

The writing in each of the five sections of *Alien Tatters* sets out with a vengeance to shed—although it might be more like *shred*—limitations. Marked by relentless non sequitur, nothing like a conventional plot appears—as Coolidge puts it, "I keep making these entries so you'll know there's no story"[13]—albeit occasional suggestions of narrative do surface. This overall disjointedness is complicated by the bizarre and jarring open class category substitutions that characterize many of Coolidge's sentences: "A moon feathering, then it all blossoms like velocities. I'll keep writing. I mean I'll just keep skipping. There are lakes of an age your bones would collapse. None of these nouns means anymore what you've been taught to think. It snaps and goes another way."[14] But while he plays with the semantics of his statements, Coolidge rarely messes with syntax in this book: the poetry's strangeness appears at the level of vocabulary, while the bulk of its sentences follow standard English order. After all, the writing in *Alien Tatters* is either based on the language in accounts of abduction delivered by American English speakers, or it is translation of alien language itself. To record this latter directly in the forms of its native grammar would be as pointless as maintaining Hopi word formation and sentence order when translating a story from Second Mesa into English. This of course was the classic Whorfian method for rendering the other exotic and strange, if not profound—gosh, their grammar makes them see the world differently!—and anyway has no relevance whatsoever for translation, which in this case is an attempt to grasp if not to understand alien speech as rendered in English.

The hallmark of this text is disorienting parataxis toggled by ambiguity and ambivalence; it is frequently difficult to visualize what exactly is being described (how does a moon feather? and then blossom like velocities?) or to follow the logic from one sentence to the next, and this indeterminacy extends to the voices in the texts: who or what is speaking; where; why, and what's the reason for? A consistently first-person singular "I" narrates much of the poetry, but whether or not this narrator is reliable or even reliably the same throughout any section is debatable; in the afterword, Coolidge speaks of "all those trapped yet oddly illuminated voices, each clinging to its own elaboration of the tale."[15] He does however drop hints and indices throughout the writing, and as each section maintains something of a coherent tone and mode of address, I will take a stab at reading distinct narratological subject positions, if not actual "characters," in the first two of the book's five long poems.

ALIEN TATTINGS

and while we're at it –
what's up with telekinesis
clairvoyance precognition
out-of-body experiences haunted houses
and those extraterrestrials next door
grilling weenies on the barbi

—Charles Borkhuis, "Dark Matter," in *Savoir-Fear*

"Alien Tatters," the eponymous first poem of *Alien Tatters*, is also its longest. Accounting for roughly half of the book, it includes fifty numbered sections, the first forty-nine of which are made up of short passages, each of which is comprised of anywhere from one to ten periodic sentences, many grammatically complete, although they are frequently punctuated by isolated noun and verb phrases. Taken together, they make for an insouciant, conversational tempo, a pricking forward and a backing up, oblique qualification built into the sonics of the prose. The writing throughout maintains an informal, personal, meditative, even intimate tone, as if someone or something were addressing us directly:

> Oh. The message came from beyond the sound of the tone. Impact loosening. The candle fuse tempts. I wore the dress down to the sound of nothing. Something simple was entering the room. The room, if it was. If it was not needed.
>
> 5
>
> Liquid blemish in the form of a human or it might be possible to extend beyond the flame. Rant here of tiny beings. Or the bronze history of the lima bean.
>
> Hear Miss Vocal? She has not yet received the point.[16]

As stated earlier, non sequitur is this text's MO: "Runic Shelves of Particle Plenty" for sure.[17] Coolidge writes later in this section that "The words are loose. . . . Under the ledge came out a babble. Relegated tongues to here."[18] And all of it "tatters," as if the writing were the runes and particles of a language arranged in shelves or ledges, interwoven and overlapped, after the manner of *tatting*, of knotting and looping lace. A trope appears in the weave and woof of the poetry—"Sonnets of hay strands being woven."[19]

The message came from beyond the tone. Perhaps what one would initially "grasp" of alien speech is precisely *tone*: humans register inflection and sonic nuance before they understand *message*, which forever lies somewhere "beyond the sound of tone." Maybe that is as far as translating takes us, to a point near the perimeter of what we hear, at the very edge of comprehension. Is tone universal? Is voice? What if "they don't even have throats, as we would understand it at least"?[20] Is it Miss Vocal or mis-vocal? One way or the other, she has not yet received the point, although the impact is loosening. Are you guys listening? "But they are hidden behind everything that you see. Tonally everything."[21] And so we loop back along the ledges and shelves of the writing, sifting for meaning and tone, on the lookout for aliens. What anyway is the difference between grasping and understanding? Dressed down to the sound of nothing, what are we mis-hearing? Liquid blemish in the form of a human . . . rant here of tiny beings.

In fact, we meet these tiny beings in the very first section of the poem, which firmly frames the text as science fiction and introduces us to the first of its "voices":

> Have you come to see us today? There have been no arrangements made, no type of thing you expect at all. We are tiny and beyond your comprehension. We landed and passed through the woods quite close to you but you barely noticed us. Our cover story was large and brown.[22]

Much if not all of "Alien Tatters" is delivered in the voice of an extraterrestrial, looking at the Earth through the fresh new eyes of first contact: "Liquids have long leashes in this furry universe. Birds beckon."[23] "The being was looking right in at me, a chipmunk loose enough from the bark for independent motion."[24] "Thoughts out of water, gas, air. Stones out of the hillside, caverns, drift hills. Unstable penetration of haunts, lobed extensions of the natural orb."[25] Where do these otherworldly creatures hail from? "This will be a blow to all positional suspicion. I come from the abandoned universe."[26] They might well be Martians: one of them swears "As Mars is my witness," and later in the book we are told "This may involve a Marsmap."[27] Their spacecraft? "A tight little ship. It's got a nozzle, there are trembles in here, a heart of light and a fumbling's oxygen. Perhaps we are bare in here."[28] What do they look like? It's hard to say since the extraterrestrials are doing the talking and they do not describe themselves. We have to piece their appearance together from what they say they do: "I came out again. I emerged blowing. I rigged the inflate genesis particular. Words here without any leveling lights."[29] Indeed. "They've been watching me glow."[30] "I thought I could crawl to the car but I couldn't flange my hands."[31] "Double faces and available antennae."[32]

> Pulling my head apart up where it's got dark.
>
> I've got a head that can't do anything about it but move from left to right. Shut that flash down. But I'm trying, I'm staring. Stand the muscles about it.
>
> Though it's only my one eye that's trying. They were aiming to draw all the blue light out of me. They were arming.[33]

By all accounts, then, the aliens are tiny, single-eyed, blowing, glowing creatures, with double faces, antennae, stiff necks, and metallic hands that they can flange to crawl and to pull their heads apart. They emit a blue light, which somebody aims to draw out of them. They seem to feel threatened; one reports, "They felt friendly but they proved no friends of ours." Another voice qualifies this: "You won't be harmed. You will probably be harmed."[34]

Is that us speaking, paranoid and blustering as usual? What are earthlings to these cosmonauts? "Spatial creatures, indelibles."[35] "Noiseless potatoes" (Alien Taters?).[36]

> I think I saw a guy's literal things, yes. Porridgelike with protrusions. The Belly called them eyes.[37]
>
> Being comes in. Thing on his back. Being in back of me. Being facing me. He's telling me to in sparkles. The same being coming over me. It's just the same matter of my word in the woods.[38]
>
> There's something around over there. But this is deep religious nonsense. Where are your hands?
>
> Blood around the woman? Holding off until the holocaust. A roofing vent for old cities. Nothing now on but further variation.[39]

The upshot: "These apes have knowledge that we must send back."[40]

Let me be clear: I am pulling these relatively straightforward passages from masses of much more obscure and opaque writing:

> Tahitic benders and their accompanying claps. Heights my sister in trust had never gained. Odds and ends for insane followers of the jewel center placement plan. Hovering has now been lifted as one of the ones.[41]

But then to bring it back to the point: these poems are not intended to be stories or narrative. They are instantiations of language that has been figuratively kidnapped by alien speech and the rhetoric of abduction. As such, they embody in their very armatures the disorientation (*Tahitic benders*), uncertainty (*accompanying claps*), surprise and fear (*insane followers*), confusion (*jewel center*), helplessness and paranoia (*placement plan*), insecurity (*hovering*), and threat (*one of the ones*) that typically accompany alien abduction and first contact. This is not the language of science fiction; it is *science fiction language*.

AREA 50

"Stop. Limits are how you look at them. No, limits are miles to go in the night."[42]

This stanza ends the first half of section 50, which marks a significant shift both in formal features and in tone. It is the only part of the whole of *Alien Tatters* where anything like conversation appears. The form is strictly dialogic, after the manner of a debriefing or an interrogation:

> What door did you find yourself coming from? None. Roof wall floor, whatever burst the interior.
>
> Did you ever come back from seeing those things? I was left with half a loaf.

> Did like a tuxedo it ease you in? I was taken badgeless and floored, dish dash whatever at incarceration speed. My ears were wadded, toes apace. It was like I was gulled, threatened with dentition by one of the same.[43]

The exchange is relentlessly surreal, approaching at times the garbled grammatical complexities of *Magnetic Fields*: "You saw them then? I mumbled but then they took me in. There were *forests* of them. A line of fire then a line of dark lake avenue fresh calm totally frosting killer singer this broken to fester the quelling automan. Get me?"[44] The difficulty of explaining an alien world leads the answerer to excruciating lengths of description; note the exasperated tone of voice: "And what about the motors, were they under somehow? How can I be expected to sing *and* see? Of course there were undefended leaden risers sponging expanding, laughs all about them they were so extended tongue-socket basic."[45] The weird technical jargon in these passages is impenetrable: we are reading what poses as the translation of a description of terrestrial machinery through the language of alien science. And as to life forms: "Carbon as basis? Numbering systems all that way, but no truth in the snap. Where vocabulary is baggage, there is no tempo."[46] The baggage of vocabulary, always the principle question in translation, makes for the heavy freight of these stanzas, the limits that are simultaneously miles to go. Coolidge uses the language to take us further out in his relentless search for the other: "If your questions were paddles then my answers would be the stream."[47]

"Alien Tatters" concludes with five long, dense paragraphs, relentlessly monologic, intensely surreal, delivered in an abrupt, declarative, even aggressive tone: "They say the heart of the weathers will be my own. Their held walls, infinite preambles to any sentence within. Just let me watch how many items they can blend out of sal ammoniac. They have something that's flat as a stinger. A sort of hoser with stained eye linings, waiter!"[48] Minus the loft that the spacing between stanzas provides in the foregoing parts of the poem, the impressions pile up breathlessly, as if the writer were traumatically accounting what they had just been through. Themes and objects from earlier sections reappear—there is that eyeliner again—but the poem ends with an aggrieved sense of rejection:

> But why won't you let me come in? I have figured the frequencies. They were even bold. I have lit whatever lights required. Logical to be local from here on out. Why have you not sounded me? Where is the treat? Skunked. Ridiculous and circular hold on not much, in fact nothing. A failure of the richest connection. Or is it just that somehow you have left me here? Dots in midst of violence, a triple Dutch treat for a killer sequenced and hidden. Not much more would be coming in. This is not the last land to be pleased in.[49]

Contact has not meant connection: while it might be logical to be local, the alien has not been *sounded*. Neither the language nor the speaker can maintain any solid grasp on what they have come to understand. The sense of disarticulation is complete; the alienated self itself double-shifts in space and time, as we learn from the last lines of the poem: "Give me other waters. Silence all but the glitch that fastens. I realize that something vital doesn't work here but, raise the volume in other rooms? I'm all senses past it. I'm charging you with nothing. Charge me with something anyway. I have to know who I was right now."[50]

DICTATION FROM THE NIGHT HOLE

> But what scared me the most was when my father would put on the gas mask. His face would disappear. This was not my father any longer. This was not a human being at all.
>
> —Philip K. Dick, *The Minority Report*

Tone, mode of address, voice, stanza length, and speaker all shift markedly in "Club in Case," the second poem in *Alien Tatters*. What is most remarkable in this section is the relentless consistency of first-person address and the many questions the narrator poses to himself. The voice is indelibly human—chatty, earnest, affable, even urbane—"Summer here on the winds, a red party hat"; "Mel dealt with Scotland and we came home to put our whole cabin on the phone"—but also agitated and searching, and concerned explicitly with *writing*:

> Sidling in and out of habits as we do, what truly comes to the writer? Here is the zoo, the aeroplanes, the elevated master then replaced and brought down. Sigh. A triplicate listing of sighs. How to get beyond the extended rod? How could the face in moving replace itself with brick?
>
> We don't have the sentiment to deal with such a wash of emotion. Were they interested? Are they interesting? Are we any different? Were they bringing the inhabiting sign? Surreptitious eye blows and elbow throttles, so what? Summer is becoming a machine for the offloading. And all the sillier implications of size.[51]

If "Alien Tatters" features the voice of the alien, "Club in Case" is delivered in the voice of the writer, ostensibly the science fiction writer, dealing with the difficulties peculiar to the genre, namely "how to get beyond the extended rod" of "cool vile expanses with the novel brothers"[52]: "Novel failure, we can't follow the patch of character anymore. The delivery does not match it."[53] We do not have the patience to deal with novels and their cathartic washes of emotion anymore—who cares about zoos or aeroplanes or tragic hubris, the eye blows and elbow throttles of sentimental literature? Especially in a writing in which "none of these nouns means anymore what you've been taught to think." Aliens are *weird*. After all, "If one came hopping up to you, how would you describe its throne? // The theater that it is? Here on earth by itself all wreathed in valuable twangers. No doubt, nothing but. Nothing left in my hand. A face, then the unspellable traces."[54] What is it that *comes* to the sci-fi writer? "There is no dearth of images. But what do they want?"[55] The questions involve how to proceed—"But why did I turn here, why didn't I just stop back there? Why am I writing so frantically from little or no source?"[56] "There is nothing to write but what remains."[57] "But why am I writing only the things I can't grasp?"[58]—and then they become existential: "But why do I recognize the man on the back of this book?"[59] "Now I keep turning the book around and there's something weird-familiar about it I don't know."[60] "I know it looks like I'm not sure of anything. I'm not but I'm in it for the life."[61] In other words, "this is not the usual form of the writing."[62] Science fiction is about encounters with the unknown, even the unknowable. How to fit language to the occasion? Who ultimately is that abducted person, the sci-fi writer?

It very possibly is Philip K. Dick. The quotation about his father's gas mask at the beginning of this section serves as the epigraph to *Alien Tatters*,[63] and at one point in "Club in Case," the speaker speculates that "It was *not* my father at the head of the stairs in the gas mask?"—suggesting that the entirety of this second poem might be read in Dick's voice.[64] If that is the case, then Dick might stand as the iconic type of the alien abductee writer club: his long struggle with schizophrenic paranoia would make of him the perfect figure for an author given over to theories of alien abduction and to hearing voices and seeing things in the shadows: "I saw the being but I didn't listen carefully enough to it. Whose wings? Whose tiny lights? Or were they huge? And then something something pharmacy I forget."[65] Home itself becomes unheimlich, uncanny:

> There is nothing but grey blends left under the razors. Grasped everything at last and stumbled up the remaining stairs. Go home. I can't. Can't seem to get there. Quite. There are loads in the way. The house of bright yellow has hindrance gadgets in its open attic, open at both ends. It will come out at me as I go by minding myself. Cut-glass ornaments in a rubble field, corner house caved into its own basement. I go by there too anxious. It'll come out at me just as I almost reach the home gate and I'll be back at the start with the whole route to be done over. And then it'll get me.[66]

In "Club in Case" the science fiction writer is a literary paranoiac, a Spicerian antenna receiving signals from the night sky, the inky hole of outer space: "I receive messages from nodules in the sun in spin in a larger darkness. There are forms of things. There were these forms tooling past."[67] But how to spell the unspellable traces of alien contact? What do the images *want*? It gets creepy: "Did you feel them twitching? They felt you. And at the drop of a hat."[68] At the end of its line, sci-fi poetics loses the plot in deadpan apocalyptic tones: the only fiction left is call and response, "what's dictated from the night hole."[69] As Charles Borkhuis puts it:

> but what's happening within
> the phantasmic figure-matrix
> that short circuits the coded gaps
> where language is an emergent
> phase transition and you can't tell
> the invisible from the visible
> or the answers from the questions[70]

Coda

Virus Alien Hoax Lasagne 2020

:.:.:.:.: alien parasites
:.:.:.:.: alien slave ship survivors,
:.:.:.:.: alien teenagers in 1950s Florida, sex
:.:.:.:.: terror and destruction, terror
:.:.:.:.: designed to part dumbass teenagers
:.:.:.:.: some now very wet
:.:.:.:.: romantic, the republican
:.:.:.:.: told me of their terror
:.:.:.:.: outfit for ?I?ma slave
:.:.:.:.: a fundraiser for republican
:.:.:.:.: and wet buns contest
:.:.:.:.: parents talking about sex
:.:.:.:.: of here 7.battle him republican 8
:.:.:.:.: 8.we are 138 9.teenagers

—K. Silem Mohammad, "Mars Needs Terrorists," in *Deer Head Nation*

The virus is a language from outer space. Infecting our very speech, COVID-19 has changed the way we communicate, what we say when we talk with one another, how and even how much we do so. A world of chronic pandemic, hazmat suits, ventilators, masks, mobile morgues, enforced isolation, paranoia: were the aliens to show up as I am writing this (Fall, 2020), they would find a planet shut down, millions ill or dead, countries upended, travel ground to a halt, social life at a standstill: multiple states of emergency; zombie plague rage; the Earth itself sick, throwing up climate catastrophes and epic storms in an increasingly savaged and pillaged natural environment; dying oceans, extreme drought, endemic flooding, raging wildfires, burning rainforests, pollution run amok; and humanity plugged into a dense Blob web of electronic communication—snagged by a network spider, itself sick with viruses, our collective nervous systems tangled and dangled into hyperspace—or relegated to the most degraded forms of material existence, battening on garbage, industrial smear, excrements of plastic and sludge. Reality either virtual or way screwed up; robots and troglodytes. We are *living science fiction.*

[flarf
—for Drew Gardner

the virus was living on a comet
which should make us rethink our desire to meet alien lifeforms
like the Space Lasagne aliens from the planet Parma
the best alien hoax in history
the Democrats' new hoax brought here by aliens, just like explorers
  years ago
first wave of the Andromeda Strain
giant lasagnes
our Alien Invasion Moment
all over the Internet aliens will be invading the earth within the
  next 18 months
world leaders created the pandemic in an effort to distract the
  world population

after discovering a doomsday asteroid was approaching Earth
the lockdown caused the highest number of sightings
since Belgium's great 'UFO wave' of 1989
speculated it could be an alien spaceship
that looked exactly like ordinary lasagne
people feel like they have no control over their lives
in the midst of a global pandemic
the comforting certainty of conspiracy
epiphanies where they start to see the big picture
no one's saying that the lasagne caused the virus
he stopped short of confessing he was a shapeshifting reptilian alien
a virus engineered to control population
bitten by an alien bug and infected with a virus
[batman]; [ninja]; [pirate]; [alien]; women with unlocked houses
they look alien, but not in a cardboard or forehead ridge sort of way
the original Alien is a hot piece of lasagne
the Alien bursts out of the guy's stomach
it was her eggs that caused it, but honestly I think I've caught a virus
a virus in my gut recently wrote a pamphlet called "Colon Sense"
like my sister, you must approach the aliens flying rainbow lasagne

techno-Satanic "space race" attack
metal rod on a rooftop in a storm, yelling FU, GOD!
Portable Lasagne
what would aliens say
Alien Gun · Arena · Arena Maps · Assault Rifles · J. Jane · Julian Lasagne · V · Version History · Virus
"nuclear pasta" found in neutron stars is 10 billion times stronger than steel
we had only the lasagne for dinner
it may not help to defeat the virus
it sure helps Aliens and secret services, communist and, of course, Jews are involved . . . Pasta al forno | baked pasta loops
Italians become even more dangerous than Alien
for all those who cant understand italian, he is saying "Pasta pasta cheese
been invaded by an alien virus, an information virus
Gnocchi, Lasagne, Vegetarian Cuisine, Pasta, space drawing, png alien
Corona Virus Disease Circle Drinkware Tableware for N95 Mask
all the richness of lasagne in a single-serving size!
Birthday quiz : Alien attack!
watch out for alien monsters jumping out of today's cake!
pasta · bang · sede · cavi · pam · sembrerebbe . . . aspettati · alien
alien hello random. :alien_hello: · alienprobe random . . . lasagne
random: lasagne: · lasagne random. :lasagne: · laser random :laser:
virus biohazard random
my lasagne coming out of the microwave evolved and developed immunity to viruses
tried to heat up my spaghetti sauce in microwave, created alien life instead
lasagne in crowds even when they have been told they are spreading
the virus they don't care because they think the virus is a hoax
—Google Search Engine, "Virus Alien Hoax Lasagne," November 9, 2020

Notes

Introduction

1. Seo-Young Chu, *Do Metaphors Dream of Literal Sleep?: A Science-Fictional Theory of Representation* (Cambridge, MA: Harvard University Press, 2011), 3.

2. William Carlos Williams, "Introduction to *The Wedge*," in *Selected Essays of William Carlos Williams* (New York: New Directions, 1969), 256.

3. Lewis Padgett, "Mimsy Were the Borogoves," in *The Science Fiction Hall of Fame*, vol. 1: *1929–1964*, ed. Robert Silverberg (New York: Orb Books, 1970), 186–87; first published in *Astounding Science Fiction Magazine* in February 1943. Lewis Padgett was the joint pseudonym of the science fiction authors and spouses Henry Kuttner and C. L. Moore.

4. Alex Preminger and T. V. F. Brogan, eds., *The New Princeton Encyclopedia of Poetry and Poetics* (Princeton, NJ: Princeton University Press, 1993), 1120.

5. Fredric Jameson, *Archaeologies of the Future: The Desire Called Utopia and Other Science Fictions* (London: Verso 2007), 18.

6. "The difficulty with identifying science fiction and proceeding from that to definition is that science fiction isn't just one thing. It has no recognizable action, like the murder mystery, or recognizable milieu, like the Western, or recognizable relationship, like the romance. It is about the future except when it is about the past or the present. It can incorporate all the other genres: one can have a science-fiction detective story, a science-fiction Western, a science-fiction romance, and, most commonly, a science-fiction adventure story. It is best characterized, as I point out in 'The World View of Science Fiction,' by an attitude, and even that is hard to define. It is the literature of change, the literature of anticipation, the literature of the human species, the literature of speculation, and more. And because it is the literature of change it is continually changing; if it remained constant, it would no longer be science fiction." James Gunn in *Speculations on Speculation: Theories of Science Fiction*, ed. James Gunn and Matthew Candelaria (Lanham, MD: Scarecrow Press, 2005), x–xi.

7. "Not all science fiction is futuristic, of course—a mistake made by many people who are familiar with the genre. Nevertheless, futuristic scenarios can be said to be the prototypical version of science fiction." Peter Stockwell, *The Poetics of Science Fiction* (Essex, UK: Pearson Education, 2000), 17.

8. "Memory becomes sedentary and sooner or later finds a physical shape (art), and this memory emerges from future time. The 'time traveler' as he advances deep into the future discovers a decrease in movement, the mind enters a state of 'slow motion' and perceives the gravel and dust of memory on the empty fringes of consciousness. Like H. G. Wells, he sees the 'ice along the sea margin'—a double perspective of past and future that follows a

projection that vanishes into a nonexistent present." Robert Smithson, *The Collected Writings*, ed. Jack Flam (Berkeley: University of California Press, 1996), 332.

9. "Nothing bores the ordinary man more than the cosmos." Walter Benjamin, *The Arcades Project*, trans. Howard Eiland and Kevin McLaughlin (Cambridge, MA: Belknap Press of Harvard University Press, 1999), 102.

10. Istvan Csicsery-Ronay Jr., *The Seven Beauties of Science Fiction* (Middletown, CT: Wesleyan University Press, 2008), 74, 118.

11. "Science fiction frequently tries to imagine what life would be like on a plane as far above us as we are above savagery; its setting is often of a kind that appears to us as technologically miraculous. It is thus a mode of romance with a strong inherent tendency to myth." Northrop Frye, *Anatomy of Criticism* (Princeton, NJ: Princeton University Press, 1957), 49.

12. "[The] oscillation of language between the technoscientific and science-fictional also explains much about the insecurity of cultural-theoretical language. . . . From this perspective sci-fi (and even the more imaginative forms of popular scientific journalism) are at any moment on the verge of tipping over into pataphysics. Contemporary critical-theoretical discourse, in contrast with Enlightenment and Romantic critical philosophy, has had only tangential connections with scientific practice (of major critical cultural theorists, only those directly involved in critical science studies seem to have been trained as scientists), but has striven to assimilate technoscience's status as the explanatory system of final appeal, by enclosing it within its own zones of concern. . . . While the community of 'Theory' seems convinced of the general applicability of its methods, its best products, nonetheless, can read as literary hoax-games that infiltrate the reality discourse of technoscience, and provoke that discourse's own literary fictions into the open." Csicsery-Ronay, *Seven Beauties*, 142–44. For an earlier assessment of science fiction and critical theory, see Carl Freedman, "Science Fiction and Critical Theory," *Science Fiction Studies* 14, no. 2, "Critical Approaches to Science Fiction: Retrospects and Prospects" (July 1987): 180–200.

13. Smithson, *Collected Writings*, 16.

14. I use the terms *science fiction* and *sci-fi* interchangeably throughout this book, even though, according to Csicsery-Ronay, "most sophisticated theoretical approaches to sci-fi tend to disparage the formulaic commodities produced solely for mass entertainment as 'sci-fi,' to be distinguished from the semantically richer and aesthetically more complex 'sf.' Csicsery-Ronay, *Seven Beauties*, 313. In the present work, I generally focus on "low" forms of science fiction. In this, I am guided not only by Smithson and his B-grade movies but by Walter Benjamin, who writes of his *Trauerspiel* that "[the research will] be guided by the assumption that what seems diffuse and disparate will be found to be linked in the adequate concepts as elements of a synthesis. And so the production of lesser writers, whose works frequently contain the most eccentric features, will be valued no less than those of the great writer" Benjamin, *The Origin of German Tragic Drama*, trans. John Osborne (London: Verso, 1998), 57–58. The question is, what does the genre of science fiction of whatever "grade" contribute to modern and contemporary poetics?

15. "Suvin's principle of 'cognitive estrangement'—an aesthetic which, building on the Russian Formalist notion of 'making strange' as well as the Brechtian Verfremdungseffekt, characterizes Sci-fi in terms of an essentially epistemological function." Jameson, *Archaeologies*, xiv.

16. Viktor Shklovsky, *Theory of Prose*, trans. Benjamin Sher (Normal: Dalkey Archive Press, Illinois State University, 1998), 5–6.

17. "Suvin argued in his seminal *Metamorphoses of Science Fiction* (1979) that Sci-fi's defining quality is 'cognitive estrangement,' a process through which publics are made to see their own social worlds, which are concealed from view by habit and ideology, with fresh eyes. Through the introduction of fictional new discoveries, inventions, or social phenomena—which Suvin calls novums—science fictional tales construct quasi-realistic alternative worlds that present the real world from an oblique, 'estranged' perspective. Because, according to Suvin, Sci-fi requires that the changes in alternative worlds fit together in a historically plausible way, readers are given indirect images of the historical and material order of their own worlds." Csicsery-Ronay, *Seven Beauties*, 396.

18. On the question of when science fiction can be said to begin historically, I go with Samuel Delaney: "There's no reason to run Sci-fi too much back before 1926, when Hugo Gernsback coined the ugly and ponderous term, 'scientifiction,' which, in the letter columns written by the readers of his magazines, became over the next year or so 'science fiction' and finally 'Sci-fi.' Ten years before or 30 years before is all right, I suppose, if you need an Ur period. It depends on what aspect of it you're studying, of course. But 50 years is the absolute outside, and that's only to guess at the faintest rhetorical traces of the vaguest discursive practices. And in practical terms, most people who extend Sci-fi too much before 1910 are waffling." Samuel Delaney, "The Semiology of Silence," interview with Sinda Gregory and Larry McCaffery, in *Science Fiction Studies* 14, no. 42, part 2 (July 1987): 137–38.

19. Darko Suvin, *Metamorphoses of Science Fiction: On the Poetics and History of a Literary Genre* (New Haven, CT: Yale University Press, 1979), 205.

20. "Unfortunately, a majority of what is published as Sci-fi is still in that prenatal or, better, regression-to-womb stage: it is simply the Western or some kindred sub-literary species masquerading its structures—generally for venal and ideological reasons—under the externals of Sci-fi: rockets, ray-guns, monsters, or in the last dozen years their slightly more sophisticated equivalents." Suvin, *Metamorphoses*, 23. Notice that this is precisely the B-grade science fiction universe that Smithson claims inspired artists of the 1960s. For comparison, see Jameson, "The Space of Science Fiction," in *Archaeologies*, 316:

I am very anxious that the texts I am going to be dealing with not be simply assimilated to the paradigms of high culture or of the literary institution. . . . These stories, however, emerge from the world of the pulps and of commercial culture whose conventions remain intimately linked to their narrative intelligibility. They cannot be read as Literature: not merely because they include much that is trash and what Adorno would have called easy reading; but above all, because their strongest effects are distinct from those of high literature, are specific to the genre, and finally are enabled only by precisely those subliterary conventions of the genre which are unassimilable to high culture. One cannot, in other words, select out a few intense "literary" effects and canonize those, since their conditions of possibility are very precisely pulp conventions. Something analogous could be said for the often strange and fascinating effects of the non-auteur film, the whole commercial underclass of the B movie.

21. Suvin, *Metamorphoses*, 15.

22. Chu, *Do Metaphors Dream*, 11.

23. Chu, *Do Metaphors Dream*, 14–15.

24. "Science fiction is a fictional universe where poetry is so nearly omnipresent that it need not take the shape of poetry to make its absent omnipresence felt." Chu, *Do Metaphors Dream*, 83. Science fiction poetry is a poetics universe where science fiction is so

nearly omnipresent that it need not take the narrative shape of fiction to make its absent omnipresence felt.

25. Chu, *Do Metaphors Dream*, 12.

26. Chu, *Do Metaphors Dream*, 65.

27. Csicsery-Ronay paraphrases Chu in his review of her book: "Question: If lyric and Sci-fi have such an affinity, why aren't there more Sci-fi poems? Answer: Because Sci-fi's use of lyric figuration obviates the need for lyric." Csicsery-Ronay, "Fantastic Mimesis: A Diamond in the Rough," *Contemporary Literature* 53, no. 2 (Summer 2012): 404.

28. Although see Csicsery-Ronay's "Fantastic Mimesis" for a nuanced and more qualified assessment of the reasonableness of Chu's argument.

29. Jameson mentions "complaints about the absence of complex and psychologically 'interesting' characters [in science fiction] (a position which does not seem to have kept pace with the postcontemporary crisis of the 'centered subject')." Jameson, *Archaeologies*, xiv. That crisis plays out in spades when it comes to lyric poetry, which decades ago become a testing ground for just such "characters."

30. Suvin calls the "empirical world naturalistic" and writes of "the corresponding 'naturalistic' or 'realistic' literature." Suvin, *Metamorphoses*, 11: "Estrangement differentiates Sci-fi from the 'realistic' literary mainstream extending from the eighteenth century into the twentieth." Suvin, *Metamorphoses*, 8. And Chu: "If the work of realistic prose is difficult, then the work of Sci-fi prose is even more so." Chu, *Do Metaphors Dream*, 32–33.

31. "It is precisely because definitions of the self have changed that the traditional genres that speak for the self (lyric poetry, for example) or of the self and its development (the novel) are either being consigned to an increasingly old-fashioned, conservative, or nostalgic position or are being subverted and reinvented to accommodate contemporary experience of being a person—a *zone*." Lyn Hejinian, *The Language of Inquiry* (Berkeley: University of California Press, 2000), 235. Cf. Khlebnikov: "Is a poem not a flight from the I?" in *The King of Time: Poems, Fictions, Visions of the Future*, ed. Charlotte Douglas, trans. Paul Schmidt (Cambridge, MA: Harvard University Press, 1985), 153; and F. T. Marinetti: "We systematically destroy the literary *I*," in *Let's Murder the Moonshine: Selected Writings*, ed. R. W. Flint, trans. R. W. Flint and Arthur A. Coppotelli. (Los Angeles: Sun and Moon Press, 1971), 106.

32. As Csicsery-Ronay puts it, Chu "relies on an implicitly Romantic and ahistorical notion of poetic discourse. . . . The result is a series of apodictic Romantic claims about the power of the lyric." Csicsery-Ronay, "Fantastic Mimesis," 402. In *Seven Beauties*, he speaks of "lyric's totality of consciousness, in which a world is constructed from personal responses" (82).

33. Csicsery-Ronay, *Seven Beauties*, 12.

34. Jakobson describes a sci-fi poem by Khlebnikov as "the projection of a literary device into artistic reality, the turning of a poetic trope into a poetic fact." Roman Jakobson, *My Futurist Years*, ed. Bengt Jangfeldt and Stephen Rudy, trans. Stephen Rudy (New York: Marsilio Publishers, 1992), 182.

35. Coolidge studied geology in college and was an avid spelunker. Both he and Smithson were interested in crystallography and thermodynamics. Science certainly plays a role in their respective works.

36. According to Stephen Rudy, "There are few instances in the history of the arts of such an intense feed-back system as existed in the artistic and theoretical praxis of the Russian avant-garde in the period 1910–1920. . . . Jakobson's early critical works must be regarded not just as an attempt to create a methodology for the literary-critical movement

known as Russian Formalism, but to defend the 'new art,' in particular Russian Futurism in its most radical form." Jakobson, *My Futurist Years*, x.

37. Jakobson, *My Futurist Years*, 186.

38. "Poetry and visual art became for Jakobson the fundamental spheres for observing how verbal phenomena work and for studying how to approach them. Poetry as a system not belonging to ordinary communication informed Jakobson's linguistic theory, especially his view on the problem of meaning, in a way similar to that of language pathology, to which he turned in later years." Roman Jakobson, *Language in Literature*, ed. Krystyna Pomorska and Stephen Rudy (Cambridge, MA: Belknap Press of Harvard University Press, 1987), 4.

39. Jakobson, *My Futurist Years*, 251.

40. Jakobson, *My Futurist Years*, 104.

41. "This work has to develop to the highest degree the art of citing without quotation marks. Its theory is intimately related to that of montage." Benjamin, *Arcades Project*, 458.

42. "A world of secret affinities opens up within [the arcades]: palm tree and feather duster, hairdryer and Venus de Milo, prostheses and letter-writing manuals. The odalisque lies in wait next to the inkwell, the priestesses raise high the vessels into which we drop cigarette butts as incense offerings. These items on display are a rebus: how one ought to read here the birdseed in the fixative-pan, the flower seeds beside the binoculars, the broken screw atop the musical score, and the revolver above the goldfish bowl—is right on the tip of one's tongue. . . . And since, to the dreaming collective itself, the decline of an economic era seems like the end of the world, the writer Karl Kraus has looked quite correctly on the arcades, which, from another angle, must have appealed to him as the casting of a dream." Benjamin, *Arcades Project*, 540.

43. "[The arcades are] structures in which we relive, as in a dream, the life of our parents and grandparents, as the embryo in the womb relives the life of animals. Existence in these spaces flows then without accent, like the events in dreams. Flanerie is the rhythmics of this slumber." Benjamin, *Arcades Project*, 106.

44. "In his Vague de rêves [Wave of dreams], Louis Aragon describes how the mania for dreaming spread over Paris. . . . The Surrealists, with a similar conviction, are less on the trail of the psyche than on the track of things. They seek the totemic tree of objects within the thicket of primal history. The very last, the topmost face on the totem pole, is that of kitsch." Walter Benjamin, "Dream Kitsch," in *Selected Writings*, vol. 2, part 1: *1927–1930*, ed. Michael W. Jennings, Howard Eiland, and Gary Smith, trans. Rodney Livingstone and others (Cambridge, MA: Belknap Press of Harvard University Press, 2005), 4.

45. "In order to understand the arcades from the ground up, we sink into the deeper stratum of the dream; we speak of them as though they had struck us." Benjamin, *Arcades Project*, 206.

46. "Our investigation proposes to show how, as a consequence of th[e] reifying representations of civilization, the new forms of behavior and the new economically and technologically based creations that we owe to the nineteenth century enter the universe of a phantasmagoria. The creations undergo this 'illumination' not only in a theoretical manner, by an ideological transposition, but also in the immediacy of their perceptible presence. They are manifest as phantasmagorias. Thus appear the arcades." Benjamin, *Arcades Project*, 14.

47. Benjamin, *Arcades Project*, 10.

48. "On the dialectical image. In it lies time. Already with Hegel, time enters into dialectic. But the Hegelian dialectic knows time solely as the properly historical, if not psy-

chological, time of thinking. The time differential in which alone the dialectical image is real is still unknown to him. Attempt to show this with regard to fashion. Real time enters the dialectical image not in natural magnitude—let alone psychologically—but in its smallest gestalt." Benjamin, *Arcades Project*, 867.

49. "[The surrealists] exchange, to a man, the play of human features for the face of an alarm clock that in each minute rings for sixty seconds." Benjamin, *Selected Writings*, vol. 2, part 1, 218.

50. Benjamin, *Arcades Project*, 25.

51. Benjamin, *Arcades Project*, 11.

52. "It was Surrealism that first opened our eyes to [the ruins of the bourgeoisie]. The development of the forces of production shattered the wish symbols of the previous century, even before the monuments representing them had collapsed. . . . From this epoch derive the arcades and intérieurs, the exhibition halls and panoramas. They are residues of a dream world. The realization of dream elements, in the course of waking up, is the paradigm of dialectical thinking. Every epoch, in fact, not only dreams the one to follow but, in dreaming, precipitates its awakening." Benjamin, *Arcades Project*, 13.

53. "There is a picture by Klee called 'Angelus Novus.' Its shows an angel who seems about to move away from something he stares at. His eyes are wide, his mouth is open, his wings are spread. This is how the angel of history must look. His face is turned toward the past. Where a chain of events appears before us, he sees one single catastrophe, which keeps piling wreckage upon wreckage and hurls it at his feet. The angel would like to stay, awaken the dead, and make whole what has been smashed. But a storm is blowing from Paradise and has got caught in his wings; it is so strong that the angel can no longer close them. This storm drives him irresistibly into the future, to which his back is turned, while the pile of debris before him grows toward the sky. What we call progress is this storm." Walter Benjamin, *Selected Writings*, vol. 4: *1938–1940*, ed. Michael W. Jennings and Howard Eiland, trans. Edmund Jephcott and others (Cambridge, MA: Belknap Press of Harvard University Press, 2003), 392.

54. Walter Benjamin, *Selected Writings*, vol. 2, part 2: *1931–1934*, ed. Michael W. Jennings, Howard Eiland, and Gary Smith, trans. Rodney Livingstone and others (Cambridge, MA: Belknap Press of Harvard University Press, 1999), 731.

55. Benjamin, *Selected Writings*, vol. 2, part 2, 732.

56. Benjamin, *Selected Writings*, vol. 2, part 2, 733.

57. Benjamin, *Selected Writings*, vol. 2, part 2, 733.

58. Paul Scheerbart, *Lesabéndio, An Asteroid Novel*, trans. Christina Svendsen (Cambridge, MA: Wakefield Press, 2012), 7.

59. I am having a bit of fun here: the German word that Scherrbart uses is *Rohre*, which means pipe as in a pipe for running water; the German word for a smoking pipe is *Pfeife*.

60. Cited in Alexander Gelley, "*Lesabéndio. An Asteroid Novel* by Paul Scheerbart. Review," *Modern Language Notes* 129, no. 3, German iss. (April 2014): 716–17.

61. Benjamin, *Selected Writings*, vol. 4, 386.

62. Benjamin, *Selected Writings*, vol. 2, part 2, 733.

63. Benjamin, *Selected Writings*, vol. 4, 387.

64. "The fact that a poet is enlisting heavenly bodies to speak on behalf of creation . . . shows to what extent the author has succeeded in shedding the dross of sentimentality. This is confirmed by his style, which has the freshness of a nursling's cheek. At the same time, Scheerbart's prose is of such transparency that one understands why he was the

first to welcome the glass architecture which, after his death, would be banished from his country as subversive." Benjamin, *Selected Writings*, vol. 4, 387.

65. Benjamin, *Selected Writings*, vol. 4, 387.

66. Benjamin, *Selected Writings*, vol. 2, part 2, 735.

67. "There is a secret agreement between past generations and the present one. For we have been expected upon this earth. Then our coming was expected on earth. Then, like every generation that preceded us, we have been endowed with a weak messianic power, a power on which the past has a claim." Benjamin, *Selected Writings*, vol. 4, 390.

68. Scheerbart, *Lesabéndio*, 194.

69. Scheerbart, *Lesabéndio*, 192–93.

70. Scheerbart, *Lesabéndio*, 193.

71. Scheerbart, *Lesabéndio*, 198.

72. Scheerbart, *Lesabéndio*, 205. And cf: "[Rhizomes are] acentered systems, finite networks of automata in which communication runs from any neighbor to any other, the stems or channels do not preexist, and all individuals are interchangeable, defined only by their state at a given moment—such that the local operations are coordinated and the final, global result synchronized without a central agency." Gilles Deleuze and Félix Guattari, *A Thousand Plateaus: Capitalism and Schizophrenia*, trans. Brian Massumi (Minneapolis: University of Minnesota Press, 1987), 17.

73. Scheerbart, *Lesabéndio*, 221–22.

74. "The rhizome connects any point to any other point, and its traits are not necessarily linked to traits of the same nature; it brings into play very different regimes of signs, and even nonsign states. The rhizome is reducible neither to the One nor the multiple. . . . It is composed not of units but of dimensions, or rather directions in motion." Deleuze and Guattari, *Thousand Plateaus*, 21.

75. "Musical form, right down to its ruptures and proliferations, is comparable to a weed, a rhizome." Deleuze and Guattari, *Thousand Plateaus*, 11–12.

76. Deleuze and Guattari, *Thousand Plateaus*, 21–22.

77. Deleuze and Guattari, *Thousand Plateaus*, 25.

78. Paul Scheerbart. *Lesabéndio, Ein Asteroiden-Roman* (München: Georg Müller, 1913), 282.

79. Translation is mine.

80. Deleuze and Guattari, *Thousand Plateaus*, 6.

81. Julius Onah, dir., *The Cloverfield Paradox*, Santa Monica, CA: Bad Robot Productions, 2018.

82. Deleuze and Guattari, *Thousand Plateaus*, 15.

83. Csicsery-Ronay, *Seven Beauties*, 7. Smithson describes illustrations of cosmic catastrophe at the Planetarium and the Museum of Natural History: "Vast monuments of total annihilation are pictured over boundless abysses or seen from dizzying heights. This is a bad-boy's dream of obliteration, where galaxies are smashed like toys. Globes of 'antimatter' collide with 'proto-matter,' billions and billions of fragments speed into the deadly chasms of space. Destruction builds on destruction; forming sheets of burning ice, violet and green, it all falls off into infinite pools of dust. A landslide of diamonds plunges into a polar crevasse of boundless dimension. History no longer exists." Smithson, *Collected Writings*, 33.

84. Smithson, *Collected Writings*, 16.

85. Smithson, *Collected Writings*, 11.

86. Smithson, *Collected Writings*, 20. Smithson quotes from P. W. Bridgman's *The Nature of Thermodynamics*: "But I think nevertheless, we do not feel altogether comfortable at being forced to say that the crystal is the seat of greater disorder than the parent liquid."

87. Csicsery-Ronay, *Seven Beauties*, 5.

88. First quote, Smithson, *Collected Writings*, 14. Smithson continues: "The description has none of the 'values' of the naturalistic 'literary' novel, it is crystalline, and of the mind by virtue of being outside of unconscious action. This very well could be an inchoate concept for a work by Judd, LeWitt, [Dan] Flavin, or [Will] Insley." Second quote, Smithson, *Collected Writings*, 10: "On rising to my feet, and peering across the green glow of the Desert, I perceived that the monument against which I had slept was but one of thousands. Before me stretched long parallel avenues, clear to the far horizon of similar broad, low pillars." This is the headnote to Smithson's "Entropy and the New Monuments."

89. Smithson, *Collected Writings*, 13.

90. Smithson, *Collected Writings*, 81.

91. Smithson, *Collected Writings*, 21.

92. Smithson, *Collected Writings*, 21.

93. Smithson, *Collected Writings*, 21.

94. "To thinking belongs the movement as well as the arrest of thoughts. Here thinking comes to a standstill in a consolation saturated with tensions—there the dialectical image appears. It is the caesura in the movement of thought. Its position is naturally not an arbitrary one. It is to be found, in a word, where the tension between dialectical opposites is greatest. Hence, the object constructed in the materialist presentation of history is itself the dialectical image. The latter is identical with the historical object; it justifies its violent expulsion from the continuum of historical process." Benjamin, *Arcades Project*, 475.

95. Csicsery-Ronay, *Seven Beauties*, 10.

96. Csicsery-Ronay, *Seven Beauties*, 5.

97. Csicsery-Ronay, *Seven Beauties*, 6.

98. Jean de La Hire, *The Nyctalope on Mars*, trans. Brian Stableford (Encino, CA: Black Coat Press, 2008), 242.

99. de La Hire, *Nyctalope on Mars*, 256.

100. de La Hire, *Nyctalope on Mars*, 277.

Chapter 1

1. Velimir Khlebnikov, *The King of Time: Poems, Fictions, Visions of the Future*, trans. Paul Schmidt, ed. Charlotte Douglas (Cambridge, MA: Harvard University Press, 1985), 127.

2. Khlebnikov, *King of Time*, 127.

3. Khlebnikov, *King of Time*, 127–28.

4. In the introduction to *King of Time*, Charlotte Douglas and Paul Schmidt make the same claim of another Khlebnikov piece from 1915: "The fantasy 'K' is, in its own way, a compendium of the devices of science fiction written well before the development of that genre." Khlebnikov, *King of Time*, 61.

5. Khlebnikov, *King of Time*, 169.

6. Khlebnikov, *King of Time*, 128

7. Khlebnikov, *King of Time*, 155.

8. Khlebnikov, *King of Time*, 140–41.

9. Marjorie Perloff in the preface to F. T. Marinetti, *Let's Murder the Moonshine*, 7.

10. Perloff, preface to Marinetti, *Let's Murder the Moonshine*, 116. The ending refrain of

"The Foundation and Manifesto of Futurism" (1909) is "Erect on the summit of the world, once again we hurl defiance to the stars!" Marinetti, *Let's Murder the Moonshine*, 52. And from "The New Religion-Morality of Speed" (1916): "Then let us join the great celestial battles, vie with the star 1830 Groombidge that flies at 241 km. a second, with Arthur that flies at 413 km. a second. Invisible mathematical artillery. Wars in which the stars, being both missiles and artillery, match their speeds to escape from a greater star or to strike a smaller one." Marinetti, *Let's Murder the Moonshine*, 104.

11. Marinetti, *Let's Murder the Moonshine*, 99.

12. Marinetti, *Let's Murder the Moonshine*, 49–50.

13. Marinetti, *Let's Murder the Moonshine*, 75.

14. Marinetti, *Let's Murder the Moonshine*, 106.

15. Marinetti, *Let's Murder the Moonshine*, 92–97.

16. Marinetti, *Let's Murder the Moonshine*, 105–11.

17. Marinetti, *Let's Murder the Moonshine*, 100.

18. Marinetti, *Let's Murder the Moonshine*, 75.

19. "Consider for instance the poem 'Incantation by Laughter.' Khlebnikov takes the Russian word for laughter, smekh, and creates a chant of new words based on it, using the Russian rules of allowable word formation. American English is much poorer in such rules than Russian, and the word 'laugh' also suffers a hopelessly outdated spelling, which helps to weaken any sound patterns we might try to make. So our translation offers neologisms excavated from the history of the word 'laugh' in the O. E. D., in an attempt to respond to the richness and complexity of the Russian text—with frankly, something funny enough to laugh at. And this process is completely in accord with Khlebnikov's intentions." Schmidt and Douglas, introduction to Khlebnikov, *King of Time*, 8.

20. Suvin, *Metamorphoses of Science Fiction*, 5.

21. L. Frank Baum, *Ozma of Oz*, ill. John R. Neill (New York: Dover Publications, 1985), 55.

22. Baum, *Ozma of Oz*, 71.

23. In the second novel in the Oz series, we learn that Ozma of Oz was transformed as an infant into a boy named Tip by the witch Mombi, who then turns him back into a girl at the end of the story.

24. Baum, *Ozma of Oz*, 70.

25. Baum, *Ozma of Oz*, 146–47.

26. Baum, *Ozma of Oz*, 44.

27. Tik-tok tells the Scarecrow that he is "fit-ted with Smith and Tin-ker's Im-proved Com-bi-na-tion Steel Brains." Baum, *Ozma of Oz*, 114–15.

28. Baum, *Ozma of Oz*, 168.

29. Baum, *Ozma of Oz*, 173.

30. Baum, *Ozma of Oz*, 174.

31. Baum, *Ozma of Oz*, 176–77.

32. "A look at the ambiguity of the arcades: their abundance of mirrors, which fabulously amplifies the spaces and makes orientation more difficult." Benjamin, *Arcades Project*, 542.

33. Benjamin, *Arcades Project*, 693.

34. *Caput-tantum*, meaning "head only" in Latin, is a term I invented, as I found no technical term for a creature that is just a head.

35. de La Hire, *Nyctalope on Mars*, 252.

36. de La Hire, *Nyctalope on Mars*, 252.

37. de La Hire, *Nyctalope on Mars*, 289.

38. Edgar Rice Burroughs, *The Chessmen of Mars* (New York: Ballantine Books, 1922), 85.

39. Burroughs, *Chessmen of Mars*, 79.

40. Burroughs, *Chessmen of Mars*, 69.

41. Burroughs, *Chessmen of Mars*, 86.

42. Burroughs, *Chessmen of Mars*, 88.

43. Marinetti, *Let's Murder the Moonshine*, 100.

44. Burroughs, *Chessmen of Mars*, 91.

45. Burroughs, *Chessmen of Mars*, 122.

46. Burroughs, *Chessmen of Mars*, 140.

47. Mina Loy, *The Lost Lunar Baedeker*, ed. Roger Conover (New York: Noonday Press, Farrar, Straus and Giroux, 1996), 40.

48. Marinetti, *Let's Murder the Moonshine*, 100.

49. Massive Astrophysical Compact Halo Object: "a compact object, such as a brown dwarf, a low-mass star, or a black hole, of a kind that is thought by some to constitute part of the dark matter in galactic halos." Google Online Dictionary.

50. Loy, *Lost Lunar Baedeker*, 59.

51. Loy, *Lost Lunar Baedeker*, 40–41.

52. Loy, *Lost Lunar Baedeker*, 41.

53. William Blake, "Eternity," in *The Complete Prose and Poetry of William Blake*, ed. David V. Erdman (New York: Doubleday, 1988), 470.

54. Loy, *Lost Lunar Baedeker*, 82.

55. Loy, *Lost Lunar Baedeker*, 6.

56. Loy, *Lost Lunar Baedeker*, 177.

57. Loy, *Lost Lunar Baedeker*, 6–7.

58. Loy, *Lost Lunar Baedeker*, 7.

59. Loy, *Lost Lunar Baedeker*, 177.

Chapter 2

1. Freedman, "Science Fiction and Critical Theory," 189.

2. Howard Eiland and Kevin McLaughlin, translators forward to Benjamin, *Arcades Project*, ix.

3. Benjamin, *Arcades Project*, 564, 864.

4. Benjamin, *Arcades Project*, 540.

5. Benjamin, *Arcades Project*, 539.

6. Benjamin, *Arcades Project*, 693, 833. And cf. André Breton: "The marvelous is not the same in every period of history: it partakes in some obscure way of a sort of general revelation only the fragments of which come down to us: they are the romantic ruins, the modern mannequin, or any other symbol capable of affecting the human sensibility for a period of time." Breton, *Manifestoes of Surrealism*, trans. Richard Seaver and Helen R. Lane (Ann Arbor: University of Michigan, 1969), 16.

7. All of these concerns are brought together by Benjamin in the following passage from the "Exposé of 1935, Early Version": "Excursus on the chthonic side of the city of Paris. Topographic traces of the prehistoric: the old bed of the Seine. The subterranean waterways. The catacombs. Legends of subterranean Paris . . . The undersea world of the arcades . . . The doll as wish symbol." Benjamin, *Arcades Project*, 895.

8. Breton, *Manifestoes of Surrealism*, 21, italics in original.

9. Breton, *Manifestoes of Surrealism*, 22.

10. Arthur B. Evans, "Surrealism and Science Fiction," rev. of *Futures of Surrealism: Myth, Science Fiction and Fantastic Art in France 1936–1969*, by Gavin Parkinson, and *Surrealism, Science Fiction and Comics*, ed. Gavin Parkinson, *Science Fiction Studies* 43, no. 2, 129 (July 2016): 351–58. For the influence of sci-fi on later surrealism, see Gavin Parkinson, ed., *Surrealism, Science Fiction and Comics* (Liverpool: Liverpool University Press, 2015).

11. "In homage to Guillaume Apollinaire, who had just died and who, on several occasions, seemed to us to have followed a discipline of this kind, without however having sacrificed to it any mediocre literary means, Soupault and I baptized the new mode of pure expression which we had at our disposal and which we wished to pass on to our friends, by the name of SURREALISM." Breton, *Manifestoes of Surrealism*, 23.

12. David Gascoyne in the introduction to André Breton and Philippe Soupault, *The Magnetic Fields*, trans. David Gascoyne (London: Atlas Press, 1985).

13. Sigmund Freud, "The Uncanny," in *The Standard Edition of the Complete Psychological Works of Sigmund Freud*, vol. 17: *1917–1919*, trans. James Strachey (London: Hogarth Press, 1955), 220, 241.

14. Freud, "Uncanny," 224, 226. "A particularly favorable condition for awakening uncanny sensations is created when there is intellectual uncertainty whether an object is alive or not, and when an inanimate object becomes too much like an animate one." Freud, "Uncanny," 233.

15. Freud, "Uncanny," 226.

16. Freud, "Uncanny," 244.

17. Quoted in Angus Fletcher, *Allegory: The Theory of a Symbolic Mode* (Ithaca, NY: Cornell University Press, 1964), 100.

18. Masahito Mori, "The Uncanny Valley [From the Field]," trans. Karl F. MacDorman and Norri Kageki, *IEEE Robotics and Automation Magazine* 19, no. 2 (June 2012): 98–100.

19. Joseph Adamson, "Science Fiction as Romance," Educated Imagination: A Website Devoted to Northrop Frye, posted June 9, 2012.

20. Adamson, "Science Fiction as Romance."

21. "A literary genre—Sci-fi or any other—ought to be understood not as a pigeon-hole into which certain texts may be filed and certain others may not, but rather as an element or, still better, a tendency, which is active to a greater or lesser degree within a literary text which is itself conceptualized as a complexly structured whole." Freedman, "Science Fiction and Critical Theory," 181–82.

22. Breton and Soupault, *Magnetic Fields*, 73.

23. Breton and Soupault, *Magnetic Fields*, 78.

24. Breton and Soupault, *Magnetic Fields*, 73.

25. Breton and Soupault, *Magnetic Fields*, 76.

26. Breton and Soupault, *Magnetic Fields*, 76.

27. Breton and Soupault, *Magnetic Fields*, 76.

28. Breton and Soupault, *Magnetic Fields*, 78.

29. Edgar Rice Burroughs, *At the Earth's Core* (New York: Grosset and Dunlap, 1922), 57–58.

30. Burroughs, *At the Earth's Core*, 63.

31. Burroughs, *At the Earth's Core*, 39.

32. Burroughs, *At the Earth's Core*, 126–27.

33. Burroughs, *At the Earth's Core*, 55.

34. Burroughs, *At the Earth's Core*, 233–34.

35. Burroughs, *At the Earth's Core*, 65.
36. Burroughs, *At the Earth's Core*, 80.
37. Burroughs, *At the Earth's Core*, 82.
38. Burroughs, *At the Earth's Core*, 93–94.
39. Burroughs, *At the Earth's Core*, 137–41.
40. Oliver Harris calls *Nova Express* "a Time Machine" that "fires the reader into textual outer space" in his introduction to William Burroughs, *Nova Express: The Restored Text* (New York: Grove Press, 2013), xii.
41. Burroughs, *Nova Express*, 41.
42. As Burroughs puts it,

> I don't know about where fiction ordinarily directs itself, but I am quite deliberately addressing myself to the whole area of what we call dreams. Precisely what is a dream? A certain juxtaposition of word and image. I've recently done a lot of experiments with scrapbooks. I'll read in the newspaper something that reminds me of or has relation to something I've written. I'll cut out the picture or article and paste it in a scrapbook beside the words from my book. Or, I'll be walking down the street and I'll suddenly see a scene from my book and I'll photograph it and put it in a scrapbook. I'll show you some of those. I've found that when preparing a page, I'll almost invariably dream that night something relating to this juxtaposition of word and image. In other words, I've been interested in precisely how word and image get around on very, very complex association lines. I do a lot of exercises in what I call time travel, in taking coordinates, such as what I photographed on the train, what I was thinking about at the time, what I was reading, and what I wrote; all of this to see how completely I can project myself back to that one point in time.

Conrad Knickerbocker, "'The Art of Fiction,' Interview with William Burroughs," *Paris Review* 36, iss. 35 (Fall 1965)

43. "*Nova Express* was definitely 'underground.' Not quite, perhaps, like the underground press of little magazines to which Burroughs contributed—since a publishing house like Grove was 'alternative' but still commercial, not aligned with the self-publishing networks that sprang up in the 1960s. Rather, it was underground in its aim to serve a resistance movement against an occupying power, its cut-up methods intended to sabotage an essential fascist above-ground world." Harris, introduction to Burroughs, *Nova Express*, xliii)
44. Harris writes that "science fiction was the ideal genre for [Burroughs's] cut-up methods." Harris, introduction to Burroughs, *Nova Express*, xiv.
45. Harris, introduction to Burroughs, *Nova Express*, xxxiii.
46. INTERVIEWER: What do cut-ups offer the reader that conventional narrative doesn't? BURROUGHS: Any narrative passage or any passage, say, of poetic images is subject to any number of variations, all of which may be interesting and valid in their own right. A page of Rimbaud cut up and rearranged will give you quite new images. Rimbaud images—real Rimbaud images—but new ones. Knickerbocker, "'Art of Fiction.'"
47. Harris, introduction to Burroughs, *Nova Express*, lii.
48. Burroughs, *Nova Express*, 7.
49. Burroughs, *Nova Express*, 53–54.
50. Burroughs, *Nova Express*, 50.

51. Burroughs, *Nova Express*, 189. And cf. "INTERVIEWER: In Nova Express, you indicate that silence is a desirable state. BURROUGHS: The most desirable state. In one sense a special use of words and pictures can conduce silence." Knickerbocker, "'Art of Fiction.'"

52. Burroughs, *Nova Express*, 60.

53. Burroughs, *Nova Express*, 39.

54. Burroughs, *Nova Express*, 29–30.

55. Knickerbocker, "'Art of Fiction.'"

56. Burroughs, *Nova Express*, 74.

57. Burroughs, *Nova Express*, 63.

58. Burroughs, *Nova Express*, 54.

59. Burroughs, *Nova Express*, 92.

60. Burroughs, *Nova Express*, 85–86.

61. Burroughs, *Nova Express*, 74.

62. Burroughs, *Nova Express*, 76.

63. Burroughs, *Nova Express*, 87–89.

64. Burroughs, *Nova Express*, 89.

65. Burroughs, *Nova Express*, 90–91.

66. Burroughs, *Nova Express*, 80–81.

67. Harris, in Burroughs, *Nova Express*, 220.

68. Burroughs, *Nova Express*, 123.

69. Burroughs, *Nova Express*, 55.

70. Burroughs, *Nova Express*, 133.

71. Burroughs, *Nova Express*, 134.

72. Burroughs, *Nova Express*, 143.

73. Burroughs, *Nova Express*, 142.

74. Burroughs, *Nova Express*, 143.

75. Burroughs, *Nova Express*, 144.

76. Burroughs, *Nova Express*, 145.

77. Burroughs, *Nova Express*, 146.

78. Burroughs, *Nova Express*, 148–49.

79. Burroughs, *Nova Express*, 151–52.

80. Burroughs, *Nova Express*, 2.

81. Burroughs, *Nova Express*, 6, 15, 127, 21.

82. Harris, introduction to Burroughs, *Nova Express*, xvi.

83. Harris writes of "The Subliminal Kid joining the ranks of Burroughs's other Western-style characters (The Intolerable Kid, The Carbonic Kid, The Heavy Metal Kid, etc.)." Harris, in Burroughs, *Nova Express*, 242.

84. Burroughs, *Nova Express*, 8.

85. Jakobson, *Language and Literature*, 69.

86. Marshall McLuhan writes, "It is amusing to read reviews of Burroughs that try to classify his books as nonbooks or as failed science fiction." Quoted by Harris, introduction to Burroughs, *Nova Express*, x. And see Harris's excellent discussion of Burroughs's cut-up poetics in "'Burroughs Is a Poet Too, Really': The Poetics of Minutes to Go," first published in the *Edinburgh Review* 114 (2005). Republished online by RealityStudio in August 2010.

87. Ted Greenwald, "Spoken," in *Bruce Andrews and Charles Bernstein's L=A=N=G=U=A=G=E: The Complete Facsimile*, ed. Matthew Hofer and Michael Golston (Albuquerque: University of New Mexico Press), 190.

88. Gilles Deleuze, *Difference and Repetition,* trans. Paul Patton (New York: Columbia University Press, 1994), xxi.

89. Ted Greenwald, *You Bet!* (San Francisco: This, 1978), 72.

Chapter 3

1. *Burroughs Live: The Collected Interviews of William S. Burroughs, 1960–1997* (Los Angeles, CA: Semiotext(e); Cambridge, MA.: Distributed by MIT Press, 2001), 73.

2. Burroughs on his Western:

> I'd use cut-ups extensively in the preparation, because they would give me all sorts of facets of character and place, but the final version would be straight narrative. I wouldn't want to get bogged down in too much factual detail, but I'd like to do research in New Mexico or Arizona, even though the actual towns out there have become synthetic tourist attractions. Occasionally I have the sensation that I'm repeating myself in my work, and I would like to do something different—almost a deliberate change of style. I'm not sure if it's possible, but I want to try. I've been thinking about the Western for years. As a boy I was sent to school in New Mexico, and during the war I was stationed in Coldspring, Texas, near Conroe. That's genuine backwoods country, and I picked up some real characters there.

Burroughs, *Live: The Collected Interviews*, 73.

3. Edward Dorn, *Gunslinger* (Durham, NC: Duke University Press, 1989), 7.

4. Dorn, *Gunslinger*, 50, 186.

5. Edgar Rice Burroughs, *A Princess of Mars* (New York: Del Rey, Ballantine Books, 1963, 1980), 19.

6. Burroughs, *Princess of Mars*, 20.

7. Burroughs, *Princess of Mars*, 21.

8. Burroughs, *Princess of Mars*, 22, 23,

9. Burroughs, *Princess of Mars*, 28.

10. Burroughs, *Princess of Mars*, 41. The American Southwest is traditionally defined as stretching from the Mexico-U.S. border to thirty-nine degrees north latitude.

11. According to the League of Extraordinary Gentlemen wiki page, "Murania is an advanced subterranean empire and outpost of the massive underground land Atvatabar, which is located 25,000' beneath the U.S. state of New Mexico. Coincidentally a ranch was built above Murania, belonging to early 20th-century gunfighter and balladeer Gene Autry."

12. Tony Hull, "The Thunderbird: A February Exhibit on a Placitas Institution," *Sandoval Signpost*, February 12, 2012, 1.http://www.sandovalsignpost.com/feb12/html/around_town.html

13. Edward Dorn, *Ed Dorn Live: Lectures, Interviews, and Outtakes*, ed. Joseph Richey (Ann Arbor: University of Michigan Press, 2007), 66.

14. Dorn, *Gunslinger*, 5.

15. Charles Olson, *Collected Prose: Charles Olson*, ed. Donald Allen and Benjamin Friedlander, with an introduction by Robert Creeley (Berkeley: University of California Press, 1997), 17.

16. Dorn, *Ed Dorn Live*, 75.

17. Dorn, *Ed Dorn Live*, 17.

18. Dorn, *Ed Dorn Live*, 66.

19. Dorn, *Ed Dorn Live*, 95.

20. Tom Clark, *Edward Dorn: A World of Difference* (Berkeley, CA: North Atlantic Books, 2002), 28.

21. Edward Dorn, *Way More West: New and Selected Poems*, ed. Michael Rothenberg (New York: Penguin Books, 2007), 180, 157.

22. Dorn, *Gunslinger*, 120.

23. Dorn, *Gunslinger*, 66.

24. Dorn, *Gunslinger*, 163.

25. Dorn, *Gunslinger*, 146.

26. Ed Dorn, "Reading at SUNY Buffalo, April 19, 1974," University of Pennsylvania, PennSound.

27. Dorn, *Way More West*, 177.

28. Dorn, *Way More West*, 173.

29. Dorn, *Gunslinger*, 130.

30. Dorn, *Gunslinger*, 129.

31. Dorn, *Gunslinger*, 146.

32. William Carlos Williams, *Imaginations* (New York: New Directions, 1979), 102.

33. Dorn, *Ed Dorn Live*, 24.

34. Dorn, *Gunslinger*, 152, 149.

35. Marjorie Perloff, introduction to Dorn, *Gunslinger*, vii.

36. Dorn, *Gunslinger*, 117.

37. Dorn, *Gunslinger*, 85, 59, 198, 168.

38. Dorn, *Gunslinger*, 198, 200.

39. Stephen Freeman and Grant Jenkins suggest a possible reference in *Gunslinger* to the Fantastic Four in "First Annotations to Edward Dorn's Gunslinger," *Sagetrieb* 15, no. 3 (Winter 1966): 71.

40. Dorn, *Gunslinger*, 111.

41. Dorn, *Gunslinger*, 13, 17, 18.

42. Dorn, *Gunslinger*, 31.

43. Dorn, *Gunslinger*, 16.

44. Dorn, *Gunslinger*, 32.

45. Dorn, *Gunslinger*, 29.

46. Dorn, *Gunslinger*, 28–29.

47. Dorn, *Way More West*, 177.

48. Dorn, *Gunslinger*, 24.

49. Dorn, *Gunslinger*, 38.

50. Dorn, *Gunslinger*, 41.

51. Dorn, *Gunslinger*, 31.

52. Dorn, *Gunslinger*, 56.

53. Olson, "Projective Verse," *Collected Prose*, 247.

54. Dorn, *Gunslinger*, 35, italics in the original.

55. Dorn, *Gunslinger*, 32–33.

56. Dorn, *Gunslinger*, 32.

57. Dorn, *Gunslinger*, 27.

58. Dorn, *Gunslinger*, 28.

59. Dorn, *Gunslinger*, 30–31.

60. Olson, *Collected Prose*, 155.

61. In a somewhat different context, Dorn explains the temporal physics behind Gunslinger's draw:

> According to the choice of inertial reference frame the accelerated linear projection of an object from a discharging muzzle assigns motion to either component indifferently; in post-Chomskyian equivalence, either "the gun fires the bullet" or "the bullet fires the gun." This last sounds like running a standard Western movie backwards or by inversion into negative space, but not so: it's standard Newtonian mechanics that the bullet throws the entire scene back into shock waves of bored trepidation, just as the "end" of any action teleologically pre-empts the motive on the trigger. Expensive on shooters but cheap on bullets and you can get a real quick draw: suicide is tricky.

Ed Dorn, "Facsimile Reprint of Bean News," *Sagetrieb*, Edward Dorn special issue 15, no. 3 (Winter 1996): inside back cover, 8.

62. Dorn, *Gunslinger*, 57.

63. Dorn, *Gunslinger*, 31.

64. Dorn, *Gunslinger*, 46, 48.

65. Dorn, *Gunslinger*, 74, 118, 78.

66. Dorn, *Gunslinger*, 48, 50.

67. Dorn, *Gunslinger*, 50–52.

68. Dorn, *Gunslinger*, 83.

69. Olson, *Collected Prose*, 158.

70. Dorn, *Gunslinger*, 162.

71. Dorn, *Gunslinger*, 72.

72. Dorn, *Gunslinger*, 114, 51.

73. Dorn, *Gunslinger*, 52.

74. Dorn, *Gunslinger*, 61.

75. Dorn, *Gunslinger*, 60.

76. Dorn, *Gunslinger*, 60–61.

77. Dorn, *Gunslinger*, 67.

78. Dorn, *Gunslinger*, 67–68.

79. Dorn, *Gunslinger*, 62.

80. Dorn, *Gunslinger*, 70. Some critics identify Universe City with Truth or Consequences, a small town in southern New Mexico, but T or C (in local parlance) has neither suburbs, nor an old town, nor a plaza, nor outdoor native vendors, nor a university. We are definitely in Albuquerque here. Everything says that the place "used to be called Truth or Consequences," which is not true, and anyway T or C was and still is called that. It appears that Dorn could not let the philosophically menacing name of the town go without mention.

81. Dorn, *Gunslinger*, 75–76.

82. Dorn, *Gunslinger*, 79.

83. Dorn, *Gunslinger*, 82.

84. Olson, *Collected Prose*, 25.

85. Olson, *Collected Prose*, 248.

86. Olson, *Collected Prose*, 162.

87. "This academic regionalism tries to make an honorable recapitulation of life in a place and bring it into the language of poetry. And really the devices between Paterson and Maximus aren't that different because they focus their material, and their documen-

tation comes from the witness of the past. And obviously *Gunslinger* doesn't do that." Dorn, *Ed Dorn Live*, 95.

88. "I am from the Midwest, which means I'm cynical. [Olson] was not. He was deep down a Catholic, so his respect for authority is much greater than mine. Those differences were basic by nature. Being a Midwesterner, I would see the unbelievably romantic and poetic values of his work, which has been slighted by people who write about it, who are much more interested in and taken by and are anxious to promote the scholarly and intellectual sources that are there. But his way of casting language and making history vibrant is extremely poetic." Dorn, *Ed Dorn Live*, 75.

89. Ed Dorn, in "An Interview with Edward Dorn," by Roy K. Okada, *Contemporary Literature* 15, no. 3 (Summer 1974): 307.

90. Michael Davidson, "To Eliminate the Draw: Edward Dorn's Slinger," *American Literature* 53, no. 3 (November 1981): 455.

91. Quoted in Davidson, "To Eliminate the Draw," 455.

92. Dorn, *Gunslinger*, 97, 95.

93. Dorn, *Gunslinger*, 98, 93, 99.

94. Dorn, *Gunslinger*, 101, 196.

95. Dorn, *Gunslinger*, 102.

96. Dorn, *Gunslinger*, 104–5.

97. See especially Peter Michelson's "Edward Dorn, Inside the Outskirts" and Grant Jenkins's "Gunslinger's Ethics of Excess," both in *Sagetrieb*, Edward Dorn special issue, 15, no. 3 (Winter 1996): 197–206 and 207–42.

98. Dorn, *Gunslinger*, 100, 152.

99. Davidson, "To Eliminate the Draw," 455.

100. Dorn, *Gunslinger*, 105.

101. Dorn, *Gunslinger*, 95.

102. Dorn, *Gunslinger*, 96.

103. Dorn, *Gunslinger*, 100. The Hughes Tool Company became Baker Hughes after merging with Baker Tools in 1987. In 2001, the company introduced the largest hydraulic fracturing vessel for deepwater work in the Gulf of Mexico. It was named after Howard Hughes.

104. Dorn, *Gunslinger*, 100. The figure of Al may point further back into the history of fracking. The grandfather of fracking is widely acknowledged to be Edward A. L. Roberts (Al/Robard?), a Civil War Union veteran who invented the Roberts exploding torpedo, patented in 1865.

105. Dorn, *Gunslinger*, 122.

106. Dorn, *Gunslinger*, 116.

107. Dorn, *Gunslinger*, 114.

108. Dorn, *Gunslinger*, 122, 123.

109. Dorn, *Gunslinger*, 163.

110. Dorn, *Gunslinger*, 117.

111. Dorn, *Gunslinger*, 121.

112. Dorn, *Gunslinger*, 128.

113. Dorn, *Gunslinger*, 129.

114. Dorn, *Gunslinger*, 179.

115. "I was also trying to work out for myself in editorials and some of the articles exactly what I meant by 'Sllab.' I was intrigued with Kubrick's use of the main deific principle in that film [*2001*]. In fact the most interesting thing in it for me was the stone with the

music." Dorn, "An Interview with Edward Dorn," 311. Dorn tells us that the AIP (American Institute of Physics) at MIT "is responsible for the gender assignment" of Sllab. Dorn, "Facsimile Reprint of Bean News," 4.

116. Interpretations vary widely. For example, Grant Jenkins claims that "this letter is mostly non-sense which yields at best only 'FLAPTRAP INFORMATION TEETOTTER,'" and he mentions Sllab only in passing (Jenkins, "Gunslinger's Ethics of Excess," 224. Peter Michelson closely reads the Nightletter, which he concludes "is a satire on what happened in the America of the sixties cast as a cryptic warning about the future"; Sllab, among other things, is "an intriguing image of a ballsy God that sets being in motion and watches what men make of it in disgust." Michelson, "Edward Dorn, Inside the Outskirts," 203, 202. On the other hand, according to Davidson, "the only recognizable information appears at the end of the letter: 'Expect Materialization at Precisely 4 Corners,' a reference to the long-anticipated incarnation of Robart. The rest of the message is in code which, as the Slinger observes, is Sllab. . . . Since the word is 'balls' spelled backwards, one can assume that this deity works through an inversion of the male sexual principle by which father is replaced by son, a transmundane God by a mortal Christ." Davidson, "To Eliminate the Draw," 459.

117. Dorn, *Gunslinger*, 131.

118. Dorn, *Gunslinger*, 132–33.

119. Dorn, *Gunslinger*, 133.

120. Dorn, "Facsimile Reprint of Bean News," 4.

121. Dorn, "Facsimile Reprint of Bean News," 4.

122. "Flat Slab Subduction," Wikipedia, updated October 28, 2022.

123. "He learned to measure the tilt of the strata, and what that told the geologist about the shape of things down below, and the probable direction of the anticline." Upton Sinclair, *Oil!* (New York: Penguin Books, 1926), 74.

124. Dorn, *Gunslinger*, 195, 185, 186.

125. Dorn, *Gunslinger*, 178.

126. All quotations from the Nightletter appear on pages 140–41 of Dorn's *Gunslinger*.

127. A *flatrap* is a Rampala fishing lure, designed to wriggle in the water when it is reeled in—that is, to "teetotter."

128. The GX-2 was a Greyhound bus introduced in 1948 that would eventually develop into the Scenicruiser. It had an observation dome, modeled after the astrodome cars popular in trains at the time, as well as a lounge, washroom, and toilet facilities, and a public address system designed both for announcements by the driver and for the playing of tape-recorded music. In many ways, the GX-2 resembles Robart's grand car, which is the last place we saw the telegram to Parmenides, hence OCCASIONS 12&3 OF JUMBLED PAST [REPT. GX + -2, WORKS]. The interior designer of the Scenicruiser was Raymond Loewy, who also designed the interior of the Boeing 307 (Stratoliner) owned by Hughes: he must be the model for Robart's interior decorator. Loewy also designed the Lucky Strike cigarette package, changing it from dark green to white: a "Lucky Strike Green" fan buys the Old Rugged Howard Hughes look-alike statue in Book II.

129. Dorn, *Ed Dorn Live*, 16.

130. Jenkins, "Gunslinger's Ethics of Excess," 216.

131. Robert Von Hallberg (in "This Marvelous Accidentalism," in *Internal Resistances: The Poetry of Edward Dorn*, ed. Donald Wesling [Berkeley: University of California Press, 1985], 76) makes something of the same point:

In the world of language, though not of men, the poet has the leverage to turn things upside down. From his new domain, as Secretary to Parmenides, "I" sees the poem as an

"ABSOLUTE LINGUATILT." The words of the poem tilt in several directions: toward the scientists with offerings like "azimuthal," "presyntactic metalinguistic urgency," "organic radicals," "epactos," and "monotremata"; toward the hallowed past with such archaic formulations as "where will you now" and "What meanst thou?"; and those tilts become formal bows with such contrivances as "a bed / will be my desire." Yet the most severe inclination of Dorn's manner is colloquial.

132. Dorn, *Gunslinger*, 178.

133. Dorn, *Gunslinger*, 149.

134. Dorn, *Gunslinger*, 124. As Dorn explains, "As most readers are surely already aware, the 4 Corners is the only purely surveyed crosshair in the world. This giant plus sign has recently gained notoriety for attracting the most negative aspects of Western industry. The smoke is so heavy it is said that this area has by far the highest incidence of missing travelers in the U.S." Dorn, "Facsimile Reprint of Bean News," 8.

135. Dorn, *Gunslinger*, 169, 178.

136. Dorn, *Gunslinger*, 179, 180.

137. Dorn, *Gunslinger*, 151, 146,

138. Dorn, *Gunslinger*, 151.

139. Dorn, *Gunslinger*, 168.

140. Dorn, *Gunslinger*, 184–85.

141. Dorn, *Gunslinger*, 157.

142. Dorn, *Gunslinger*, 162.

143. Dorn, *Gunslinger*, 166.

144. Dorn, *Gunslinger*, 200.

145. Dorn, *Gunslinger*, 179.

146. Dorn, *Gunslinger*, 182.

147. Dorn, *Gunslinger*, 185.

148. Dorn, *Gunslinger*, 194.

149. Dorn, *Gunslinger*, 195.

150. Dorn, *Gunslinger*, 196.

151. Dorn, *Gunslinger*, 200.

152. Clark Coolidge, *Smithsonian Depositions and Subject to a Film* (Clark Coolidge, 1980), 15.

Chapter 4

1. Dorn, *Gunslinger*, 104.

2. "He found in entropy or the measure of disorganization for a closed system an adequate metaphor to apply to certain phenomena in his own world. . . . He found himself, in short, restating Gibbs' prediction in social terms, and envisioned a heat-death for his culture in which ideas, like heat-energy, would no longer be transferred, since each point in it would ultimately have the same quantity of energy; and intellectual motion would, accordingly, cease." Thomas Pynchon, *Slow Learner* (New York: Little Brown, 1984), 81–98.

3. Clark Coolidge, "Arrangement: July 19, 1977," in *Talking Poetics from Naropa Institute*, ed. Anne Waldman and Marilyn Webb (Boulder: Shambala, 1978), 146–47.

4. Coolidge, "Arrangement," 147.

5. Coolidge, "Arrangement," 149.

6. Coolidge, *Space* (New York: Harper and Row, 1970), 69.

7. Coolidge, "Arrangement," 145. Coolidge gos on to summarize the story for his audience: "In the story, in the beginning a little boy named Scott, who's ten years old, is play-

ing down by a creek and finds these strange objects, and these objects are toys, they're instructional toys from another planet in the future. He doesn't know that, but he takes them home and he and his sister Emma, who's about five years old, start playing with them, and these toys start working on their minds and changing them from human beings into . . . what?" The children eventually vanish, while "on the carpet lay a pattern of markers, pebbles, an iron ring—junk. A random pattern."

8. Smithson, *Collected Writings*, 20–21.

9. Christian Bök's *Crystallography*, I would argue, is just such a project. Scrupulously designed after the dynamics of crystal structures, the poems in this volume are modeled purely on science; there is nothing of science fiction in them. See Bök, *Crystallography* (Toronto: Coach House Books, 2003, 2013).

10. Coolidge says of one of the poems in *Space* (and by extension, all of them), "I was really trying to work with the words, look at the words, try to use all their qualities. There's no question of meaning, in the sense of explaining and understanding this poem. Hopefully, it's a unique object, not just an object. Language isn't just objects, it moves." Coolidge, "Arrangement," 161.

11. "The writing of Quartz Hearts overlaps work on both the last section of Polaroid (completed August 1973) and the beginning of my long (as yet untitled) 'prosoid' work (first section completed November 1973). It is in every sense a hinge work, reflecting a fresh interest in sentence structure as axial armature." Clark Coolidge, *Quartz Hearts* (San Francisco: THIS, 1978), 56.

12. Coolidge, *Quartz Hearts*, 9.

13. The only titled poem in *Quartz Hearts* is "The Blocks," which ends, "A house closed to the ground onto a / square the length of a street to the next town." Coolidge, *Quartz Hearts*, 10. *Block* is a frequent noun in the book, appearing six times.

14. Coolidge, *Quartz Hearts*, 4, 5, 8, 11.

15. Smithson, *Collected Writings*, 91.

16. Coolidge, *Quartz Hearts*, 53.

17. Coolidge, *Quartz Hearts*, 6, 12, 19, 20.

18. Smithson, *Collected Writings*, 8.

19. Smithson, *Collected Writings*, 91.

20. Coolidge, *Quartz Hearts*, 57.

21. Coolidge, *Quartz Hearts*, 32–35.

22. Coolidge, *Quartz Hearts*, 57. Coolidge could also be referring to Carleton Coon's *The Seven Caves: Archaeological Explorations in the Middle East* (1957).

23. Smithson, *Collected Writings*, 8.

24. Coolidge, *Quartz Hearts*, 54.

25. Coolidge recounts a conversation with Aram Saroyan wherein the latter declared that reading a Coolidge text is like looking at "a big cliff of rock." Coolidge agrees, with the proviso that "the way I look at it, because I've had geological interests and some training, is that geologists read the rocks. They can read the layers by the fossils in them and what ages and what came first and sometimes there are very complicated arrangements of strata and faults and things." Coolidge, "Arrangement," 154.

26. Smithson, *Collected Writings*, 6.

27. Smithson, *Collected Writings*, 111–12.

28. Smithson, *Collected Writings*, 249, 254, 255.

29. Smithson, *Collected Writings*, 110.

30. "The amazing thing about Clark Coolidge is that all the time I believed he was a conceptual artist, making impersonal structures of words, he was probably in fact writing

a very deep, very American, very spacey autobiography, which he continues to do." Aram Saroyan, "Clark Coolidge and I," in *Stations # 5: A Symposium on Clark Coolidge*, ed. Ron Silliman (Wisconsin: Membrane Press, 1978), 6–7.

31. Coolidge, *Smithsonian Depositions*, 12–13. Coolidge recalls a childhood excursion to caverns in "Arrangement": "Jumping back a bit, I became a cave explorer, and that sort of came out of my interest in minerals. My folks took me to Luray Caverns in Virginia when I was about ten years old. Well, it's a beautiful cave full of orange and red stalactites, totally covered with these beautiful and weird formations." Coolidge, "Arrangement," 152.

32. Coolidge, *Smithsonian Depositions*, 19–21.

33. Coolidge, *Smithsonian Depositions*, 20–23.

34. Coolidge, *Smithsonian Depositions*, 17–18. And cf. "I had spent my junior high school years in the early '50s devouring hundreds of science fiction stories. Starting with the Robert Heinlein juveniles (*Red Planet* [1949], *Farmer in the Sky* [1950], etc.), I soon moved on through the gamut of originators: Ray Bradbury, Theodore Sturgeon, Isaac Asimov, Henry Kuttner, et al." Coolidge, "After Tomorrow," in *Art Forum International* 48, iss. 2 (2009): 206.

35. "Then Passaic Center loomed like a dull adjective. Each 'store' in it was an adjective unto the next, a chain of adjectives disguised as stores." Coolidge, *Smithsonian Depositions*, 9, from Smithson, "A Tour of the Monuments of New Jersey," in *Collected Writings*, 72; "Science is a shack in the lava flow of ideas" and "In other words, there's nothing to grasp onto except the cinders." Coolidge, "Discussion with Heizer, Oppenheim, Smithson" in *Smithsonian Depositions*, 17, 21, from Smithson, *Collected Writings*, 249.

36. Coolidge claims that he actually discovered Ballard through Smithson: "I first encountered J. G. Ballard in the epigraph to an essay by Robert Smithson. 'Quasi-Infinities and the Waning of Space,' which appeared in the November 1966 issue of Arts Magazine, begins with a brief but intriguing quote from 'The Overloaded Man,' a story in Ballard's 1962 collection *The Voices of Time*: 'Without a time sense consciousness is difficult to visualize.'" Coolidge, "After Tomorrow," 206.

37. Coolidge, *Smithsonian Depositions*, 27–28.

38. Coolidge, *Smithsonian Depositions*, 27.

39. Coolidge, *Smithsonian Depositions*, 26–27.

40. Coolidge, *Smithsonian Depositions*, 28. And cf. Smithson and Mel Bochner's essay on planetariums, "The Domain of the Great Bear," in Smithson, *Collected Writings*, 26–43.

41. Coolidge, *Smithsonian Depositions*, 32.

42. Smithson, *Collected Writings*, 17.

43. Coolidge, *Smithsonian Depositions*, 33.

44. Smithson, *Collected Writings*, 340.

45. Coolidge writes that "the Ballard hero finds himself once again abandoned in the overlit decor and stray apparatus of a diminished civilization. Most of the others are now elsewhere as he roams and reports from those spectral bleaks, holding fast to a wan normalcy. He leaves us with a strange but habitable world, just a few suburban fences over from our own backyard. Who or what has he almost glimpsed? Could it be that at last even the future has passed him by?" Coolidge, "After Tomorrow," 206. With Ballard, we are never far from the attenuated housing blocks of *Quartz Hearts*, "just a few suburban fences over from our own backyard."

46. Coolidge, *Smithsonian Depositions*, 33. This series of passages is followed by one line from the Cretaceous level of Smithson's "Strata A Geophotographic Fiction": "The classical attitude toward mountains is gloomy." Smithson, *Collected Writings*, 75.

47. Coolidge, *Smithsonian Depositions*, 40.

48. Coolidge, *Smithsonian Depositions*, 22.

49. "Lightbulbs over Paradise." Coolidge, *Smithsonian Depositions*, 40.

50. Coolidge, *Smithsonian Depositions*, 43.

51. Coolidge, *Smithsonian Depositions*, 28–31.

52. Edgar Rice Burroughs, *Synthetic Men of Mars* (New York: Ballantiune Books, 1967), 21.

53. "After the 'structural film' there is the sprawl of entropy." Smithson, "A Cinematic Atopia," in *Collected Writings*, 139. Cf. Adorno: "Every visit to the cinema leaves me, against all my vigilance, stupider and worse." Theodor W. Adorno, *Minima Moralia: Reflections from Damaged Life*, trans. E. F. N. Jephcott (London: Verso, 1978), 25.

54. Burroughs, *Synthetic Men of Mars*, 33.

55. Burroughs, *Synthetic Men of Mars*, 33.

56. Roland Barthes, "Plastic," in *Mythologies*, selected and trans. Annette Lavers (New York: Noonday Press, 1972), 97–99.

57. Burroughs, *Synthetic Men of Mars*, 67.

58. Burroughs, *Synthetic Men of Mars*, 72.

59. This whole scenario is itself something of a Hollywood science fiction: "The carbon dioxide (CO2) extinguisher was invented by the Walter Kidde Company in 1924. CO2 is still popular today as it is an ozone-friendly clean agent and is used heavily in film and television production to extinguish burning stuntmen. Carbon dioxide extinguishes fire mainly by displacing oxygen. It was once thought that it worked by cooling, although this effect on most fires is negligible." "Fire Extinguisher," Wikipedia, update October 18, 2022. Is the Blob a stuntman?

60. Quoted in Evelyn Reilly, *Styrofoam* (New York: Roof Books, 2009), 58.

61. Burroughs, *Synthetic Men of Mars*, 78–79.

62. Reilly, *Styrofoam*, 58.

63. Reilly, *Styrofoam*, 10, 28, 42–43.

64. Reilly, *Styrofoam*, 63.

65. Burroughs, *Synthetic Men of Mars*, 105.

66. For excellent descriptions and discussions of *Styrofoam*, see Lynn Keller, *Recomposing Ecopoetics: North American Poetry of the Self-Conscious Anthropocene* (Charlottesville: University of Virginia Press, 2017), 19–24, 61–67, and 76–97; and Heather Milne, *Poetry Matters: Neoliberalism, Affect, and the Posthuman in Twenty-First Century North American Feminist Poetics* (Iowa City: University of Iowa Press, 2018), 133–51.

67. Reilly, *Styrofoam*, 48.

68. Reilly, *Styrofoam*, 55.

69. Reilly, *Styrofoam*, 15.

70. Burroughs, *Synthetic Men of Mars*, 105.

71. Keller notes that the poetry's "disjunctive construction" is ameliorated by its "proliferating links" and what she calls elsewhere "collage nets." Keller, *Recomposing Ecopoetics*, 20, 23. Milne argues in the same vein: "Rather than using fragmentation to illustrate a lack of unity or wholeness, Reilly uses fragmentation in these poems to explore the interconnectedness of things. In other words, it is precisely through this radically fragmented form that Reilly is able to powerfully but somewhat paradoxically articulate a poetics of radical interconnectivity and trans-corporeality." Milne, *Poetry Matters*, 133–34.

72. Deleuze and Guattari bring the rhizome back to Burroughs's practice in *Nova Express*: "Take William Burroughs's cut-up method: the folding of one text onto another, which constitutes multiple and even adventitious roots (like a cutting), implies a sup-

plementary dimension to that of the texts under consideration. In this supplementary dimension of folding, unity continues its spiritual labor." Deleuze and Guattari, *Thousand Plateaus*, 6.

73. Reilly, *Styrofoam*, 23.

74. Reilly, *Styrofoam*, 26, 13. And cf. Adorno: "All post-Auschwitz culture, including its urgent critique, is garbage." Theodor W. Adorno, *Negative Dialectics*, trans. E. B. Ashton (New York: Seabury, 1973), 367.

75. Reilly, *Styrofoam*, 57.

76. Milne, *Poetry Matters*, 146.

77. Keller characterizes plastic as "a plague" that nevertheless produces "an astonishingly useful array of hyperobjects." Keller, *Recomposing Ecopoetics*, 861.

78. Reilly, *Styrofoam*, 56.

79. Burroughs, *Synthetic Men of Mars*, 110.

80. Bruce Andrews, *Paradise and Method: Poetics and Praxis* (Evanston: Northwestern University Press, 1996), 259, 262, 266.

81. Andrews, *Paradise and Method*, 262.

82. "We may approach abstraction in writing by launching an infinity, a promise of infinity on the spectrum of reference—by carrying ourselves to the very limits of reference in order to reveal something of its mechanisms and methods. . . . Syllable by phrase by word cluster or word constellation tightrope walking without the net that customary or normative grammar gives it: syntax and sound as laboratories of breakage and reconvening." Andrews, *Paradise and Method*, 259.

83. "Infinity—or paradise—leads us to its home, our reference, outside of the confines of any tight system. A decriminalizing of all the minute particulars of word by word movement (inching) forward as read, to be read—these motions of lexical & acoustic intimacy. Immediacy returns—as breakage. Chargings and rechargings & dischargings are subject matter—to shake down identity into a diaspora, a multiplicity, an evanescing." Andrews, *Paradise and Method*, 259.

84. "Time is frozen into the shape of a system—history disheveled by a spatial fix. All the internal complexity in the world can't make it budge. Choke on all this differentiation. Less of a motor than a panopticon. Even the contentlessness is jerrybuilt." Andrews, *Paradise and Method*, 259. Peter Quartermain succinctly summarizes Andrews's compositional procedures in *Lip Service*:

> Drawing on materials he began generating in 1986, and written from 1989 to 1992, *Lip Service* is divided into what Andrews calls ten "planets" corresponding to the ten "bodies" of the Paradiso, and each is divided into ten parts: Earth, Moon, Mercury, Venus, Sun, Mars, Jupiter, Saturn, Fixed Stars, and Primum Mobile. The complete poem is in two large sections, the five "planets" of Part One corresponding with Dante's cantos 1–13, and the five of Part Two—"a little less critical & more optimistic" than Part One ("Paradise" 252)—corresponding with cantos 14–33. In "Paradise and Method" (252–4) Andrews maintains that he is using "thematic cues" from Dante as well as "resonances" between his own materials, topics, imagery, and sound-patterns and those found in Singleton's edition of Dante, including "cognates or so-called 'false-friend' relations with the Italian," as well as punctuation and paragraphing based "strictly on Dante's punctuation & tercet structure." . . . In "Paradise and Method," written when he was about two-thirds of the way through writing *Lip Service*, Andrews outlines the great intricacy of its structure. In writing the poem he superimposed the de-

> tailed thematic outline of "Tips for Totalizers," a projected book on poetics, not only onto the overall organization of the complete work, but also in "increasingly detailed" form onto the "internal organization" of each of its one-hundred parts, "sometimes" using the three-part breakdown of that poetics project "even to organize a fifty- or one-hundred word paragraph." The intricacy, that is to say, echoes something of the intricacy of Dante's poem, and provided him with a set of technical difficulties to work with and against.

Peter Quartermain, "Paradise as Praxis: A Preliminary Note on Bruce Andrews's *Lip Service*," *Witz: A Journal of Contemporary Poetics* 6, no. 2 (Summer 1998): 5–18, University of Pennsylvania, Electronic Poetry Center, Authors.

85. Bruce Andrews, *Lip Service* (Toronto: Coach House Books, 2001), 108.

86. "A VOLATILIZING & CAPACITATING AESTHETICS OF LANGUAGE & THE SUBLIME: 'TO NEVER SAY—WE ARE WHO WE ARE'" (sections 7 to 12). Talk given at "Im/Possibility: On the Production, Distribution, and Articulation of the Possible and Impossible," September 30–October 1, 2016, University of Kiel.

87. Andrews, *Lip Service*, 110.

88. Geoffrey Chaucer, *The Riverside Chaucer*, ed. F. N. Robinson (Boston: Houghton Mifflin, 1987), 34, ll. 2129–51.

89. Chaucer, 135, ll. 2214–31.

90. I would like to acknowledge Aled Roberts here, who alerted me to the medieval scholastic debate regarding the impossible in "The Summoner's Tale."

91. Aristotle, *The Pocket Aristotle*, ed. Justin D. Kaplan, trans. Ingram Bywater (New York: Washington Square Press, 1968), 377.

92. Andrews, *Lip Service*, 112.

93. Conklin Groff, ed., *Possible Worlds of Science Fiction* (New York: Vanguard Press, 1951), vii.

94. Andrews, *Lip Service*, 115.

95. Andrews, *Lip Service*, 116.

96. Mike Allen, *Strange Wisdoms of the Dead* (Rockville, MD: Wildside Press, 2006), 22.

97. Andrews, *Lip Service*, 119.

98. Dante Alighieri, *Paradiso: The Divine Comedy of Dante Alighieri*, vol. 3, part 1, trans. Charles S. Singleton (Princeton, NJ: Princeton University Press, 1975), 83–85. This is the translation that Andrews uses for *Lip Service*.

99. Dante, Divine Comedy, 83. My translation.

100. Andrews, *Lip Service*, 108–9.

101. Andrews, *Paradise and Method*, 258.

102. Andrews, *Paradise and Method*, 236.

103. Andrews, *Lip Service*, 123.

104. Bob Perelman, "This Just In: Past Haunts *Lip Service*," *Jacket* 22 (May 2003).

105. Greg Biglieri, "Invitation to a Misreading: Andrews' *Lip Service*," *Jacket* 22 (May 2003).

106. Bill Friend, "Modernism, Advertising, and *Lip Service*," *Jacket* 22 (May 2003).

107. Peter Quartermain, "Paradise as Praxis: Bruce Andrews's Lip Service," in *Stubborn Poetries: Poetic Facticity and the Avante-Garde* (Tuscaloosa: University of Alabama Press, 2013), 247.

108. Barbara Cole, "Bruce Andrews's Venus: Paying Lip Service to Écriture Féminine," *Jacket* 22 (May 2003).

109. Friend, "Modernism, Advertising, and *Lip Service*."

110. Roberto Tejada, "Becoming Bruce Andrews: A User's Guide to Starting Over Stars," *Jacket* 22 (May 2003).

111. Joel Bettridge, "Bruce Andrews's Language of Belief," *Jacket* 22 (May 2003).

112. Andrews, *Lip Service*, 125.

113. Andrews, *Lip Service*, 128.

Chapter 5

1. For a reading of the impossible in Sun Ra's poetry, see Brent Edwards, "The Race for Space," in Sun Ra, *Sun Ra: The Immeasurable Equation, The Collected Poetry and Prose*, comp. and ed. James L. Wolf and Hartmut Geerken (Norderstedt: WAITAWHILE Books, 2205), 29–55.

2. See Mark Dery's "Black to the Future: Interviews with Samuel R. Delaney, Greg Tate, and Tricia Rose," in *Flame Wars: The Discourse of Cyberculture*, ed. Mark Dery (Durham, NC: Duke University Press, 1994), 179–222. See especially his interview with Greg Tate therein. Dery coined the term *Afrofuturism* in his introduction to the interviews. For further elaboration and deeper explication, see Alondra Nelson's "Introduction: Future Texts," in *Afrofuturism*, ed. Alondra Nelson, in *Social Text* 20, no. 2 (71) (Summer 2002): 1–15.

3. W. E. B. Du Bois, "The Comet," in *Darkwater: Voices from within the Veil*, ed. W. E. B. Du Bois and William Edward Burghardt (New York: Harcourt, Brace, 1920), 253–74.

4. For analysis, see Adriano Elia, "W. E. B. Du Bois's Proto-Afrofuturist Short Fiction: 'The Comet,'" *Il Tolomeo* 18 (December 2016): 173–86.

5. Lisa Yaszek, "Afrofuturism, Science Fiction, and the History of the Future," *Socialism and Democracy* 20, no. 3 (2006): 41–60.

6. Kodwo Eshun, "Further Considerations of Afrofuturism," *New Centennial Review* 3, no. 2 (Summer 2003): 298.

7. Sun Ra, *Immeasurable Equation*, 142, 120, 452, 69.

8. Le Sony'r Ra was the name Sun Ra took before he changed it to the latter.

9. Baraka also wrote several sci-fi short stories. See Amiri Baraka, "Answers in Progress" and "God and Machine," in *The Fiction of LeRoi Jones/Amiri Baraka* (Chicago: Lawrence Hill Books, 2000), 219–25.

10. Amiri Baraka, "An Agony. As Now," in *SOS: Poems 1961–2013*, selected by Paul Vangelisti (New York: Grove Press, 2014), 57. All citations hereafter are from pages 57–58.

11. Amiri Baraka, "How You Sound??" in *The LeRoi Jones / Amiri Baraka Reader*, ed. William J. Harris (New York: Basic Books, 2009), 16.

12. Baraka himself published Olson's "Projective Verse" as a pamphlet in 1959, nine years after it was written and five years before "An Agony. As Now" appeared in *The Dead Lecturer* (1964), his second book of poetry.

13. Baraka, "How You Sound??" 16.

14. Olson, *Collected Prose*, 245–46.

15. Baraka, *SOS*, 12.

16. Baraka, *SOS*, 39.

17. Charles Olson, "La Préface," in *The Collected Poems of Charles Olson*, ed. George F. Butterick (Berkeley: University of California Press, 1987), 46–47.

18. Charles Olson, "I, Maximus of Gloucester, to You," in *The Maximus Poems*, ed. George F. Butterick (Berkeley: University of California Press, 1983), 5.

19. Olson, *Maximus Poems*, 5.

20. Baraka, *SOS*, 420.

21. "First of all I express sincerity. There's also that sense of humor, by which people sometimes learn to laugh about themselves. I mean, the situation is so serious that the people could go crazy because of it. They need to smile and realize how ridiculous everything is. A race without a sense of humor is in bad shape. A race needs clowns." Sun Ra, *Immeasurable Equation*, 43.

22. Edgar Rice Burroughs, *The Gods of Mars* (New York: Ballantine Books, 1974), 68.

23. Sun Ra, *Immeasurable Equation*, 235.

24. Sun Ra, *Immeasurable Equation*, 452, 141, 101.

25. Sun Ra, *Immeasurable Equation*, 171.

26. Edgar Rice Burroughs, *Gods of Mars*, 57.

27. Sun Ra, *Immeasurable Equation*, 235.

28. Sun Ra, *Immeasurable Equation*, 301.

29. Omar Khayyam, *The Rubaiyat* (Cleveland: Imperial Press, 1903), 17.

30. Sun Ra, *Immeasurable Equation*, 163.

31. Sun Ra, *Immeasurable Equation*, 106.

32. Sun Ra, *Immeasurable Equation*, 452, 350.

33. Sun Ra, *Immeasurable Equation*, 448.

34. All items in this italicized passage are derived from titles of Sun Ra tunes.

35. Sun Ra, *Immeasurable Equation*, 397.

36. "Every dissonance is in a certain sense a remembrance of the suffering that domination, and ultimately a dominating society, inflict on nature. Only in the shape of this suffering, the shape of longing—and dissonance is essentially longing and suffering—does the oppressed nature find its voice." Theodor W. Adorno, quoted in Espen Hammer, *Adorno's Modernism: Art, Experience, and Catastrophe* (Cambridge: Cambridge University Press, 2015), 68. The translation is Hammer's.

37. Edgar Rice Burroughs, *Gods of Mars*, 71.

38. Sun Ra, *Immeasurable Equation*, 443.

39. Sun Ra, *Immeasurable Equation*, 447.

40. Sun Ra, *Immeasurable Equation*, 225.

41. Sun Ra, *Immeasurable Equation*, 405.

42. Sun Ra, *Immeasurable Equation*, 232.

43. Sun Ra, *Immeasurable Equation*, 278.

44. Sun Ra, *Immeasurable Equation*, 460.

45. Sun Ra, *Immeasurable Equation*, 352.

46. Sun Ra, *Immeasurable Equation*, 286.

47. Sun Ra, *Immeasurable Equation*, 64.

48. Sun Ra, *Immeasurable Equation*, 433.

49. Sun Ra, *Immeasurable Equation*, 460.

50. Sun Ra, *Immeasurable Equation*, 232.

51. Sun Ra, *Immeasurable Equation*, 90.

52. Edgar Rice Burroughs, *Gods of Mars*, 98.

53. Sun Ra, *Immeasurable Equation*, 63.

54. Sun Ra, *Immeasurable Equation*, 171.

55. Sun Ra, *Immeasurable Equation*, 155.

56. Sun Ra, *Immeasurable Equation*, 451.

57. Sun Ra, *Immeasurable Equation*, 306.

58. Sun Ra, *Immeasurable Equation*, 82.

59. Sun Ra, *Immeasurable Equation*, 433.

60. Sun Ra, *Immeasurable Equation*, 438.

61. Olson, *Collected Prose*, 246.

62. Olson, *Collected Prose*, 107.

63. Edgar Rice Burroughs, *Gods of Mars*, 188.

64. I should point out here that, if it is not already obvious, I am not trained as a musicologist, although like every other serious buff, I can describe what I hear. Since the focus of this book is poetry, in this section I look primarily at song lyrics, both in their interactions with the music in which they are embedded and as they are themselves estranged in the service of sci-fi *ostranenie*.

65. Jimi Hendrix Experience, *Axis, Bold as Love* (London: Olympic Studio, 1967).

66. Jimi Hendrix Experience, *The City of Love* (New York: Electric Lady Studios, 1971).

67. Jimi Hendrix Experience, *Are You Experienced* (London: Track Records, 1967).

68. At the time of this writing, the segment can be viewed online at Yusef Lateef, About, and Yusef Lateef, "Robot Man," YouTube.

69. Bill Milkowski, "Ornette Coleman: The Complete Science Fiction Sections," *Jazz Times*, September 1, 2000.

70. Steve Huey, "*Science Fiction* Review by Steven Huey," AllMusic, *Point 2*.

71. Ornette Coleman, *Science Fiction* (New York: Columbia Records, 1972).

72. See, most recently, Alexandra Alter, "'We've Already Survived an Apocalypse': Indigenous Writers Are Changing Sci-Fi," *New York Times*, August 14, 2020. The term *Indigenous futurism* is often attributed to Grace L. Dillon, whose "Imagining Indigenous Futurisms" is the title to her introduction to the anthology *Walking the Clouds*: "In the end, *Walking the Clouds* returns us to ourselves by encouraging Native writers to write about Native conditions in Native-centered worlds liberated by the imagination. These stories display features of self-reflexivity, defamiliarization, and the hyperreal present that Veronica Hollinger explains undergirds postmodern science fiction." Grace L. Dillon, ed., *Walking the Clouds: An Anthology of Indigenous Science Fiction* (Tucson: University of Arizona Press, 2012), 11.

73. "The images and subjects [in my poems] may appear 'surreal' to a Westerner, but in my Indigenous perspective, the world has a much wider field of experiences to draw from. I write from multiple vantage points. Poetry gives me the ability to compress opposing worldviews and attempt to harmonize those seemingly disparate energies." Sherwin Bitsui, "A Landscape Is Never Still: An Interview with Sherwin Bitsui," *Superstition [Review], an Online Literary Magazine*, iss. 23 (Spring 2019), conducted via e-mail by interview editor, Savannah Yates.

74. Sherwin Bitsui, *Shapeshift* (Tucson: University of Arizona Press, 2003), 6, 8.

75. Bitsui, *Shapeshift*, 33.

76. Samuel R. Delany, *Trouble on Triton: An Ambiguous Heterotopia* (Middletown: Wesleyan University Press, 1996), 285.

77. All quotations from "Asterisk" come from pages 3 and 4 of *Shapeshift*.

Chapter 6

1. Jakobson, *Language in Literature*, 69, 70.

2. Cf. Benjamin Lee Whorf's essay "An American Model of the Universe," *ETC: A Review of General Semantics* 8, no. 1 (December 1950): 27–33.

3. Christian Bök, "The Alien Argot of the Avant-Garde," *Cabinet Magazine*, iss. 1, Invented Languages (Winter 2000–2001).

4. "The timeless Hopi verb does not distinguish between the present, past and future

of the event itself but must always indicate what type of validity the speaker intends the statement to have." Benjamin Lee Whorf, "Science and Linguistics," in *Language, Thought, and Reality: Selected Writings of Benjamin Lee Whorf*, ed. J. B. Carroll (Cambridge, MA: MIT Press, 1956), 217.

5. Bök, "Alien Argot."

6. Bök, "Alien Argot."

7. Clark Coolidge, *Alien Tatters* (Berkeley: Atelos, 2000), 32.

8. Coolidge, *Alien Tatters*, 199.

9. Coolidge, *Alien Tatters*, 199. And he writes in the book's second section, "But why am I writing only the things I can't grasp?" (110).

10. "In the fifties, you'd just see disks in the sky and that was it. And then it began to be—they used to call them 'contactees,' people who have walked out into their backyard and met some Venusian woman in a skisuit. Or something a little more realistic. And then finally we have the abduction scenario, which is very involved, and that's what really got *Alien Tatters* going, because suddenly there were all these hypnosis tapes. I actually got a hold of some tapes that Budd Hopkins had recorded of people describing their experiences under hypnosis, and the language is interesting." "An Interview with Clark Coolidge," by Tom Orange, *Jacket* 13 (April 2001).

11. For instance, lines from several Bob Dylan songs appear at various points: cf, *Alien Tatters*, 50: "I promise to go wandering"; 59: "why and what's the reason for"; 92: "Blind Willie McTell haunts me"; 111: "Maybe I'll return along the cove." Coolidge also includes a reference to the Grateful Dead song "New Potato Caboose" on page 106: "To do with the new potato caboose, mongrel levels, benign carrier dwellers."

12. Coolidge, *Alien Tatters*, 145.

13. Coolidge, *Alien Tatters*, 39.

14. Coolidge, *Alien Tatters*, 112.

15. Coolidge, *Alien Tatters*, 199.

16. Coolidge, *Alien Tatters*, 19.

17. Coolidge, *Alien Tatters*, 21.

18. Coolidge, *Alien Tatters*, 55.

19. Coolidge, *Alien Tatters*, 104.

20. Coolidge, *Alien Tatters*, 35.

21. Coolidge, *Alien Tatters*, 48.

22. Coolidge, *Alien Tatters*, 15.

23. Coolidge, *Alien Tatters*, 25.

24. Coolidge, *Alien Tatters*, 23.

25. Coolidge, *Alien Tatters*, 31.

26. Coolidge, *Alien Tatters*, 32.

27. Coolidge, *Alien Tatters*, 23, 170.

28. Coolidge, *Alien Tatters*, 61.

29. Coolidge, *Alien Tatters*, 37.

30. Coolidge, *Alien Tatters*, 63.

31. Coolidge, *Alien Tatters*, 68.

32. Coolidge, *Alien Tatters*, 65.

33. Coolidge, *Alien Tatters*, 76–77.

34. Coolidge, *Alien Tatters*, 18.

35. Coolidge, *Alien Tatters*, 17.

36. Coolidge, *Alien Tatters*, 16.

37. Coolidge, *Alien Tatters*, 74.
38. Coolidge, *Alien Tatters*, 21.
39. Coolidge, *Alien Tatters*, 22.
40. Coolidge, *Alien Tatters*, 23.
41. Coolidge, *Alien Tatters*, 38.
42. Coolidge, *Alien Tatters*, 90.
43. Coolidge, *Alien Tatters*, 81–82.
44. Coolidge, *Alien Tatters*, 83.
45. Coolidge, *Alien Tatters*, 87.
46. Coolidge, *Alien Tatters*, 85.
47. Coolidge, *Alien Tatters*, 86.
48. Coolidge, *Alien Tatters*, 91.
49. Coolidge, *Alien Tatters*, 97.
50. Coolidge, *Alien Tatters*, 97.
51. Coolidge, *Alien Tatters*, 102.
52. Coolidge, *Alien Tatters*, 101
53. Coolidge, *Alien Tatters*, 108.
54. Coolidge, *Alien Tatters*, 104.
55. Coolidge, *Alien Tatters*, 103.
56. Coolidge, *Alien Tatters*, 106.
57. Coolidge, *Alien Tatters*, 119.
58. Coolidge, *Alien Tatters*, 110.
59. Coolidge, *Alien Tatters*, 107.
60. Coolidge, *Alien Tatters*, 110.
61. Coolidge, *Alien Tatters*, 116.
62. Coolidge, *Alien Tatters*, 121.
63. The quotation is taken from the footnote to a short story. Dick clarifies: "I was only four years old. After that my mother and father got divorced and I did not see my father for years. But the sight of him wearing his gasmask, blending as it did with his accounts of men with their guts hanging from them, men destroyed by shrapnel—decades later, in 1963, as I walked alone day after day along that country road with no one to talk to, no one to be with, that metal, blind, inhuman visage appeared to me again, but now transcendent and vast, and absolutely evil." Philip K. Dick, "The Days of Perky Pat," in *The Minority Report and Other Classic Stories* (New York: Kensington Publishing, 1987), 378.
64. Coolidge, *Alien Tatters*, 118. At an earlier point in the poem, he asks, "Could it really have been my father in that guise? He's still coming up into the light where I lurk. But what's that thing on him?" (109).
65. Coolidge, *Alien Tatters*, 101–2.
66. Coolidge, *Alien Tatters*, 118.
67. Coolidge, *Alien Tatters*, 101.
68. Coolidge, *Alien Tatters*, 123.
69. As Coolidge puts it, "This is only what can be said, what's dictated from the night hole." Coolidge, *Alien Tatters*, 121.
70. Borkhuis, "Dark Matter."

Bibliography

Adamson, Joseph. "Science Fiction as Romance." Educated Imagination: A Website Devoted to Northrop Frye. Posted June 9, 2012.

Adorno, Theodor W. *Minima Moralia: Reflections from Damaged Life*. Translated by E. F. N. Jephcott. London: Verso, 1978.

———. *Negative Dialectics*. Translated by E. B. Ashton. New York: Seabury, 1973.

Allen, Mike. *Strange Wisdoms of the Dead*. Rockville, MD: Wildside Press, 2006.

Alter, Alexandra. "'We've Already Survived an Apocalypse': Indigenous Writers Are Changing Sci-Fi." *New York Times*, August 14, 2020.

Andrews, Bruce. "Im/Possibility: On the Production, Distribution, and Articulation of the Possible and Impossible." Talk given September 30–October 1, 2016, University of Kiel.

———. *Lip Service*. Toronto: Coach House Books, 2001.

———. *Paradise and Method: Poetics and Praxis*. Evanston, IL: Northwestern University Press, 1996.

Aristotle. *The Pocket Aristotle*. Edited by Justin D. Kaplan. Translated by Ingram Bywater. New York: Washington Square Press, 1968.

Baraka, Amiri. *The Fiction of LeRoi Jones/Amiri Baraka*. Chicago: Lawrence Hill Books, 2000.

———. "How You Sound??" In *The LeRoi Jones/Amiri Baraka Reader*. Edited by William J. Harris, 16. New York: Basic Books, 2009.

———. *SOS: Poems 1961–2013*. Selected by Paul Vangelisti. New York: Grove Press, 2014.

Barthes, Roland. *Mythologies*. Selected and translated by Annette Lavers. New York: Noonday Press, 1972.

Baum, L Frank. *Ozma of Oz*. Illustrated by John R. Neill. New York: Dover Publications, 1985.

Benjamin, Walter. *The Arcades Project*. Translated by Howard Eiland and Kevin McLaughlin. Cambridge, MA: Belknap Press of Harvard University Press, 1999.

———. *The Origin of German Tragic Drama*. Translated by John Osborne. London: Verso, 1998.

———. *Selected Writings*. Vol. 2, part 1: *1927–1930*. Edited by Michael W. Jennings, Howard Eiland, and Gary Smith. Translated by Rodney Livingstone and others. Cambridge, MA: Belknap Press of Harvard University Press, 2005.

———. *Selected Writings*. Vol. 2, part 2: *1931–1934*. Edited by Michael W. Jennings, Howard Eiland, and Gary Smith. Translated by Rodney Livingstone and others. Cambridge, MA: Belknap Press of Harvard University Press, 1999.

——. *Selected Writings*. Vol. 4, *1938–1940*. Edited by Michael W. Jennings and Howard Eiland. Translated by Edmund Jephcott and others. Cambridge, MA: Belknap Press of Harvard University Press, 2003.

Bettridge, Joel. "Bruce Andrews's Language of Belief." *Jacket* 22 (May 2003).

Biglieri, Greg. "Invitation to a Misreading: Andrews' *Lip Service*." *Jacket* 22 (May 2003).

Bitsui, Sherwin. "A Landscape Is Never Still: An Interview with Sherwin Bitsui." In *Superstition [Review], an Online Literary Magazine*, iss. 23 (Spring 2019), conducted via e-mail by interview editor, Savannah Yates.

Blake, William. *The Complete Prose and Poetry of William Blake*. Edited by David V. Erdman New York: Doubleday, 1988.

——. *Shapeshift*. Tucson: University of Arizona Press, 2003.

Bök, Christian. *Crystallography*. Toronto: Coach House Books, 2003.

——. "The Alien Argot of the Avant-Garde." *Cabinet Magazine*, iss. 1, Invented Languages (Winter 2000–2001).

Borkhuis, Charles. *Savoir-Fear*. New York: Spuyten Duyvil, 2003.

Breton, André. *Manifestoes of Surrealism*. Translated by Richard Seaver and Helen R. Lane. Ann Arbor: University of Michigan, 1969.

Breton, André, and Philippe Soupault. *The Magnetic Fields*. Translated by David Gascoyne. London: Atlas Press, 1985.

Brower, Otto, and B. Reeves Eason, dirs. *The Phantom Empire*. Los Angeles, Mascot Pictures, 1935.

Burroughs, Edgar Rice. *At the Earth's Core*. New York: Grosset and Dunlap, 1922.

——. *The Chessmen of Mars*. New York: Ballantine Books, 1922.

——. *A Princess of Mars*. New York: Del Rey, Ballantine Books, 1980.

——. *The Gods of Mars*. New York: Ballantine Books, 1963.

——. *Synthetic Men of Mars*. New York: Ballantine Books, 1967.

Burroughs, William. *Burroughs Live: The Collected Interviews of William S. Burroughs, 1960–1997*. Los Angeles, CA : Semiotext(e).

——. *Nova Express: The Restored Text*. New York: Grove Press, 2013.

Chaucer, Geoffrey. *The Riverside Chaucer*. 3rd ed. Edited by F. N. Robinson. Boston: Houghton Mifflin, 1987.

Cole, Barbara. "Bruce Andrews's Venus: Paying Lip Service to Écriture Féminine." *Jacket* 22 (May 2003).

Chu, Seo-Young. *Do Metaphors Dream of Literal Sleep? A Science-Fictional Theory of Representation*. Cambridge, MA: Harvard University Press, 2011.

Clark, Tom. *Edward Dorn: A World of Difference*. Berkeley, CA: North Atlantic Books, 2002.

Coleman, Ornette. *Science Fiction*. New York: Columbia Records, 1972.

Coolidge, Clark. "After Tomorrow." In *Art Forum International*, 48, iss. 2 (2009): 206.

——. *Alien Tatters*. Berkeley, CA: Atelos, 2000.

——. "Arrangement: July 19, 1977." In *Talking Poetics from Naropa Institute*, edited by Anne Waldman and Marilyn Webb, 143–69. Boulder: Shambala, 1978.

——. "An Interview with Clark Coolidge." Interview with Tom Orange. *Jacket* 13 (April 2001).

——. *Quartz Hearts*. San Francisco: THIS, 1978.

——. *Smithsonian Depositions and Subject to a Film*. New York: Vehicle Editions, 1980.

——. *Space*. New York: Harper and Row, 1970.

Csicsery-Ronay, Istvan, Jr. "Fantastic Mimesis: A Diamond in the Rough." *Contemporary Literature* 53, no. 2 (Summer 2012): 387–405.

——. *The Seven Beauties of Science Fiction*. Middletown, CT: Wesleyan University Press, 2008.

Dante Alighieri. *Paradiso: The Divine Comedy of Dante Alighieri*. Vol. 3, part 1. Translated by Charles S. Singleton. Princeton, NJ: Princeton University Press, 1975.

Davidson, Michael. "To Eliminate the Draw: Edward Dorn's Slinger." *American Literature* 53, no. 3 (November 1981): 443–64.

de La Hire, Jean. *The Nyctalope on Mars*. Translated by Brian Stableford. Encino, CA: Black Coat Press, 2008.

Delaney, Samuel. "The Semiology of Silence." Interview with Sinda Gregory and Larry McCaffery. *Science Fiction Studies* 14, no. 42, part 2 (July 1987): 134–64.

——. *Trouble on Triton: An Ambiguous Heterotopia*. Middletown, CT: Wesleyan University Press, 1996.

Deleuze, Gilles. *Difference and Repetition*. Translated by Paul Patton. New York: Columbia University Press, 1994.

Deleuze, Gilles, and Félix Guattari. *A Thousand Plateaus: Capitalism and Schizophrenia*. Translated by Brian Massumi. Minneapolis: University of Minnesota Press, 1987.

Dery, Mark, ed. *Flame Wars: The Discourse of Cyberculture*. Durham, NC: Duke University Press, 1994.

Dick, Philip K. *The Minority Report and Other Classic Stories*. New York: Kensington Publishing, 1987.

Dillon, Grace L., ed. *Walking the Clouds: An Anthology of Indigenous Science Fiction*. Tucson: University of Arizona Press, 2012.

Dorn, Edward. *Ed Dorn Live: Lectures, Interviews, and Outtakes*. Edited by Joseph Richey. Ann Arbor: University of Michigan Press, 2007.

——. *Views*. Edited by Donald Allen. San Francisco: Four Seasons Foundation, 1980.

——. "Facsimile Reprint of Bean News." Published as an insert in *Sagetrieb*, Edward Dorn special issue 15, no. 3 (Winter 1996).

——. *Gunslinger*. Durham, NC: Duke University Press, 1989.

——. "An Interview with Edward Dorn." By Roy K. Okada." *Contemporary Literature* 15, no. 3 (Summer 1974): 297–314.

——. "Reading at SUNY Buffalo, April 19, 1974." University of Pennsylvania, PennSound.

——. *Way More West: New and Selected Poems*. Edited by Michael Rothenberg. New York: Penguin Books, 2007.

Du Bois, W. E. B. "The Comet." In *Darkwater: Voices from within the Veil*. Edited by W. E. B. Du Bois and William Edward Burghardt, 253–74. New York: Harcourt, Brace, 1920.

Elia, Adriano. "W. E. B. Du Bois's Proto-Afrofuturist Short Fiction: 'The Comet.'" *Il Tolomeo* 18 (December 2016): 173–86.

Evans, Arthur B. "Surrealism and Science Fiction." Review of *Futures of Surrealism: Myth, Science Fiction and Fantastic Art in France 1936–1969*, by Gavin Parkinson, and *Surrealism, Science Fiction and Comics*, edited by Gavin Parkinson. *Science Fiction Studies* 43, no. 2, 129 (July 2016): 351–58.

Eshun, Kodwo. "Further Considerations of Afrofuturism." *New Centennial Review* 3, no. 2 (Summer 2003): 287–302.

"First Annotations to Edward Dorn's *Gunslinger*." Compiled by Stephen Freeman and Grant Jenkins. *Sagetrieb* 15, no. 3 (Winter 1966).

Fletcher, Angus. *Allegory: The Theory of a Symbolic Mode*. Ithaca, NY: Cornell University Press, 1964.

Freedman, Carl. "Science Fiction and Critical Theory." *Science Fiction Studies* 14, no. 2, "Critical Approaches to Science Fiction: Retrospects and Prospects" (July 1987): 180–220.

Friend, Bill. "Modernism, Advertising, and *Lip Service*." *Jacket* 22 (May 2003).

Freud, Sigmund. *The Standard Edition of the Complete Psychological Works of Sigmund Freud*. Vol. 17: *1917–1919*. Translated by James Strachey. London: Hogarth Press, 1955.

Frye, Northrop. *Anatomy of Criticism*. Princeton, NJ: Princeton University Press, 1957.

Gelley, Alexander. "*Lesabéndio. An Asteroid Novel* by Paul Scheerbart. Review." *Modern Language Notes* 129, no. 3, German iss. (April 2014): 716–18.

Greenwald, Ted. "Spoken," in *Bruce Andrews and Charles Bernstein's L=A=N=G=U=A=G=E: The Complete Facsimile*. Edited by Matthew Hofer and Michael Golston, 190. Albuquerque: University of New Mexico Press.

———. *You Bet!* San Francisco: This, 1978.

Groff, Conklin, ed. *Possible Worlds of Science Fiction*. New York: Vanguard Press, 1951.

Gunn, James. *Speculations on Speculation: Theories of Science Fiction*. Edited by James Gunn and Matthew Candelaria, x–xi. Lanham, MD: Scarecrow Press, 2005.

Hammer, Espen. *Adorno's Modernism: Art, Experience, and Catastrophe*. Cambridge: Cambridge University Press, 2015.

Harris, Oliver. "'Burroughs Is a Poet Too, Really': The Poetics of Minutes to Go." *Edinburgh Review* 114 (2005). Republished online by RealityStudio, August 2010.

Hejinian, Lyn. *The Language of Inquiry*. Berkeley: University of California Press, 2000.

Hendrix, Jimi. *Starting at Zero: His Own Story*. New York: Bloomsbury, USA, 2015.

Huey, Steve. "*Science Fiction* Review by Steve Huey." AllMusic, *Point 2*.

Hull, Tony. "The Thunderbird: A February Exhibit on a Placitas Institution." *Sandoval Signpost*, February 12, 2012, 1.

Jakobson, Roman. *Language in Literature*. Edited by Krystyna Pomorska and Stephen Rudy. Cambridge, MA: Belknap Press of Harvard University Press, 1987.

———. *My Futurist Years*. Edited by Bengt Jangfeldt and Stephen Rudy. Translated by Stephen Rudy. New York: Marsilio Publishers, 1992.

Jameson, Fredric. *Archaeologies of the Future: The Desire Called Utopia and Other Science Fictions*. London: Verso 2007.

Jenkins, Grant. "Gunslinger's Ethics of Excess." *Sagetrieb*, Edward Dorn Special Issue, 15, no. 3 (Winter 1996): 207–242.

Jimi Hendrix Experience. *Are You Experienced*. London: Track Records, 1967.

———. *Axis, Bold as Love*. London: Olympic Studio, 1967.

———. *The City of Love*. New York: Electric Lady Studios, 1971.

Keller, Lynn. *Recomposing Ecopoetics: North American Poetry of the Self-Conscious Anthropocene*. Charlottesville: University of Virginia Press, 2017.

Khayyam, Omar. *The Rubaiyat*. Cleveland: Imperial Press, 1903.

Khlebnikov, Velimir. *The King of Time: Poems, Fictions, Visions of the Future*. Edited by Charlotte Douglas. Translated by Paul Schmidt. Cambridge, MA: Harvard University Press, 1985.

Knickerbocker, Conrad. "'The Art of Fiction.' Interview with William Burroughs." *Paris Review* 36, iss. 35 (Fall 1965).

Loy, Mina. *The Lost Lunar Baedeker*. Edited by Roger Conover. New York: Noonday Press, Farrar, Straus and Giroux, 1996.

Marinetti, Filippo Tommaso. *Let's Murder the Moonshine: Selected Writings*. Edited by

R. W. Flint. Translated by R. W. Flint and Arthur A. Coppotelli. Los Angeles: Sun and Moon Press, 1971.

Michelson, Peter. "Edward Dorn, Inside the Outskirts." *Sagetrieb*, Edward Dorn Special Issue, 15, no. 3 (Winter 1996): 197–206.

Milkowski, Bill. "Ornette Coleman: The Complete Science Fiction Sections." *Jazz Times*, September 1, 2000.

Milne, Heather. *Poetry Matters: Neoliberalism, Affect, and the Posthuman in Twenty-First Century North American Feminist Poetics*. Iowa City: University of Iowa Press, 2018.

Mohammad, K. Silem. *Deer Head Nation*. Oakland, CA: Tougher Disguises, 2003.

Mori, Masahito. "The Uncanny Valley [From the Field]." Translated by Karl F. MacDorman and Norri Kageki. *IEEE Robotics and Automation Magazine* 19, no. 2 (June 2012): 98–100.

Nelson, Alondra, ed. *Afrofuturism*. *Social Text* 20, no. 2 (71) (Summer 2002).

Onah, Julius, dir., *The Cloverfield Paradox*. Santa Monica, CA: Bad Robot Productions, 2018.

Olson, Charles. *The Collected Poems of Charles Olson*. Edited by George F. Butterick. Berkeley: University of California Press, 1987.

———. *Collected Prose: Charles Olson*. Edited by Donald Allen and Benjamin Friedlander. Introduction by Robert Creeley. Berkeley: University of California Press, 1997.

———. *The Maximus Poems*. Edited by George F. Butterick. Berkeley: University of California Press, 1983.

Padgett, Lewis. "Mimsy Were the Borogoves." In *The Science Fiction Hall of Fame 1, 1929–1964*, edited by Robert Silverberg, 181–210. New York: Orb Books, 1970.

Parkinson, Gavin, ed. *Surrealism, Science Fiction and Comics*. Liverpool: Liverpool University Press, 2015.

Perelman, Bob. "This Just In: Past Haunts *Lip Service*." *Jacket* 22 (May 2003).

Preminger, Alex, and T. V. F. Brogan, eds. *The New Princeton Encyclopedia of Poetry and Poetics*. Princeton, NJ: Princeton University Press, 1993.

Pynchon, Thomas. *Slow Learner*. New York: Little Brown, 1984.

Quartermain, Peter. "Paradise as Praxis: A Preliminary Note on Bruce Andrews's *Lip Service*." *Witz: A Journal of Contemporary Poetics* 6, no. 2 (Summer 1998): 5–18.University of Pennsylvania, Electronic Poetry Center, Authors.

———. *Stubborn Poetries: Poetic Facticity and the Avante-Garde*. Tuscaloosa: University of Alabama Press, 2013.

Reilly, Evelyn. *Styrofoam*. New York: Roof Books, 2009.

Saroyan, Aram. "Clark Coolidge and I." In *Stations # 5: A Symposium on Clark Coolidge*, edited by Ron Silliman, 6–7. Milwaukee, WI: Membrane Press, 1978.

Scheerbart, Paul. *Lesabéndio, Ein Asteroiden-Roman*. München: Georg Müller, 1913.

———. *Lesabéndio, An Asteroid Novel*. Translated by Christina Svendsen. Cambridge, MA: Wakefield Press, 2012.

Shklovsky, Viktor. *Theory of Prose*. Translated by Benjamin Sher. Normal: Dalkey Archive Press, Illinois State University, 1998.

Sinclair, Upton. *Oil!* New York: Penguin Books, 1926.

Smithson, Robert. *The Collected Writings*. Edited by Jack Flam. Berkeley: University of California Press, 1996.

Stockwell, Peter. *The Poetics of Science Fiction*. Essex, UK: Pearson Education, 2000.

Sun Ra. *Sun Ra: The Immeasurable Equation, The Collected Poetry and Prose*. Compiled and edited by James L. Wolf and Hartmut Geerken. Norderstedt: WAITAWHILE Books, 2005.

Suvin, Darko. *Metamorphoses of Science Fiction: On the Poetics and History of a Literary Genre.* New Haven, CT: Yale University Press, 1979.

Tejada, Roberto. "Becoming Bruce Andrews: A User's Guide to Starting Over Stars." *Jacket* 22 (May 2003).

Von Hallberg, Robert. "This Marvelous Accidentalism." In *Internal Resistances: The Poetry of Edward Dorn,* edited by Donald Wesling, 66–80. Berkeley: University of California Press, 1985.

Whorf, Benjamin Lee. "An American Model of the Universe." *ETC: A Review of General Semantics* 8, no. 1 (December 1950): 27–33.

——. *Language, Thought, and Reality: Selected Writings of Benjamin Lee Whorf.* Edited by J. B. Carroll. Cambridge, MA: MIT Press, 1956.

Williams, William Carlos. *Imaginations.* New York: New Directions, 1979.

——. *Selected Essays of William Carlos Williams.* New York: New Directions, 1969.

Yaszek, Lisa. "Afrofuturism, Science Fiction, and the History of the Future." *Socialism and Democracy* 20, no. 3 (2006): 41–60.

Index

Page numbers in italics refer to figures.